IMAGES
of America

EVERGLADES NATIONAL PARK

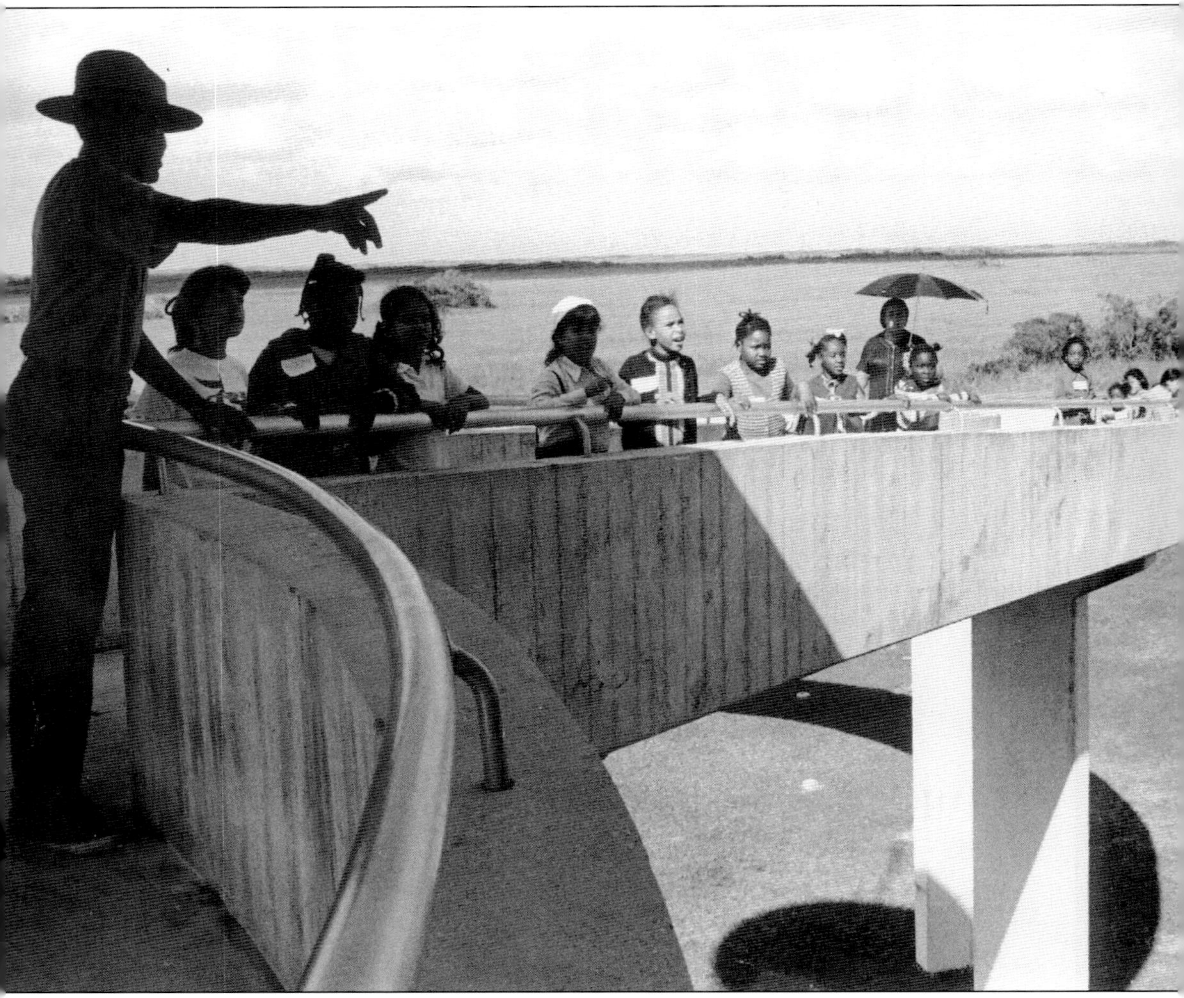

Reached by tram, bicycle, or a hike, Everglades National Park's 65-foot-tall Shark Valley observation tower seven miles south of Tamiami Trail provides a uniquely expansive bird's-eye view of the Everglades. This photograph from the tower's viewing platform shows ranger Edward Meadows with a 1972 school group, pointing out the sawgrass marshes and islands of trees that characterize the Everglades. (HM.)

On the Cover: Everglades National Park protects the plants and animals of the southern Everglades as well as those of Florida Bay, tropical mangrove swamps, and endangered pine forests. Anhinga Trail is the park's most popular wildlife viewing location. In this mid-1960s image, visitors, encouraged by a park ranger, are looking at nesting anhingas, the waterbird for which the nature trail was named. (NPS.)

IMAGES
of America

Everglades National Park

James A. Kushlan and Kirsten Hines

ARCADIA
PUBLISHING

ISBN 978-1-4671-0728-0

Published by Arcadia Publishing
Charleston, South Carolina

Printed in the United States of America

Library of Congress Control Number: 2021945984

For all general information, please contact Arcadia Publishing:
Telephone 843-853-2070
Fax 843-853-0044
E-mail sales@arcadiapublishing.com
For customer service and orders:
Toll-Free 1-888-313-2665

Visit us on the Internet at www.arcadiapublishing.com

Dedicated to the memories of four seminal chroniclers of Everglades National Park: Daniel Beard, Frank Craighead Sr., William B. Robertson Jr., and Charlton W. Tebeau.

Contents

ACKNOWLEDGMENTS

As a student and later Everglades National Park wildlife biologist, senior author James Kushlan had the privilege of learning about the Everglades from those who knew it well, including some who are now historic figures mentioned in this book, such as Taylor Alexander, Frank Craighead, Willard Dilley, Walt Dineen, Burt Hunt, Rich Klukas, Art Marshall, Ralph Miele, Oscar Owre, Barney Parker, Bill Robertson, Durban Tabb, Charlton Tebeau, and Erwin Winte. He also wishes to acknowledge National Park Service mentors Gary Davis, Dennis Fenn, John Good, Bob Lynn, Nathaniel Reed, and Ted Sudia. We thank Everglades National Park for encouraging this project in celebration of the park's 75th anniversary, especially Supt. Pedro Ramos, chief of resource education and interpretation Alan Scott, and museum curator Jim Williams and archivist Bonnie Ciolino at the South Florida Collections Management Center. We especially thank historian and author Robert W. Blythe and National Park Service archivist Nancy Russell. Bob's masterful administrative history, *Wilderness on the Edge*, provides exceptional background on the park's story. We thank him for his encouragement, sharing his knowledge, and his help with images. Nancy offered her deep knowledge of Everglades National Park, providing encouragement and exceptional guidance in so many ways. Both Bob and Nancy also endured our interminable questions. We thank Kelly Balmes for use of her photograph. At HistoryMiami, we thank executive director Jorge Zamanillo, archives manager Ashley Trujillo, and archives assistant Jeremy Salloum. We also thank the following institutions and staff: American Museum of Natural History, Matthew Heenan; Denver Public Library; Everglades Foundation chief science officer Steven Davis and Tom Van Lent; Florida Keys Public Library; Library of Congress; Miami-Dade Public Library System digital collections manager Margarita Mirabal; State Archives of Florida archivist assistant Dixon Gutierrez; University of Florida, George A. Smathers Libraries digital services specialist Terrence Phillips and digital production manager Laura Perry; University of Utah, J. Willard Marriott Library assistant photograph archivist Sara Davis; US National Archives; and US National Library of Medicine. We thank our editor at Arcadia Publishing, Stacia Bannerman, for her guidance. We especially thank reviewers of earlier drafts Robert Blythe, Gary Bremen, Philip Kushlan, Nancy Russell, and Alan Scott.

INTRODUCTION

The Everglades—dark, swampy, mysterious, glassy-eyed snakes draped from overhead branches, murky tea-colored water, giant alligators ready to pounce on the unwary traveler. This is what many think; yet, none of it is so. The Everglades is subtle, appearing two-dimensional, its water crystal clear, its great native predators mostly asleep during the daytime visits of tourists. It is not a dark forbidding swamp; it is a seasonally flooded grassy prairie, shimmering in the bright South Florida sunlight.

A national park—surely a place of formidable geological formations, geysers, awe-inspiring three-dimensional vistas, mountaintop glaciers, herds of megafauna and their toothsome predators, landscapes to gaze upon from roadside overlooks, well-kept trails to be strolled dry-shod, or views from air-conditioned comfort while riding between rustic restaurants. Not this national park. Everglades National Park is an environment to be experienced from a single dead-end road, a tram ride, elevated boardwalks, or by hip-deep wading through marshes, canoeing through mangrove-lined creeks, or boating across extremely shallow bays. Everglades is not your usual national park. It is the first US national park designated primarily for its biological significance. It is a biological park.

Although situated in North America, many of the plants and animals in this national park come from the tropics. Mahogany and mangroves, orchids and bromeliads, tropical birds and butterflies, manatees and crocodiles, and spiders and snails all came from the West Indies. These tropical species flourished in South Florida's tropical environment. The region often is referred to as subtropical because frosts do occur, but by accepted climatological classification, it indeed is tropical. By whatever classification, the plants and animals formed natural communities in South Florida like those of their Caribbean ancestors. Everglades National Park is not only a biological park, but a tropical one.

The Everglades is unique within the United States. Once, it stretched as an unbroken marshy plain 50 miles wide and 100 miles long, from the south shore of Lake Okeechobee to Florida's southern coast. That Everglades is no more. Overall, the Greater Everglades Ecosystem covers 18,000 square miles, but the Everglades marsh itself is half the size it once was. Over a century of ditches, levees, pumping stations, over-drying and over-flooding, and manipulating the natural surface water primarily for flood control and agricultural and urban water supply has changed it fundamentally. Its waters are now controlled and managed; that is, except when nature decrees otherwise, as it does every once in a while through floods, droughts, frosts, and hurricanes, all quite natural events in the Everglades but events that can overwhelm human planning. It is the unencumbered, downstream tip of the Everglades marshland that is encompassed by Everglades National Park. Beyond being the southern terminus of the great Everglades, the park is also mangrove swamps and mangrove-lined rivers, beaches and dunes, islands of pinelands and tropical forest, coastal lagoons, and Florida Bay. Beyond its biology, it is a park of history and the human stories of Archaic peoples, Tequesta, Spanish and British colonialists, American pioneers, Mikasuki-speaking Indians, soldiers, settlers, activists, public servants, scientists, residents, and visitors.

Everglades National Park's origin story traces to the conservation movements of the early 1900s that aimed, among other causes, to protect birds and to set aside special places for people's edification. At the time, feathers, sometimes whole birds, were being fashionably worn on women's hats and garments. Although feathers have decorated the garb of many a culture, the impact of this particular fad was near-global, leading to the worldwide destruction of millions of birds every year. One of the early hot spots for plume hunting was South Florida, where the Everglades hosted seemingly endless populations of waterbirds. Chief among these, from the plume hunter's perspective, were the egrets that sported long frilly plumes during their breeding season. They nested in colonies that, although hard to get to, were easily shot out. For South Florida's residents, both settlers and Seminoles, pluming was one of the few, and the most lucrative, money-making opportunities available. Beyond the hunters, profits were immense as plumes traveled through trading posts and middlemen to factories and finally haberdashery shops, supporting a nationally significant number of jobs. The carnage was brought to national attention by naturalists and conservationists. Numerous Audubon societies were formed. An Everglades bird with the longest plumes, the great egret—then known as the American egret—became a poster child for the movement. Wardens were hired privately to patrol, including in what is now Everglades National Park. Guy Bradley, who lived in Flamingo, was murdered by plume hunters in Florida Bay. The murder created a national martyr for the conservation cause. Laws were passed in New York and Florida throttling the trade; tariffs inhibited imports, fashion changed, and a world war began, but the memory of the Everglades' wading birds remained. The idea of conservation in the Everglades from the beginning was about protecting its birds.

Everglades National Park's origin story also is about its becoming appreciated as a special place worth preserving. The initial highlight was a tiny forest, locally called a hammock. It was called Paradise Key, then Palm Hammock, and in 1916, officially named Royal Palm State Park. This hammock was recognized for its distinctive plants, epitomized by its tall, stately royal palms, a plant that in North America is found only in South Florida. The cause of preserving the hammock led by Mary Munroe and May Jennings was taken up by Florida's women's clubs. Setting aside Royal Palm Hammock for the enjoyment and education of the people was the seed that three decades later would germinate into a national park.

Everglades National Park covers 1.5 million acres, or 7,800 square miles. It is not small; it is larger than three US states. The boundaries suggested by its proponents, such as Ernest F. Coe, would have encompassed much of South Florida's natural ecological diversity; its approved boundaries did not. Yet over time, the wisdom of the proposed boundaries came to be appreciated as the park was expanded and much of its originally-proposed landscapes and seascapes eventually became protected in Biscayne National Park, John Pennekamp Coral Reef State Park, Crocodile Lake National Wildlife Refuge, Ten Thousand Islands National Wildlife Refuge, Big Cypress National Preserve, and Water Conservation Area 3. There are over 20 reserved areas in the Greater Everglades Ecosystem, a matrix of protected lands with Everglades National Park as its heart.

On its east, Everglades National Park abuts developed southeast Florida, nearly all of which used to be Everglades before it was drained. Over five million people live within a few dozen miles of the park's boundary. In many years, about a million people visit the park. So, as well as being about wildlife and its tropical character, Everglades National Park is a place for and about people. People are not some new intrusion into a pristine, uninhabited Everglades. Humans have always been there. People of Paleo-Indian cultures were in South Florida twice as long as there has been an Everglades, which began forming only after the last ice age about 5,000 years ago. Over thousands of years, the Indigenous peoples became finely adapted to their increasingly watery South Florida environment. The Everglades' marsh and pinelands that developed over millennia require fire for persistence, a landscape management process long used by humans.

At the time of European contact, the Spanish called the native peoples then living in southeastern Florida Tequesta. A main village was at the eastern edge of the Everglades on the Miami River. The people of the Ten Thousand Islands were called Muspa by the Spanish. Well north of the eventual park, the Mayaimi lived around Lake Okeechobee and the Calusa had their major villages around Charlotte Harbor. At the time of contact, the Calusa were politically and culturally dominant, having achieved cultural influence over the people of the Ten Thousand Islands. South

Florida was mostly wetland, and the people lived on the limited patches of higher ground along lakes, rivers, and coastal lagoons. The resources of the Everglades complemented more heavily used marine resources. Excavated canals accessed towns and canoe trails connected camps on Everglades tree islands.

South Florida's Indigenous peoples persisted through the 250 years of Spanish colonialism, relatively apart and relatively independent, continuing their traditions as hunters, fishers, and gatherers but also becoming shipwreck salvors and traders, accepting Spanish overlordship but firmly maintaining isolation while adapting to the Spanish presence. Populations nonetheless declined, concluding when the British set loose parties of slave-raiding Indians from their more northern colonies on the remaining Indigenous people of South Florida. When Spain turned over Florida to Britain in 1763, some Spanish-acculturated people were taken to Cuba and others were left behind, but South Florida was effectively depopulated. By this time, immigrating segments of other southeastern Indigenous people had arrived in Florida, encouraged by the Spanish, British, and then Spanish again. Separating themselves from northern tribes, over time they became known as the Seminole.

When the United States acquired Florida in 1821, its policies of eliminating all Indigenous people east of the Mississippi led to prolonged wars of removal that pushed Florida's Seminoles ever further south and finally into the Big Cypress and Everglades. They were then the people of the Everglades, an environment to which they quickly and successfully adapted. During the Seminole Wars, the American military followed them into the marshes, learning their trails, cutting new ones, and establishing forts on Cape Sable and other sites. For the first time, non-Indigenous people traversed the Everglades. By the end of the war of removal, the Everglades, Big Cypress Swamp, coastal rivers, Ten Thousand Islands, and Florida Bay were well known to the American government.

The early to mid-1800s also saw Americans, as well as Cubans and Bahamians, moving into South Florida. They were wreckers and farmers, hunters and trappers, turtlers and eggers, outlaws and carpetbaggers, tuberculosis sufferers, and men and families seeking a new place to start. Most came and went, leaving no trace. Pioneers, immigrants, and homesteaders brought to South Florida the trappings and expectations of 19th-century American society, with first a barter economy and then money. The remnant Seminole families, not a coastal people, tended to the interior, while American home sites and settlements claimed the coasts. Nearly all transport was by water. Pioneers farmed as well as they could, fished and hunted for food, guided adventuresome visitors and gentlemen-sportsmen, and made moonshine. They hunted for plumes, alligator hides, and otter and raccoon fur to sell at trading posts, some of which eventually became towns and cities, such as Miami, Fort Lauderdale, and Everglades City. They transported charcoal, sea turtles and their eggs, and fish, first salted and then iced, to Key West or later Fort Myers.

Beyond wrecking and small-scale farming of sugarcane, tomatoes, melons, cabbage, and peppers for the Key West market, the early South Florida economy was based on exploiting natural resources, including those of the Everglades. But this pioneer world and its perceived stash of unlimited exploitable resources were not to endure. The mucklands under the Everglades proved irresistible to those looking for farmland or speculative land to sell. Draining began in the late 1800s around Lake Okeechobee, expanding from there in the decades following. In 1896, the railroad arrived three miles from the Everglades' eastern edge. South Florida's new economic opportunities proved as irresistible as Everglades muckland. Better drainage provided land for farming, housing, and real estate ventures. The population expanded exponentially, edging inexorably inland into the former Everglades. In short order, native animal populations such as wading birds, alligators, otters, sea turtles, and clams collapsed.

For centuries, the Everglades and its coast were only accessible, and hardly that, by boat. The glades remained uncrossable, unless by a Seminole or backwoods gladesman. That is, until land development interests pushed a road from Miami to Tampa by way of Marco. Tamiami Trail changed everything by allowing access to the previously inaccessible Everglades marshes. It enticed resident Indians out of the difficult wetlands with opportunities to live on the higher ground of the roadside, to travel by canal and road, and to engage in the money economy. And it opened lands, however flooded, for sale. The new road also impeded the flow of surface water southward. Tamiami Trail took 15 years to build, but on April 25, 1928, cars rolled across the previously formidable southern Everglades.

Led by indefatigable organizations and charismatic spokespersons, the attention of conservationists turned to creating a grand tropical park in the Everglades, a process that took decades. Committees, delegations, and studies followed. In 1934, a tropical park in the Everglades was authorized by the federal government, and about a decade later it became a reality. Pres. Harry S. Truman dedicated the park in the town of Everglades on December 6, 1947. The job of protecting, preserving, accessing, and interpreting fell to the National Park Service, especially to the park's first superintendent, Daniel B. Beard.

Protecting and managing a tropical wetland dependent on the seasonal flow of low-nutrient surface water from upstream turned out not to be an easy task. Landholdings needed to be acquired, destructive access limited, poaching stopped, bird colonies protected, and visitor facilities developed. The main road running through the park needed improving, or maybe replacing. Visitor centers, ranger stations, campsites, trails, boardwalks, and vantage points needed to be built. Ranger patrols needed boats, airboats, and airplanes. And nature was not quiescent. Hurricanes caused large and unanticipated impacts. It came to be understood that a natural periodic fire regime needed to be restored. The existential issue of the impedance of surface water flow into the park needed to be dealt with, ironically a problem with origins in the same year as the park's dedication. It also came to be understood that the Everglades was naturally nutrient-poor, and water coming into the Everglades was not. Water needed to flow into the southern Everglades from the north in the wet season, but the Everglades also needed to dry in the dry season. It was not simple.

Whereas Tamiami Trail impeded the flow of surface water into the southern Everglades as early as the 1920s, by the 1960s, water management had gained the capability to cut flow off completely. The Everglades marshes north of the park were surrounded by levees so as not to flood places (mostly former Everglades) that people no longer wanted wet. In the otherwise dry years of the early 1960s, with its upstream water cut off, Everglades National Park overly dried. It burned deeply, and once again, alligator populations crashed and wading birds stopped nesting successfully. Iteratively over time, with public concern and increasing environmental awareness, water management processes changed. Water flow to the park was restored, although not necessarily within the natural flow-ways or with natural timing or quantities. It came to be realized that issues of protecting the park's environment lay also beyond the park's boundaries. The park's boundaries were expanded and scientific investigations learned more and more about the Everglades. The remnant management-controlled Everglades needed to be re-plumbed. In 2000, the state and federal governments agreed, and Everglades restoration was born. Some of the engineered Everglades began to be taken apart and put back together.

The Everglades, mangrove coast, and Florida Bay of Everglades National Park may not be what they once were, but what part of nature is? The park continues to protect its expansive natural montage of sawgrass and prairies, pine rocklands and tropical hammocks, mangrove swamps and coastal prairie, rivers and lagoons, and bays and keys. Bald eagles, osprey, and great white herons continue to nest in Florida Bay. Populations of Florida panthers, American alligators, and American crocodiles, once much reduced, have rebounded. White ibis and wood stork populations have expanded. Everglades restoration is proceeding with increasing success. Places to experience Everglades National Park—Anhinga Trail, Royal Palm Hammock, Shark Valley, Flamingo, Everglades City, the Ten Thousand Islands, the Wilderness Waterway, and Florida Bay—remain on the visiting and adventure agendas of residents and visitors alike. Challenges do continue. Everglades restoration awaits completion. Non-native species such as pythons, tropical fish, and Brazilian pepper pose ongoing threats, and the sea level is rising. Yet despite over a century of environmental change, Everglades National Park continues to protect this special environment while encouraging its enjoyment and edification by present and future generations.

One

A Biological Park

If neither glaciers nor geysers, what then is the southern Everglades and its national park? To be understood, the Everglades needs to be experienced, in person or through images such as those in this chapter. The Everglades is a marsh of sawgrass growing thickly in strands elongated in the direction of water flow, impenetrable to humans unless they are willing to endure the slice of its serrated blades. The Everglades also is made up of strands of deeper marshes called wet prairies or sloughs (pronounced "slew") dotted with white water lilies and carnivorous yellow-flowered bladderworts. Its marsh bottom is covered by an organic ooze of decaying plant material. Plant stems are encapsulated by an algae-based blanket called periphyton. Its water is gin-clear, home to mosquitofish, gar, bass, bluegill, crayfish, prawns, and apple snails. In the Everglades, tree branches are covered with epiphytic orchids, bromeliads, and resurrection ferns. Islands perched on slight limestone projections are covered by hammocks of tropical gumbo limbo and pigeon plum and temperate willow and hackberry. They are more or less dry places for barred owls, pygmy rattlesnakes, cottonmouths, and deer, as well as, in turn, the camps of Tequesta, Seminoles, and gladesmen. The marsh is punctuated by gator holes—ponds made by alligators. In addition to alligators, the Everglades is home to herons and egrets of plume-hunting fame, ibises, spoonbills, Everglade snail kites, and Cape Sable seaside sparrows. Adjacent to the true Everglades are marshes of slightly higher elevation, palm-lined hammocks of mahogany trees, forests of dwarf cypress trees, and pinelands. Mangrove swamps and coastlines of Everglades National Park are populated by tropical salt-tolerant trees: black mangroves, once harvested for mosquito-fending smudge fires; red mangroves, supported by sprawling debris-catching roots with tannin-infused bark that tints the nearby water brown; and buttonwoods, its charcoal once fueling the fires of pioneers. The mangrove-lined estuaries and coastal lagoons are home to manatees, crocodiles, snook, tarpon, and mangrove snappers. Further seaward is Florida Bay, its islands low and its shallow waters supporting bonefish, tarpon, mullet, and redfish. In the Everglades, the depth of water and salinity of its estuaries fluctuate with the rainy and dry seasons, a process that drives its biology.

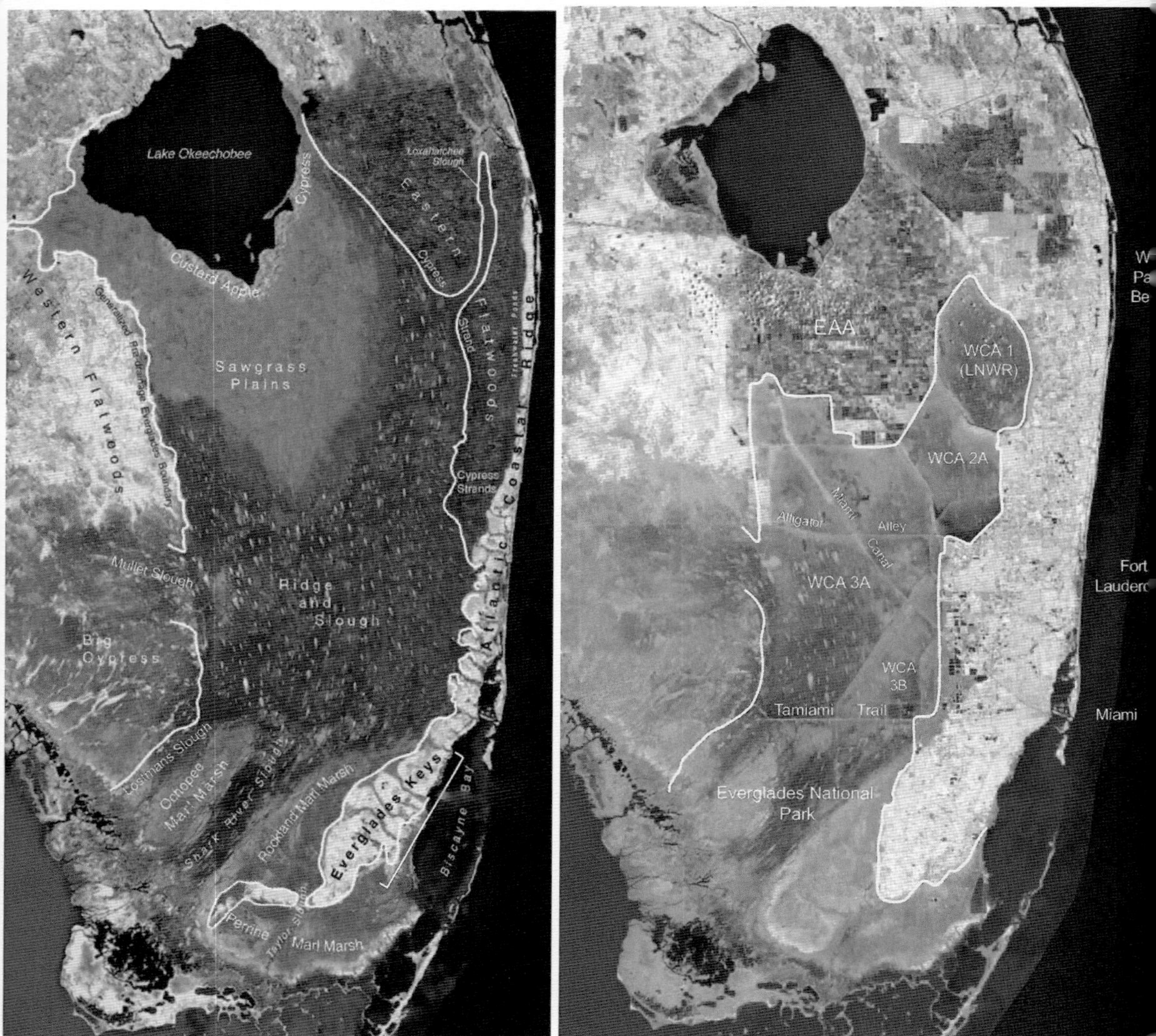

Viewing the Everglades from the ground provides a limited impression. A view from above is required. At left is a depiction of the original Everglades. Impenetrable sawgrass plains south of Lake Okeechobee gave way to the ridge and slough topography of the core Everglades drainage. To the west is the Big Cypress Swamp. To the east is the somewhat elevated Atlantic Coastal Ridge and Everglades Keys. In the south, the glades are compressed into Shark River Slough flanked by higher marl marshes as it bends southwest into coastal marshes, mangrove forests, and streams flowing into the Gulf of Mexico. At right is a current depiction. The sawgrass plains south of Lake Okeechobee were converted to farming, called the Everglades Agricultural Area (EAA). The eastern Everglades is drained and built over. The remaining northern portions of the Everglades are impounded in water conservation areas (WCA); levees and canals impede or move surface water as managers choose. The swampland to the west is now Big Cypress National Preserve. Everglades National Park occupies the bottom of the drainage basin south of Tamiami Trail. (EF.)

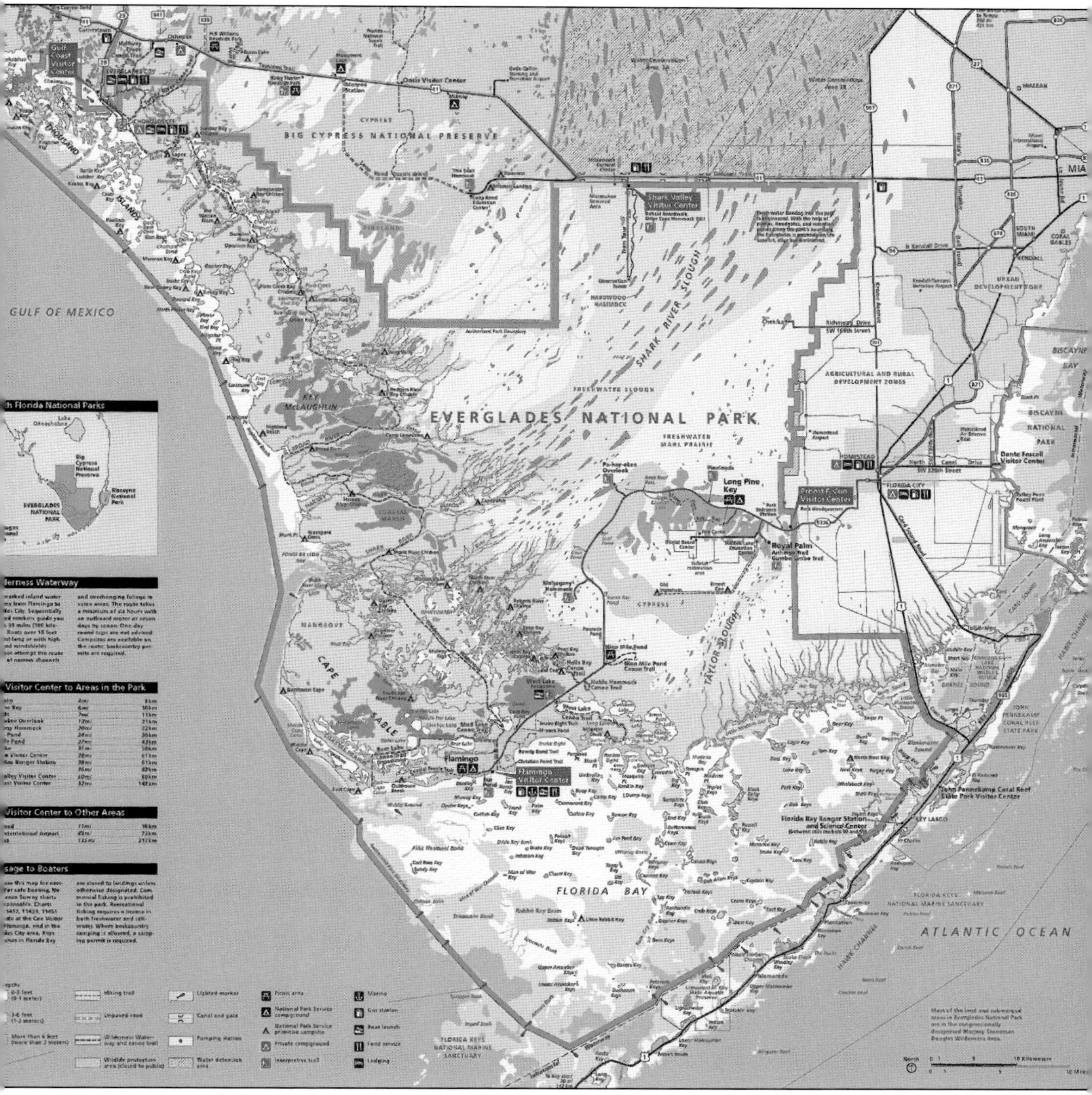

The boundaries of Everglades National Park embrace the core of the southernmost portion of the Everglades as well as part of the Ten Thousand Islands and coastal rivers to the west and Cape Sable and the marine shallows and keys of Florida Bay to the south. Developed Miami-Dade County looms to the east and Water Conservation Area 3 to the north. This map shows the main park road running from the Ernest F. Coe Visitor Center to the Flamingo Visitor Center on Florida Bay. At its northern boundary is the Shark Valley Visitor Center and road to the Shark Valley observation tower. The Gulf Coast Visitor Center provides access to the Ten Thousand Islands area. Everglades National Park is famous worldwide. It has been recognized as a world heritage site, a biosphere reserve, and a wetland of international importance. It is the third-largest national park in the lower 48 states. In 1997, 1.3 million of its acres were dedicated as the Marjory Stoneman Douglas Wilderness. (NPS.)

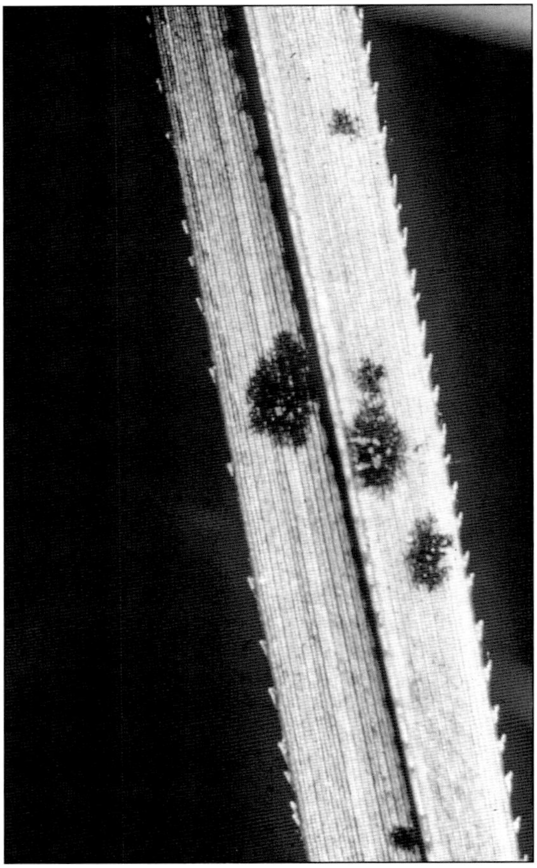

Sawgrass is the iconic plant of the Everglades. Historically a significant impediment to traversing the glades, sawgrass's serrated edge can knife through skin and clothes if rubbed the wrong way. A sedge rather than a grass, it can reach 10 feet tall in deep peat soil but is shorter in shallower soil. Sawgrass depends for its persistence on being dry for two months of the year and being burned periodically. It is a plant that grows best under nutrient-poor conditions, a salient characteristic of the Everglades. The 1978 aerial image below shows the Everglades covered by dense strands of sawgrass surrounding tree islands elongated in the direction of water flow. (Both, KH.)

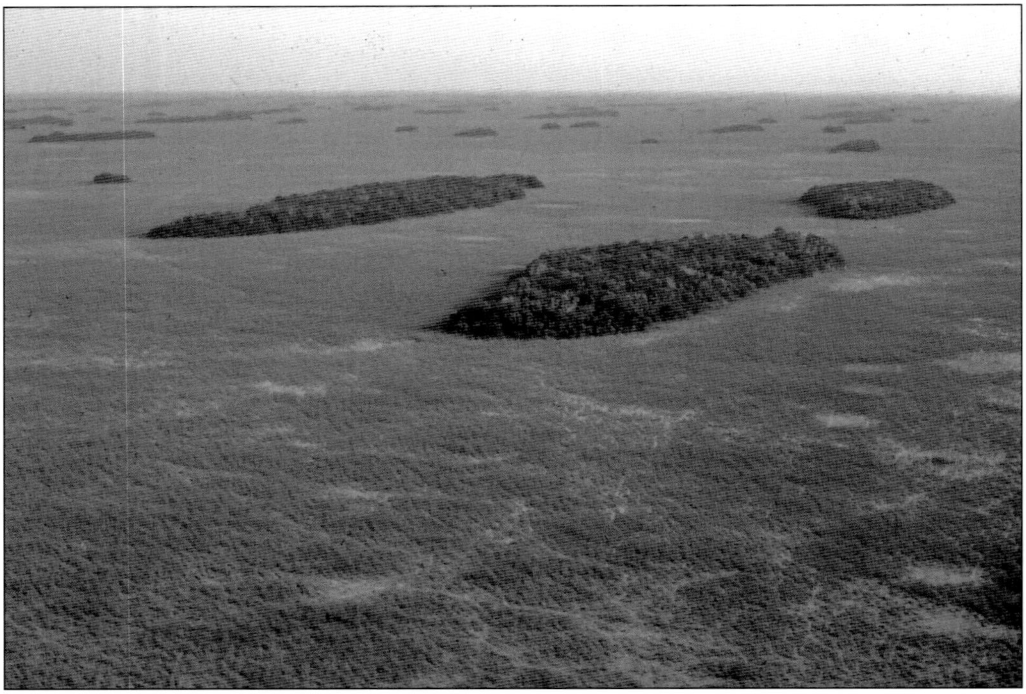

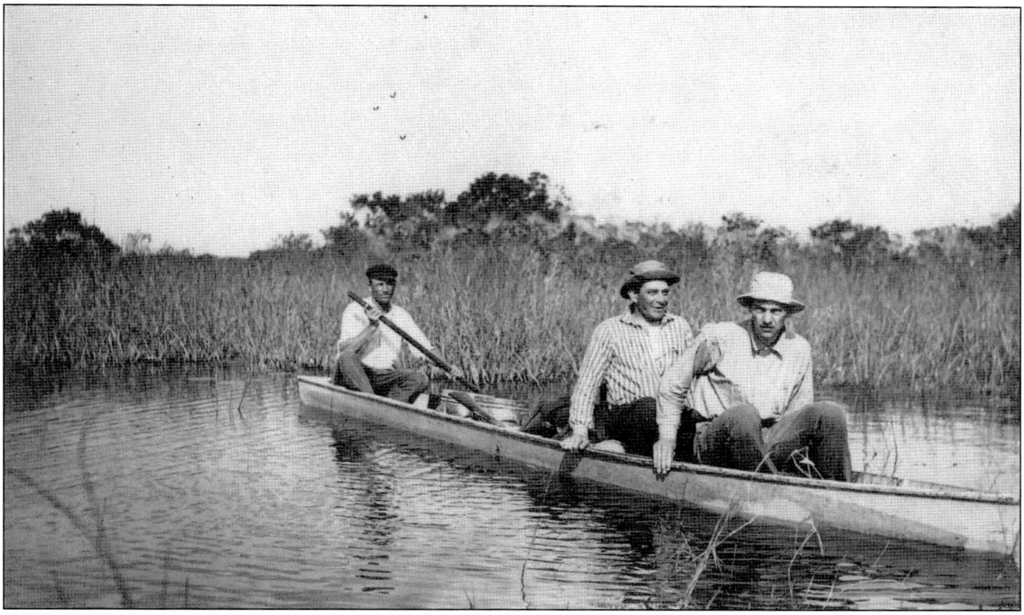

Indigenous people, soldiers, and pioneers crossed the dense stands of sawgrass using well-worn canoe trails. Sawgrass strands are intermixed with slightly deeper, less densely vegetated marshes, called wet prairies, also elongated in the direction of water flow, that were easier to canoe. This 1910 photograph shows a canoeing party led by a salesman for the Everglade Land Sales Company, selling Everglades land by the gallon, it was said. (HM.)

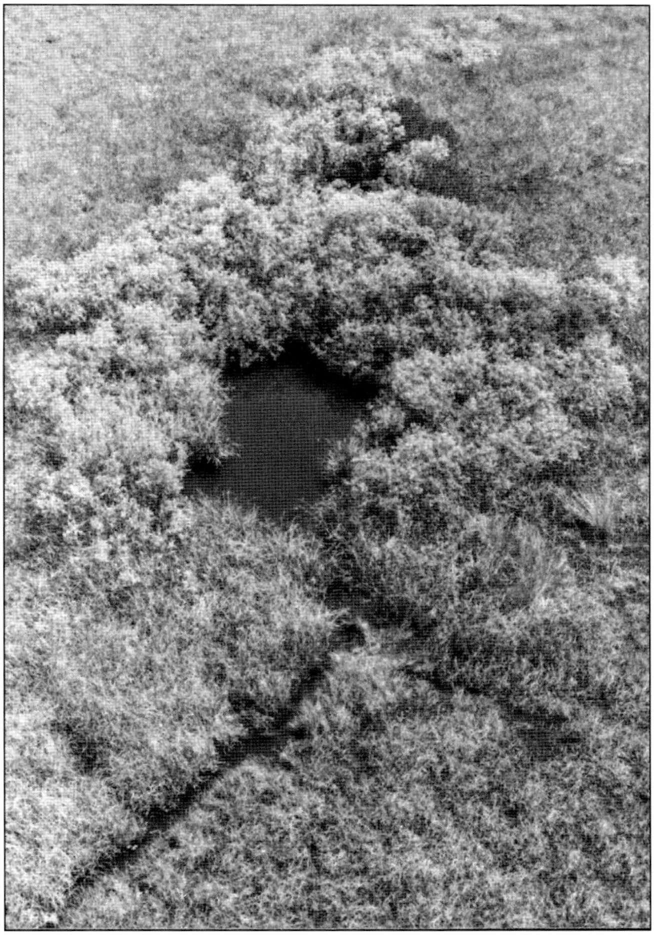

During the 1970s, it became understood how important ponds, called gator holes, were to the Everglades. Maintained by American alligators, during the annual drying season these ponds provide refugia for aquatic animals that repopulate the marsh when water levels rise again in the following wet season. This 1980 photograph shows a pond edged by willow trees with an alligator trail leading from the pond into the surrounding sawgrass marsh. (KH.)

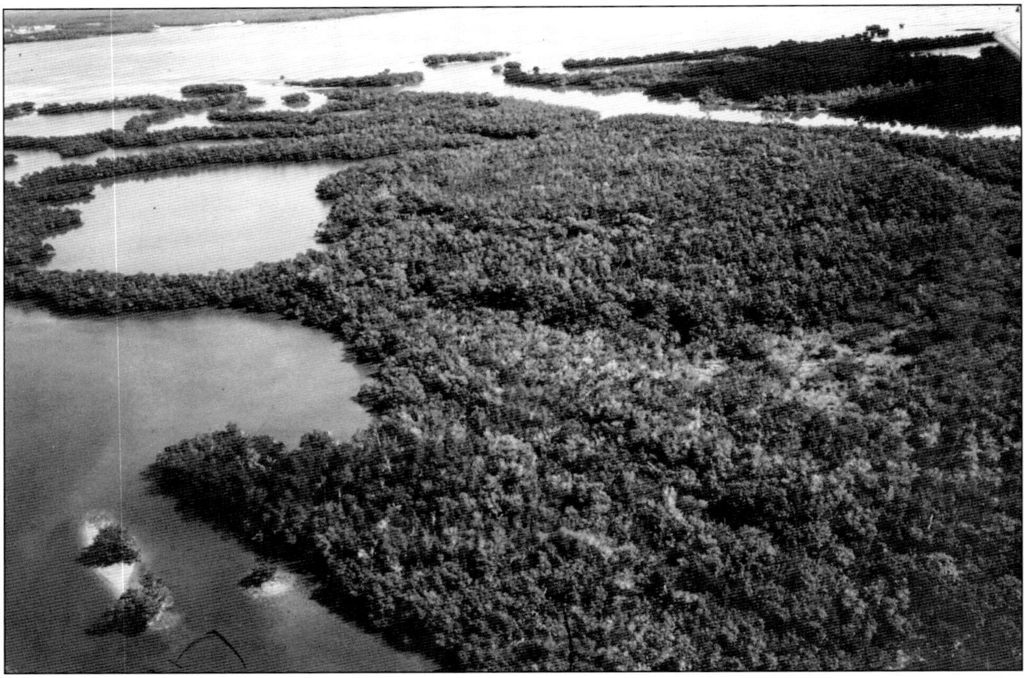

The coastline of Everglades National Park is lined with tropical mangrove forests, as shown in the 1950s aerial photograph above. These are forests of trees that can grow in saltwater. The image below from 1950 provides an impression of a red mangrove forest as a skiff makes its way down a mangrove-lined creek in what recently had become Everglades National Park. Mangroves occur only south of freezing temperatures and so in North America only in coastal South Florida. The mangrove forests bordering the Everglades were some of the finest examples in the Americas. Mangroves along its coasts are as iconic of Everglades National Park as sawgrass is in the interior. (Both, NPS.)

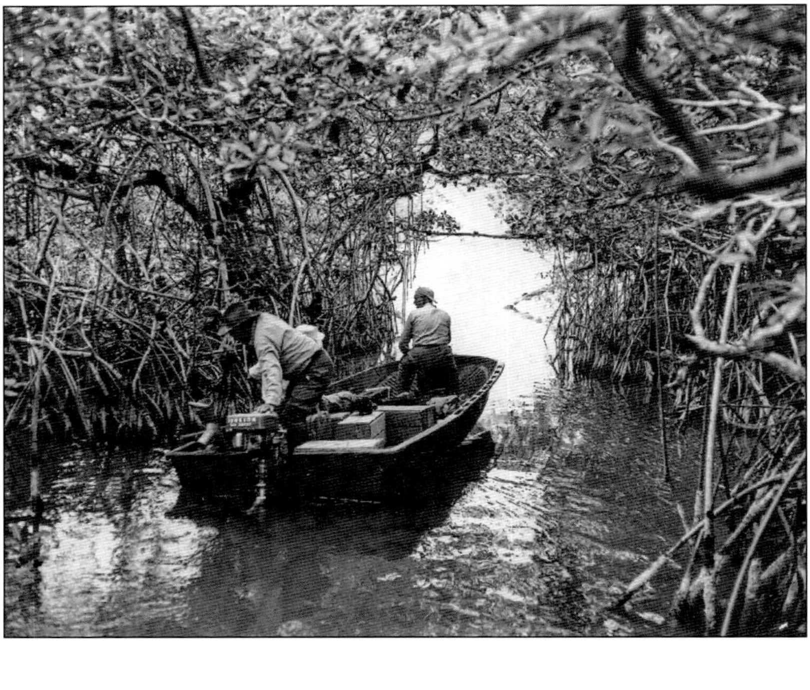

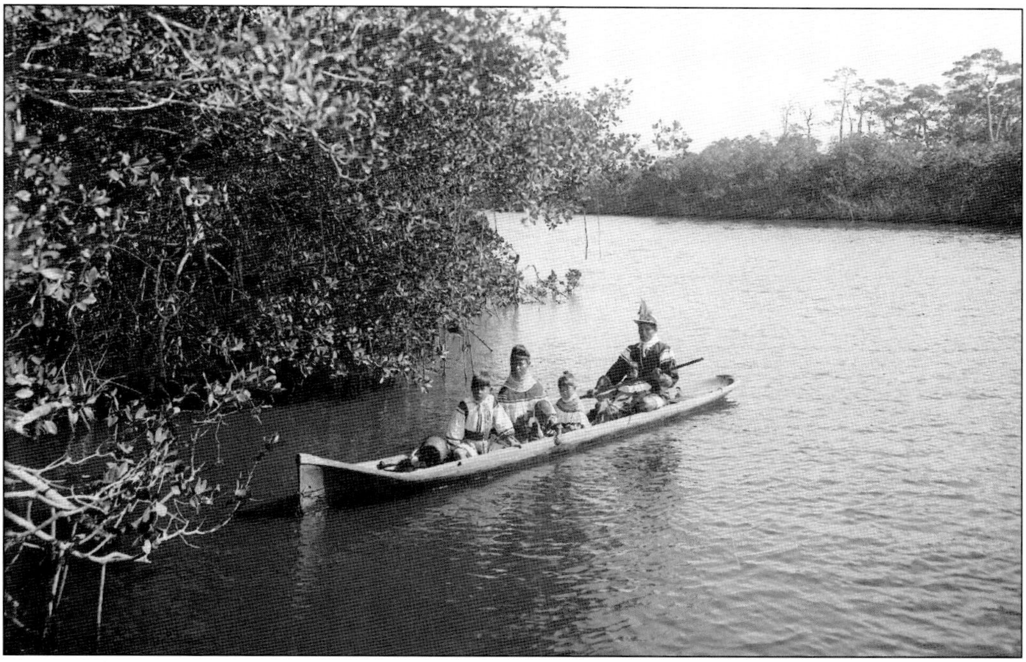

Historically, the Indigenous people and then pioneers accessed the Everglades by its coastal rivers, notably the Lostmans, Harney, Broad, Rodgers, Shark, Taylor, Miami, Little, Snake (now Oleta), and New Rivers. The image above from the early 1900s shows a Seminole family canoeing from the Everglades down the Miami River. The 1979 aerial image below shows dendritically interlacing, mangrove-lined rivers cutting through the marsh. Coastal rivers are estuarine environments; salinity varies seasonally. Water is fresher nearer the Everglades, especially in the high-water rainy season, and saltier toward the coast, especially in the low-water dry season. Tidal influence can extend well upriver, more so in the dry season. Freshwaters support large-mouth bass and alligators. Snook, tarpon, and crocodiles can deal with various salinities. Dolphins may occur throughout. In the winter, manatees travel up the rivers to warm water. (Above, LOC; below, NPS.)

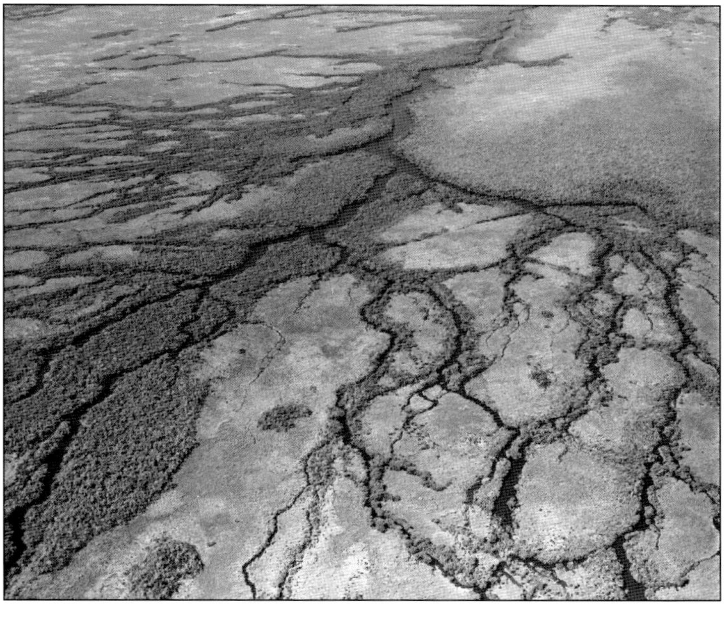

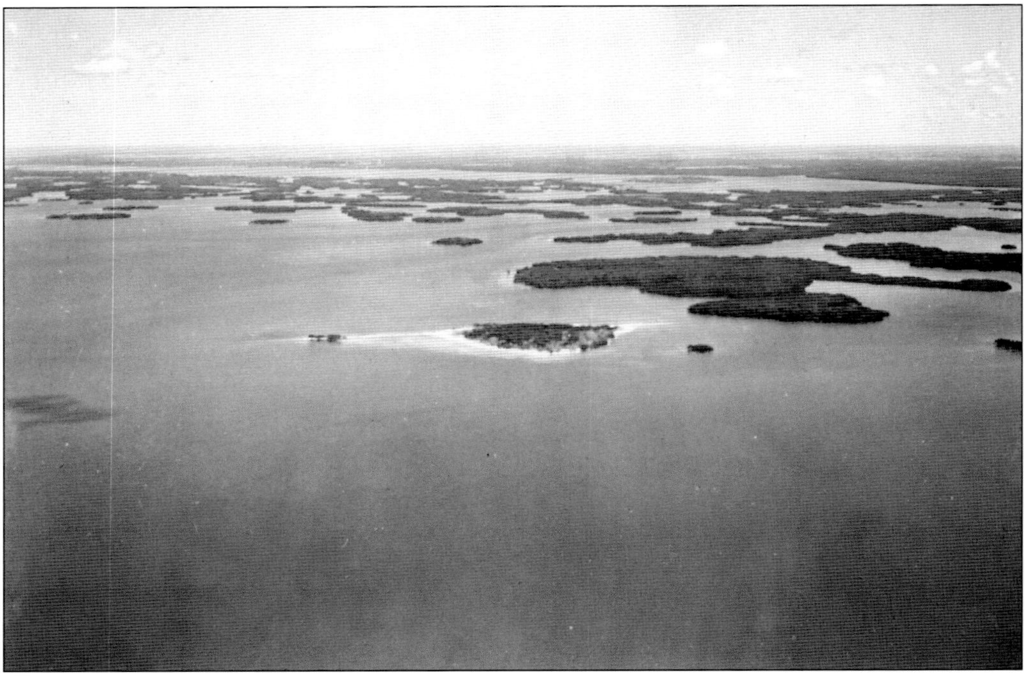

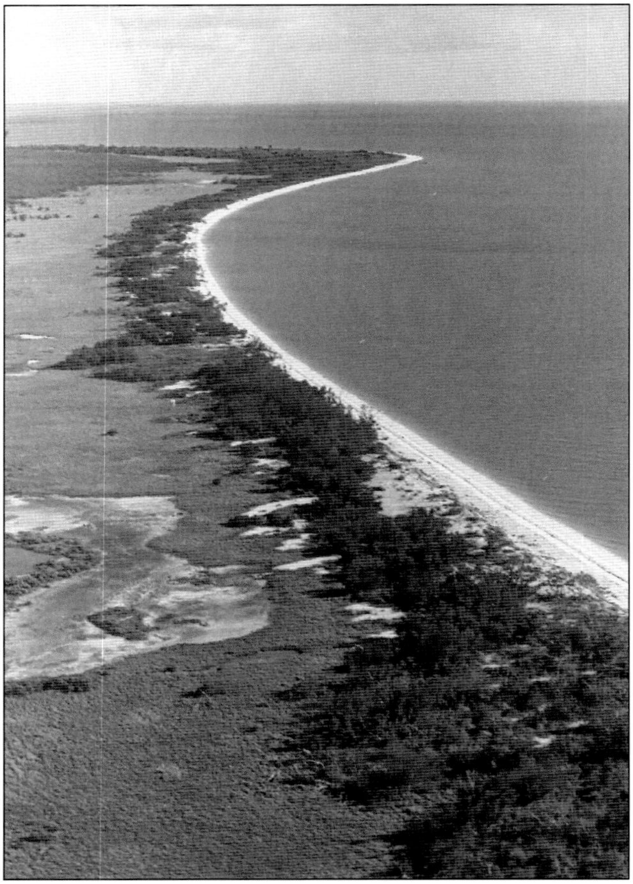

The Gulf Coast and Ten Thousand Islands have been a place of history and legends. This 1947 image provides an aerial view of islands, channels, and treacherous shallows between. Scattered mounds of shell and soil rising above the islands' peaty floors provided home sites for Indigenous people and then for pioneers. The Ten Thousand Islands Archeological District, listed in the National Register of Historic Places, includes over 70 such sites. (NPS.)

Cape Sable, where the shallows of Florida Bay meet the Gulf of Mexico, is the southernmost point of the US mainland. Its beachfront formed from the accretion of storm-built dunes. The cape was used by Indians, soldiers, pioneer settlers, plantation owners, and a plant introducer. It was once the dream of land developers. The cape's marl prairies were farmed by pioneers until hurricanes determined otherwise. (NPS.)

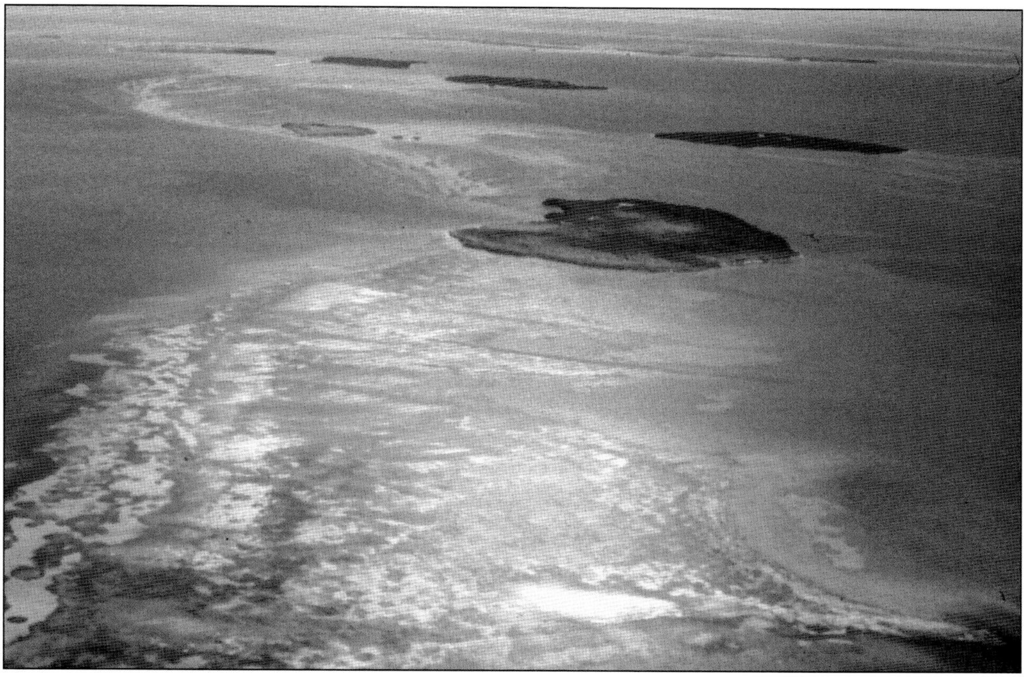

Florida Bay was included in the park to protect waterbird colonies and roosts on its islands. This late-1970s image shows its shallow banks, punctuated by low, mangrove-fringed islands. The banks divide the bay into basins supporting meadows of seagrass and also impede water circulation while evaporation raises salinity. Before drainage and development around the park, freshwater flowed into Florida Bay from the Everglades, especially through Taylor Slough. (NPS.)

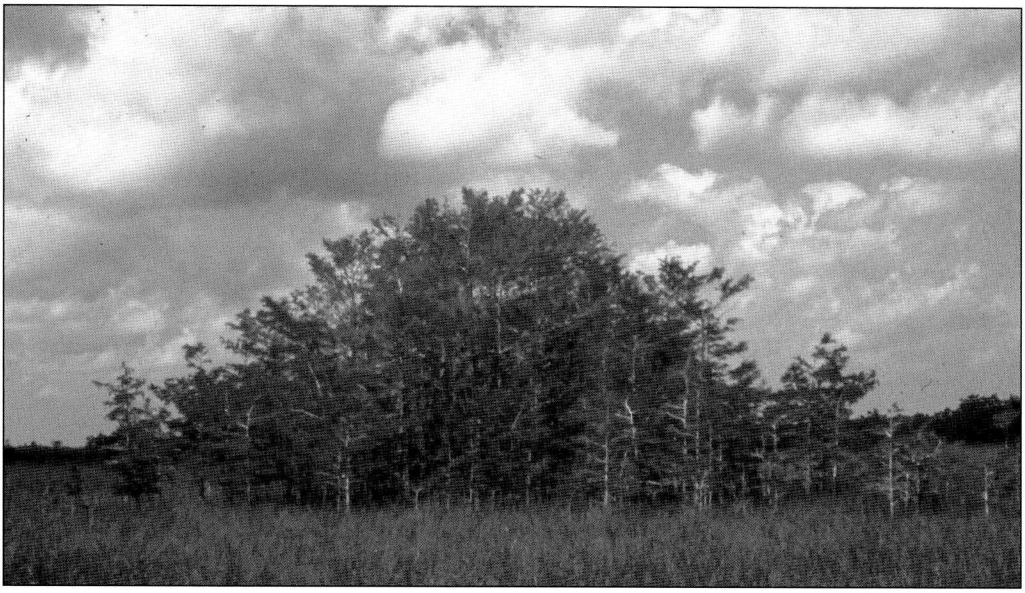

Forests of cypress trees edging the Everglades provided Indigenous people with building materials and their source of transportation, dugout canoes. Tree height depends on the depth of the soil. Much of the park's forest is composed of dwarf or scrub cypress trees. This image shows dwarf cypress in shallow soil in front of taller cypress growing in deeper soil, forming what is locally called a cypress head or dome. (NPS.)

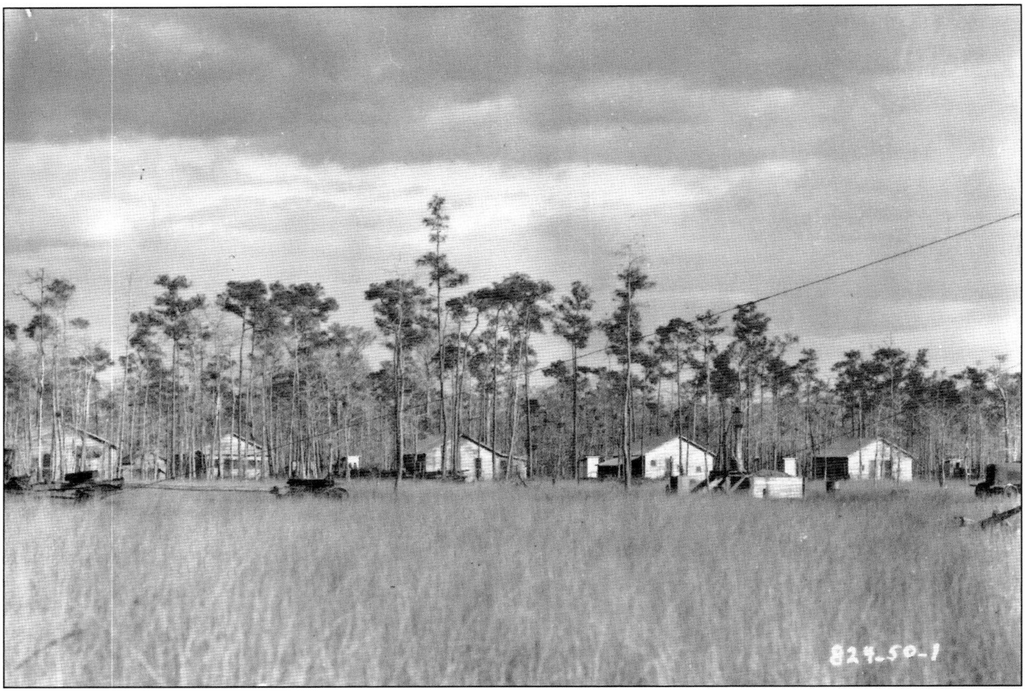

Long Pine Key is the westernmost extension of the pine-covered Atlantic Coastal Ridge, the elevated feature confining the Everglades on its east. Everglades National Park protects most remnants of these now endangered pine rocklands. Adapted to wet conditions, slash pine grew slowly. Locally called "Dade County Pine," it was hard, dense, termite-proof, nail-resistant, and heavily lumbered. This image shows the Clancy Lumber Company on Long Pine Key. (HM.)

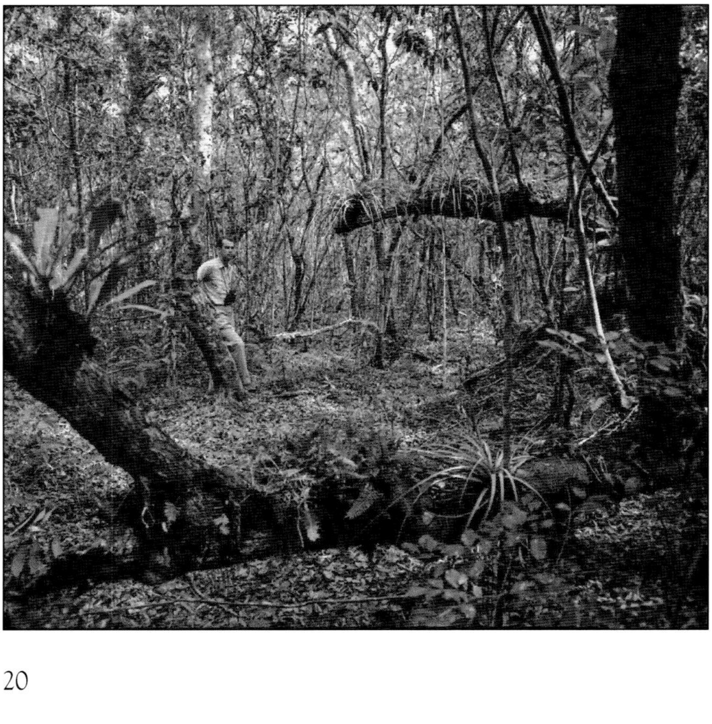

Patches of forest, called hammocks, are populated mostly by plants also found in the West Indies. Hammocks occur on elevations such as tree islands, within high pinelands, and along the coast. This image, with a man for scale, shows a hammock's dense interior. Ferns and bromeliads grow on the tree branches. Typical plants have such exotic names as gumbo limbo, mastic, cocoplum, mahogany, royal palm, and paurotis palm. (NPS.)

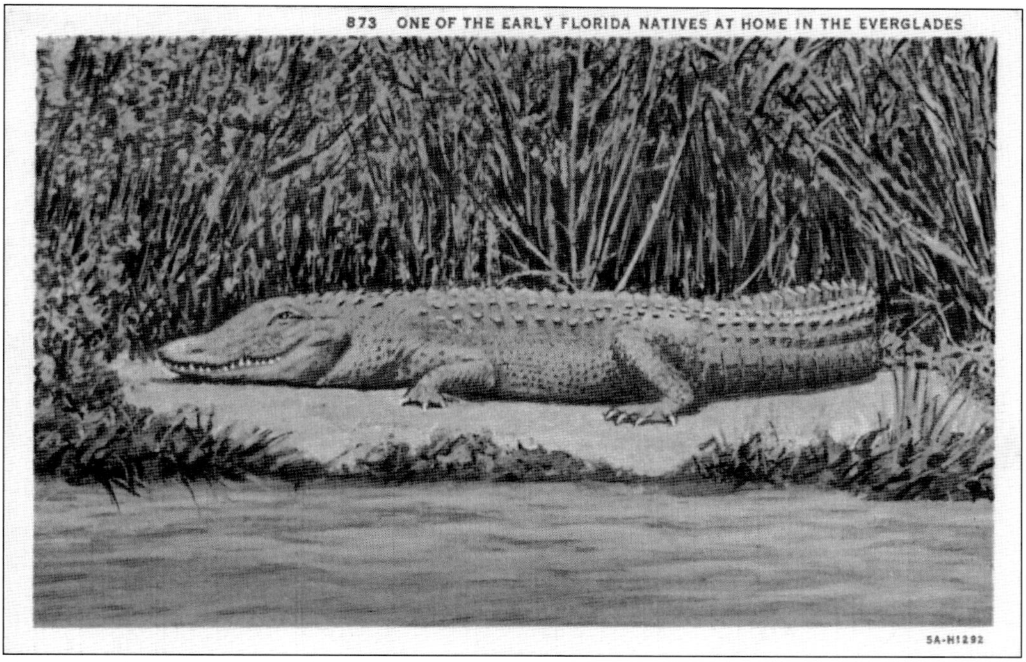

A creature (and caricature) of tourist postcards, the American alligator has always been the park's most popular attraction. During drying season, these large, ancient-looking reptiles gather at pools near visitor viewing sites. The drying season is also when their natural ponds serve their vital ecological function. When the park was established, alligators were still being hunted for their hides. The new park's enforcement was instrumental in protecting them. (SLAF.)

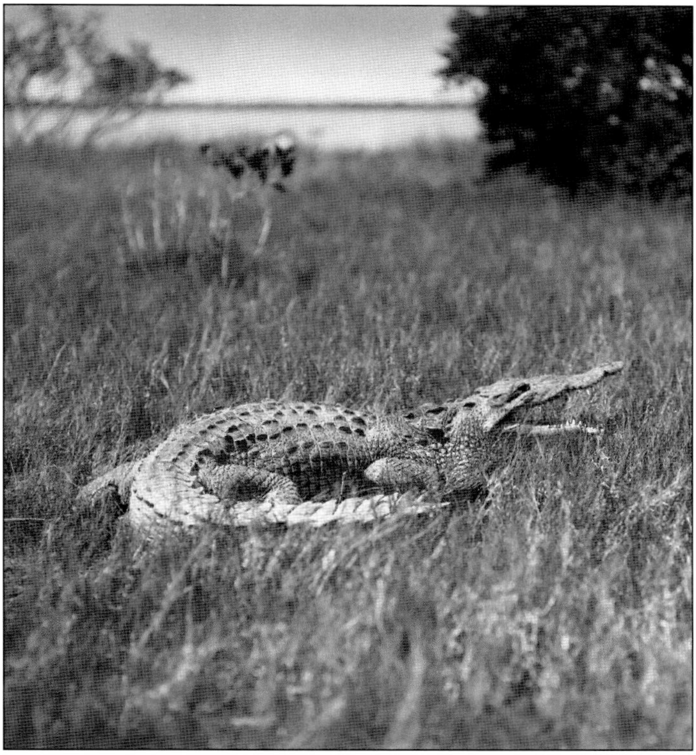

Everglades National Park protects another crocodilian, the American crocodile, a tropical species occurring in North America only in extreme South Florida. This 1905 photograph was taken by Julian Dimock near Little Madeira Bay off Florida Bay. The crocodile was captured for the Bronx Zoo and was shipped there from Key West. Crocodiles are marine and estuarine animals occurring in the mangrove swamps and coastal lagoons of the park. (AMNH.)

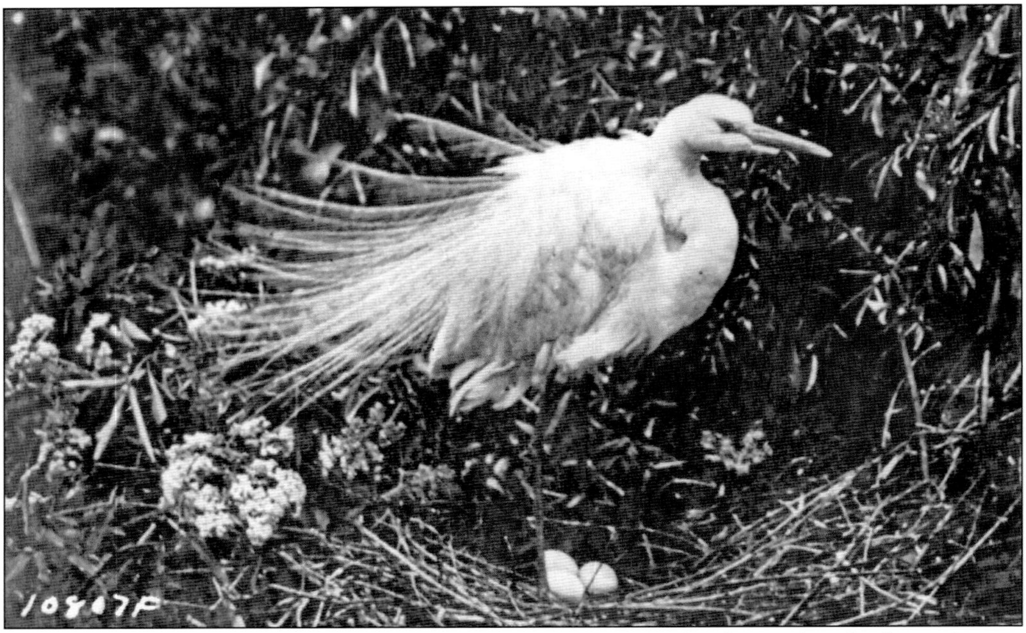

By the time Everglades National Park was established, South Florida's wading bird populations had been severely reduced from plume hunting followed by effects of drainage. During the plume hunting era, a primary target was the great egret—known then as the American egret and called the "long white" by hunters after its long, frilly courtship plumes—shown in this 1929 image. Snowy egrets were called "short whites." (HM.)

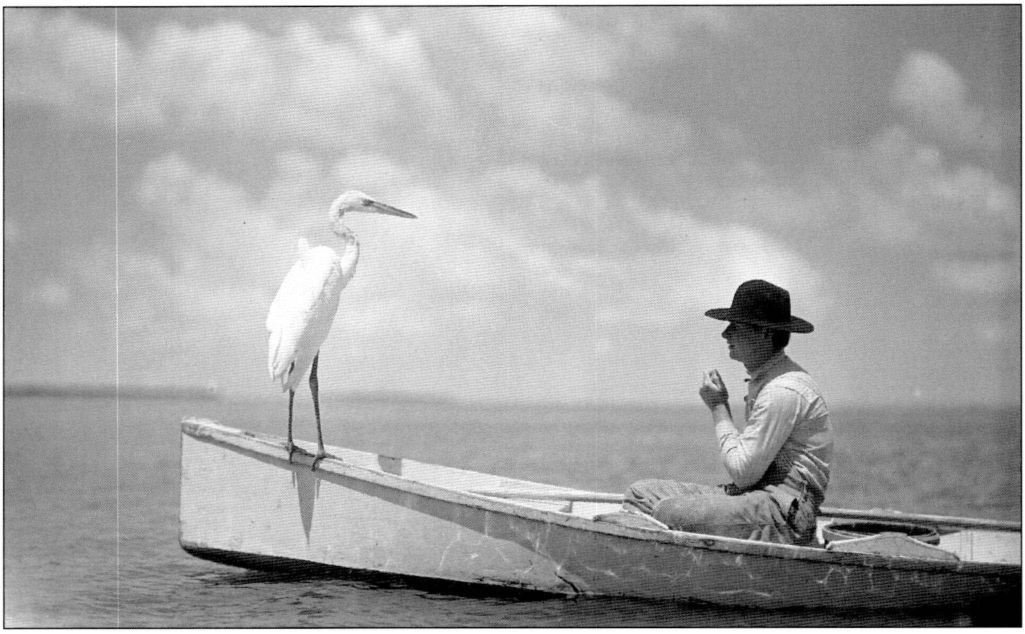

The great white heron was discovered for science in 1832 by John James Audubon in Florida Bay, now part of Everglades National Park. This 1906 image shows the size of this huge bird. Historically, within North America, it occurred almost entirely in Everglades National Park and the nearby lower Florida Keys. It feeds on the flooded flats of the bay and is now considered globally endangered. (AMNH.)

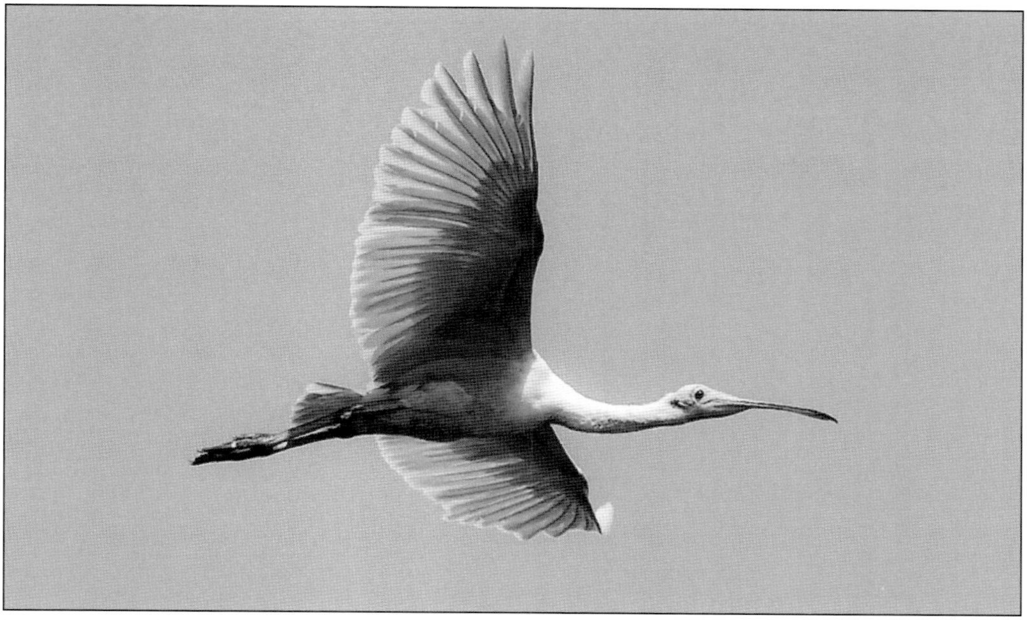

Roseate spoonbill feathers, like egret feathers, were sought after by hunters, who called them pink curlew. The spoonbill uses its remarkably flattened bill to catch fish by waving it from side to side in the water. It historically nested on Florida Bay islands and fed on marine flats and along the mangroves. The American flamingo, another pink bird, also historically seasonally frequented what is now the park. (NPS.)

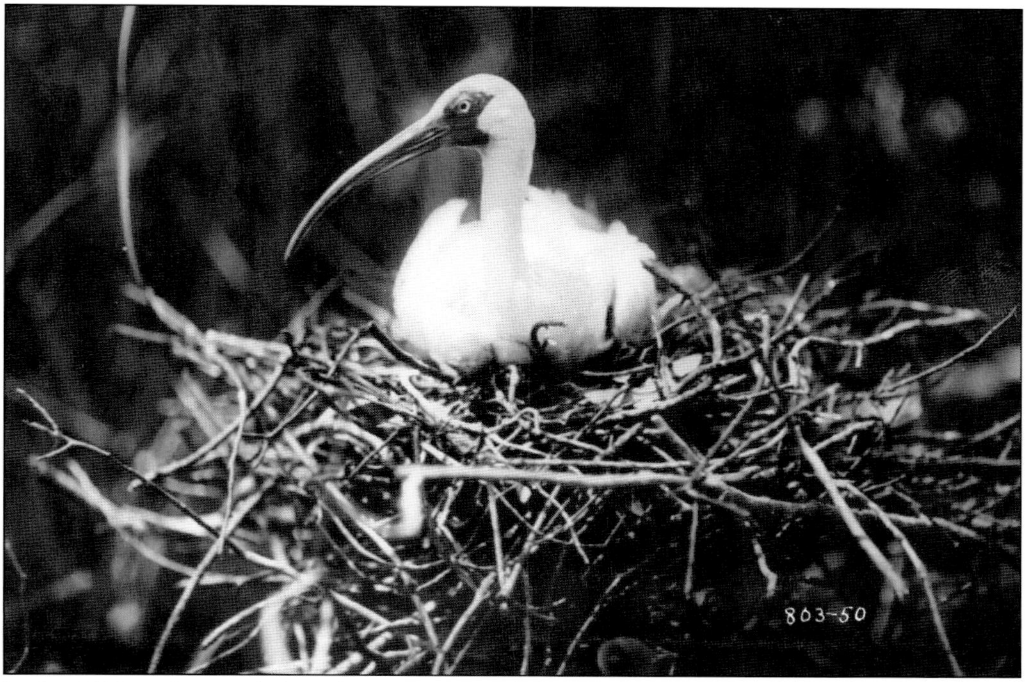

In the 1930s, colonies of white ibis were reported numbering in the tens of thousands. This 1933 photograph shows an adult white ibis sitting on its nest. The long bill is used to probe in the water and mud for food. Unlike egrets, ibises were not hunted for plumes but rather for food. Called curlew by locals, it is said that residents also referred to them as "Chokoloskee Chicken." (HM.)

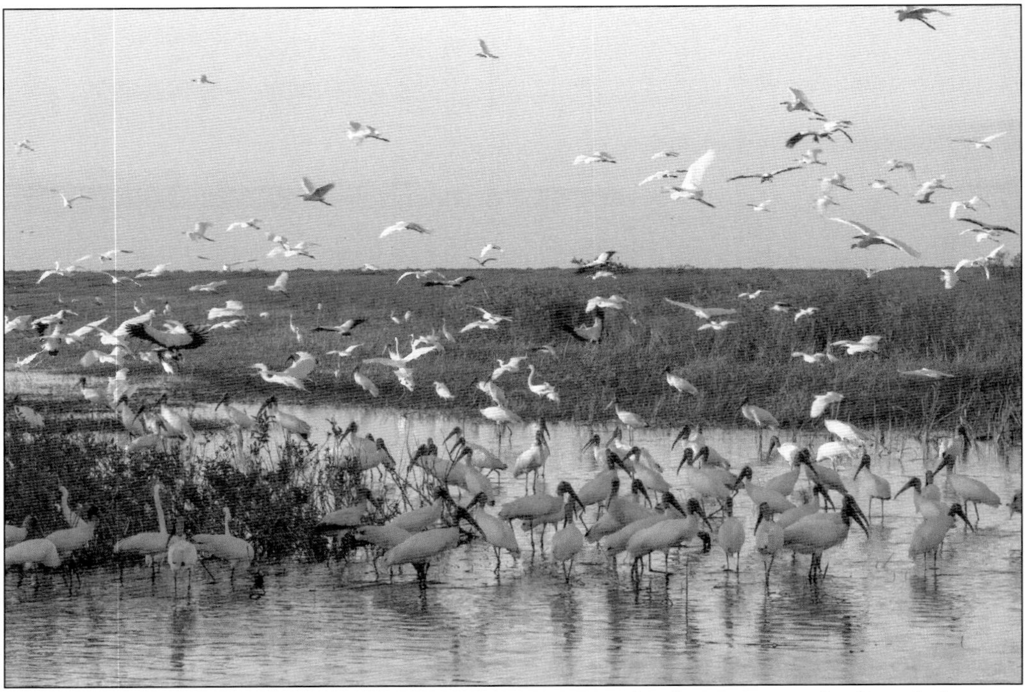

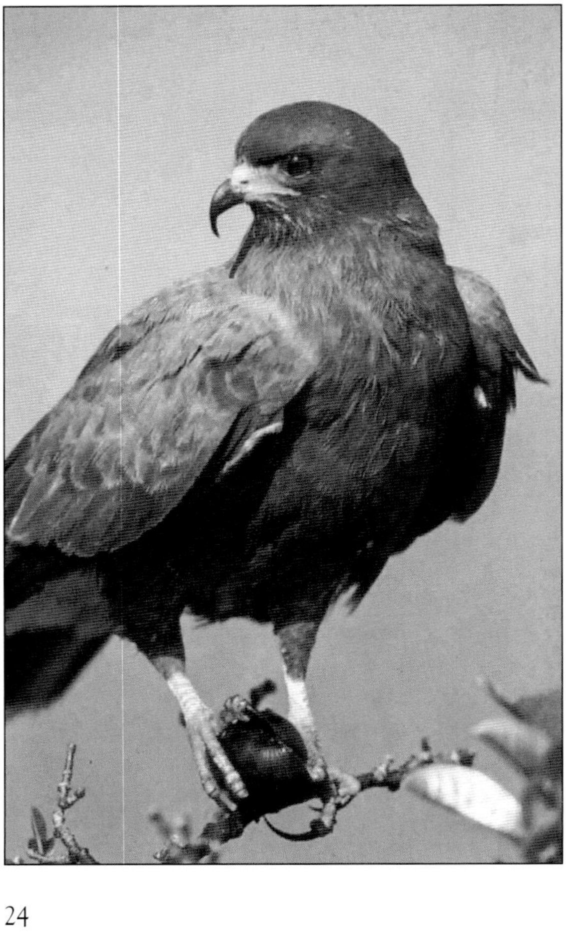

In the dry season in the Everglades, herons, egrets, ibis, storks, and spoonbills all gather to feed together in impressive aggregations. As water levels decrease in the drying season, fish and other aquatic animals become concentrated in drying pools where these birds assemble to feed on them. Such prey concentrations, dependent on the natural seasonal fluctuation of Everglades waters, are required for the perpetuation of its wildlife. (KH.)

The Everglades has a hawk that eats snails. The snail kite, historically called the Everglade kite, is a tropical bird that feeds entirely on large aquatic mollusks, called apple snails. It hovers over the marsh to grab the snail with its talons and then takes it to a perch where it uses its long, thin, curved bill to extract the snail from its shell. (NPS.)

The Cape Sable seaside sparrow occurs almost entirely within Everglades National Park. It was discovered for science in 1918, as its name suggests, on Cape Sable. This bird's habitat lies on slightly higher ground on either side of the southern Everglades. It remains a controversial concern because water management practices can flood its habitat in the dry season, keeping it from nesting successfully. (NPSLO.)

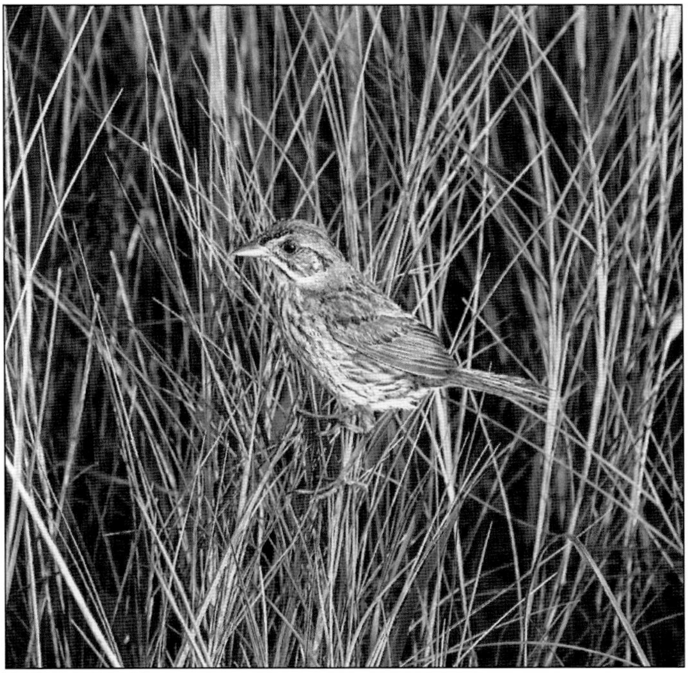

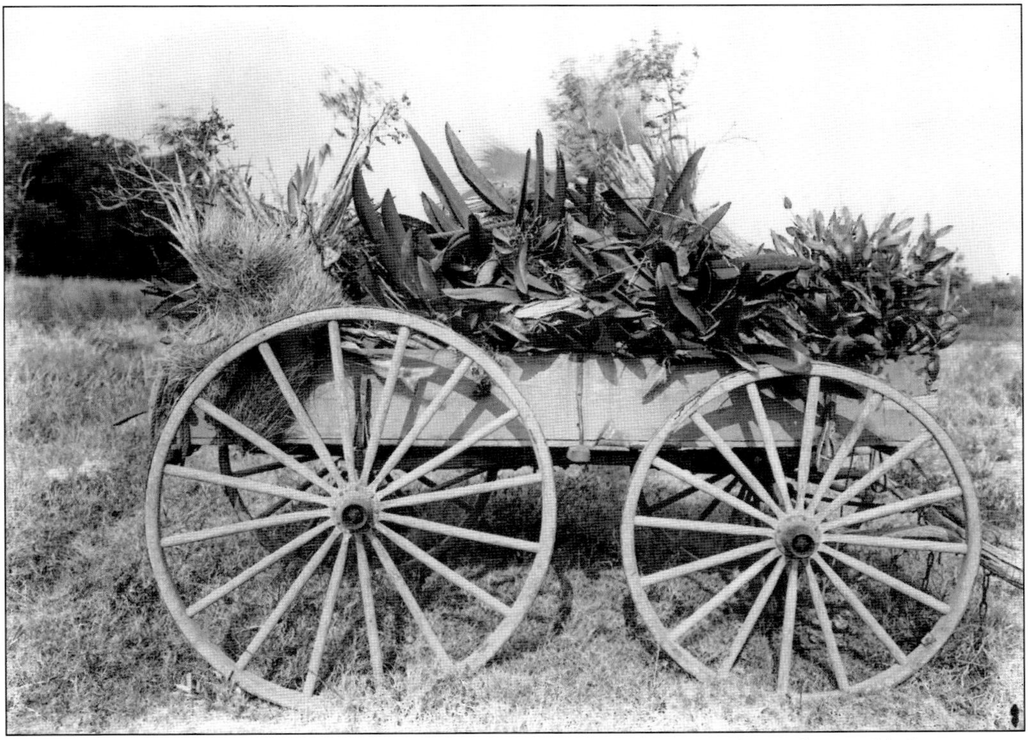

Egrets were not the only resource once threatened by hunting prior to the park's establishment—so were plants. Orchids, bromeliads (sometimes called air plants), ferns, lichens, and other tropical plants were the quarry of plant collectors, naturalists, and nurseries. This 1916 image shows wagonloads of orchids being hauled out of the Flamingo Prairie. Such massive collecting seriously depleted natural populations. (SLAF.)

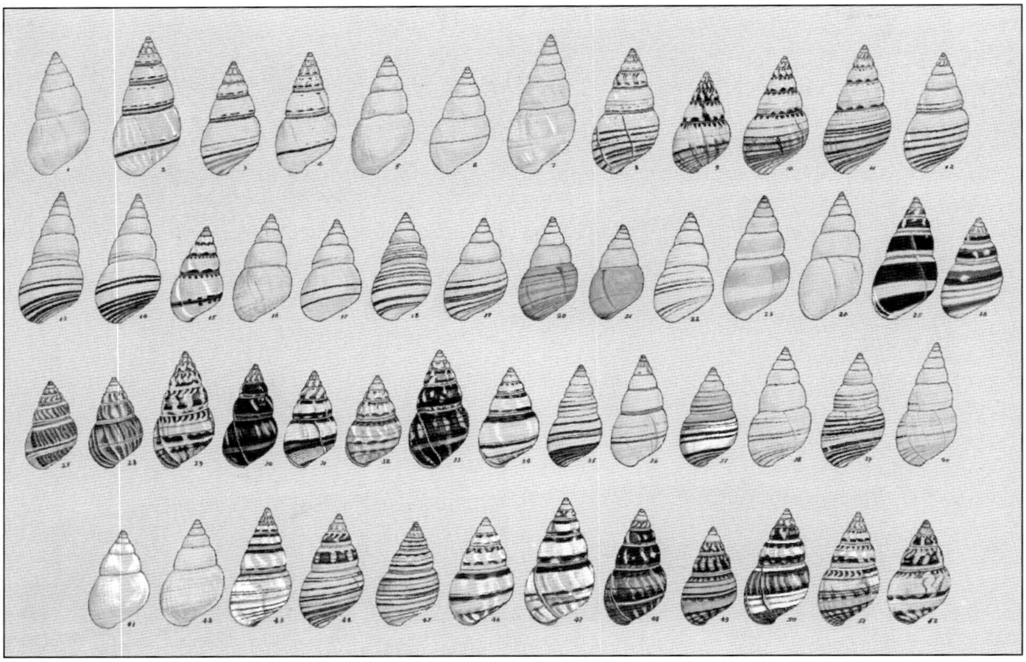

Tree snails, having remarkably diverse shell coloration, were the gems of South Florida hammocks. Liguus, or "lig," populations were decimated by collectors, and most of their hammocks were destroyed by fire, drainage, and development. To save them, color forms were introduced into the park by early ranger Erwin Winte and collaborators. This plate is by outstanding biological illustrator and painter Richard Deckert. (NPS.)

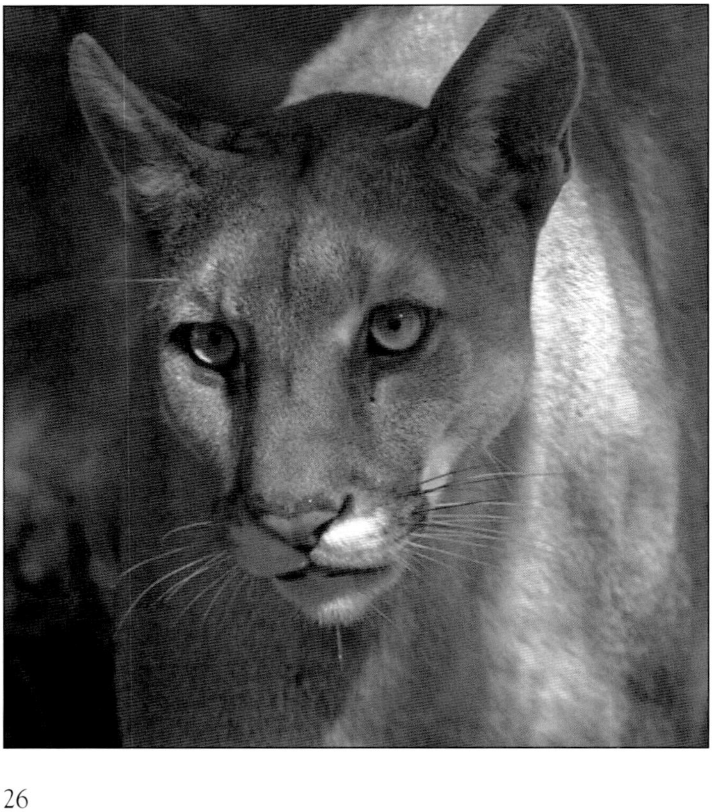

The Florida panther is an animal deeply ingrained into South Florida's history in both Seminole culture and pioneer tales. Called *coowahchobe* in Mikasuki, the panther was chosen to be the first animal to walk the earth and its clan was granted possession of knowledge and leadership. An endangered species and the Florida state mammal, it has greatly benefitted from the security of the park and nearby protected areas. (NPS.)

Two

Native Peoples of the Everglades

The Indigenous people of what is now the Everglades arrived 10,000–12,000 years ago, gradually changing culturally in tandem with their similarly changing post-glacial environment. By about 2,500 years ago, they were developing into geographically distinct nations led by chiefs. Not needing to farm, they instead lived off the land and waters, creating nearly unprecedented sophisticated hunter-fisher-gatherer cultures. Five centuries ago, at the time of European contact, the people of the Everglades, called Tequesta and Muspa by the Spanish, lived primarily along the coast but also made use of the Everglades, its tree islands, and its food resources. Geographic isolation, persistent resistance to engagement, and rejecting the Spanish desire that they farm their missions, allowed the people to maintain their separateness over the Spanish centuries. But inevitably, populations declined, and many of those remaining left Florida before the British took over. From the 1760s into the 1830s, for the first time ever, no one is known to have lived in or around the Everglades.

Welcomed by the colonial governments, southeastern Indians, who eventually came to be known as Seminoles, began settling in northern Florida in the 1700s, and were a presence in South Florida as well. But for 40 years starting in 1818, the American military campaigned against them, including through the Everglades and Big Cypress Swamp. Facing relentless American pressure, most ended up being removed to the West, but the few who successfully resisted remained in the southern Florida wetlands. Adapted to a new lifestyle, they lived in small group camps on patches of high ground, including on tree islands in the Everglades. Meanwhile, settlers occupied the coasts, and a city grew in Key West. By the late 19th century, native people of the Everglades began engaging in the nearby economy, traveling by canoe from their camps to trading posts. But they also faced increasing challenges as settlers moved inland, rifle-bearing hunters killed the wildlife, the plume trade ended, wildlife laws were passed, drainage took away the water, and Tamiami Trail opened. In 1961, many of the Indians living in the southern Everglades gained federal government recognition as the Miccosukee Tribe of Indians of Florida. Others were recognized as the Seminole Tribe of Florida; some never accepted government recognition.

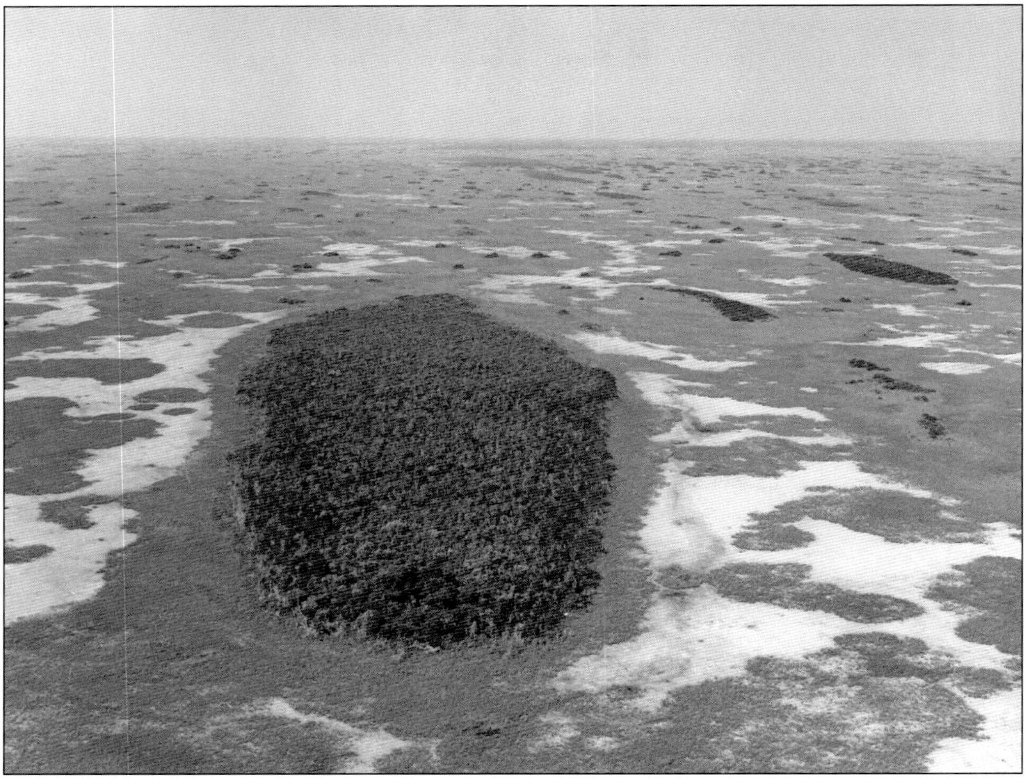

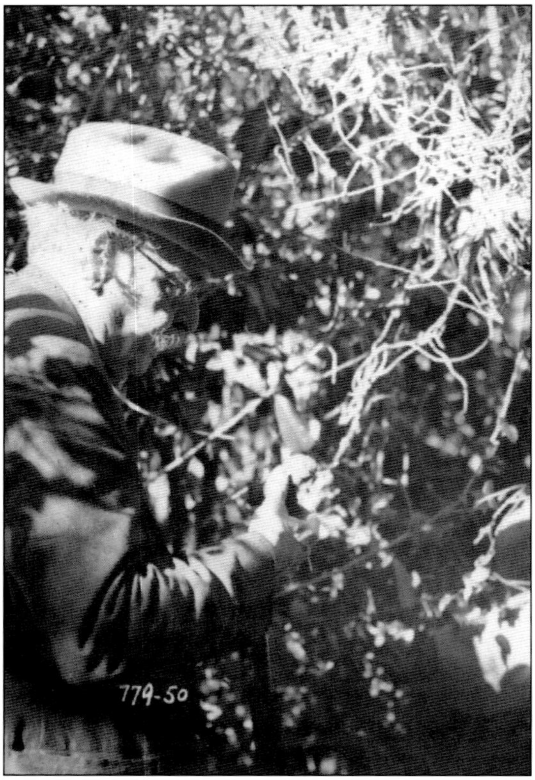

The high-ground sites used by the Indigenous peoples were built up with shells, sand, soil, and refuse into mounds. Their use of Everglades tree islands even predated deposition of the upper layers of limestone. Panther Mound, seen above in the 1960s is a large historically occupied tree island. Bear Lake mound complex dates back over 1,500 years. The 1932 image at left shows archeologist Carlos de la Torre examining pottery from the mounds, which adjoin an indigenous canal almost 4 miles long and 20 feet wide that provided a shortcut around Cape Sable. The Canepatch site on Shark River is listed in the National Register of Historic Places. Sites used by Indigenous people along the Gulf Coast include Chatham Bend, Camp Lonesome on Broad River, and Onion Key. Turner River shell mounds were a population center dating back over 2,000 years. (Above, NPS; left, HM.)

South Florida's soft limestone did not provide stone hard enough for tools, so Indigenous people used materials such as shell, bone, shark teeth, and stingray spines. They manufactured pottery (right), baskets, fabric, ornaments (below), nets, hooks, spears, and net weights. Axes made of conch shell, traded as far as the Midwest, were as good as ones made of chert. Remains at the Panther Mound and Bear Lake archeological sites reveal that they gathered seasonal fruit of tropical plants, such as mastic, hog plum, cocoplum, seagrape, and palms. Tubers were ground into flour. In the Everglades, they caught bowfin, gar, catfish, sunfish, turtles, and snakes. At Bear Lake, they secured an evolving mostly marine diet of sea catfish, jacks, sharks, rays, sea turtles, and mollusks, including oysters, clams, conchs, and whelks. (Both, NPS.)

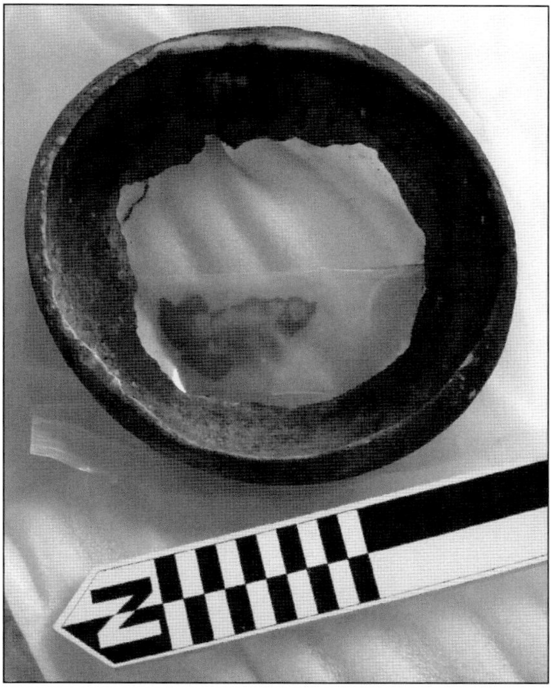

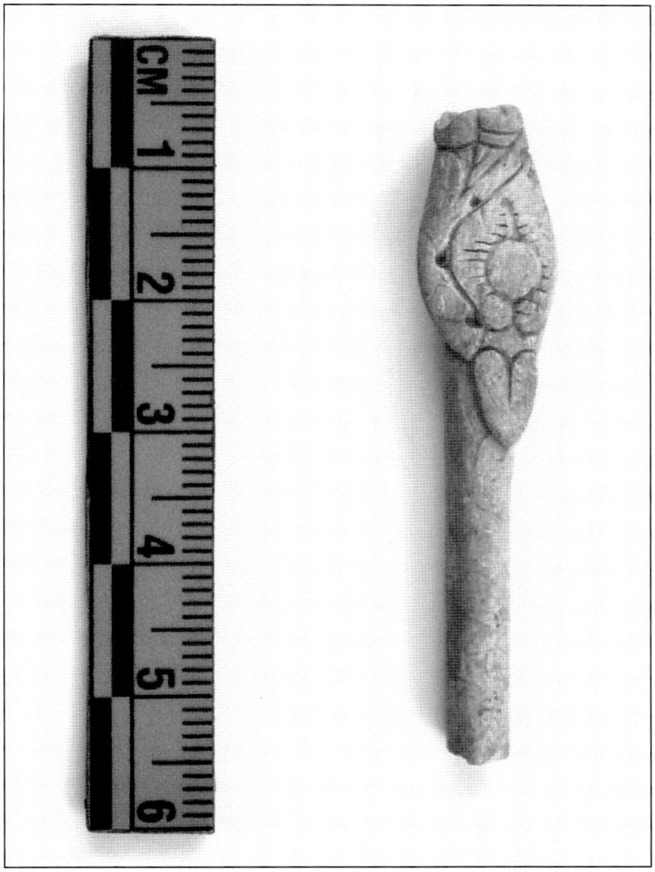

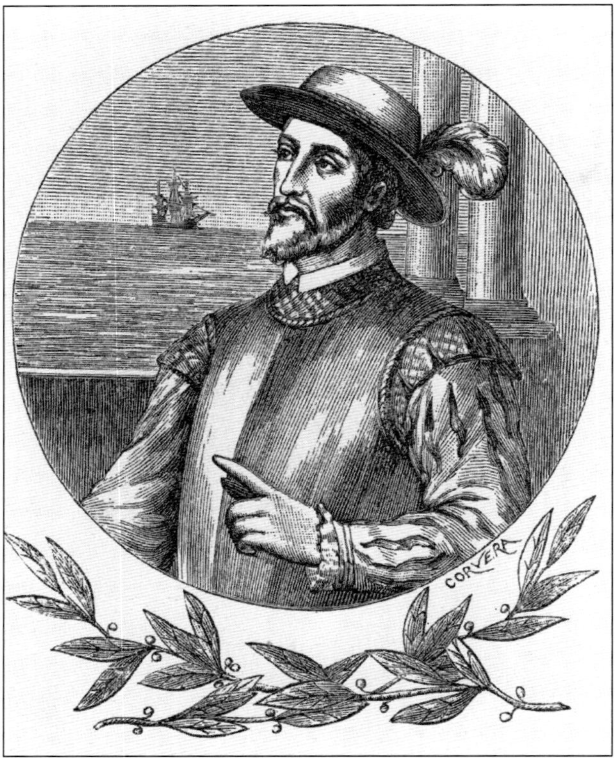

South Florida's Indigenous people were first officially contacted by Europeans in 1513, by Juan Ponce de León in Biscayne Bay and along the Gulf Coast. In the process, he discovered freshwater outflows of the Everglades including Shark River drainage emptying into the bay that today bears his name. Ponce de León's contacts were not peaceful. Returning a decade later, he was repelled from southwestern Florida, fatally. (SLAF.)

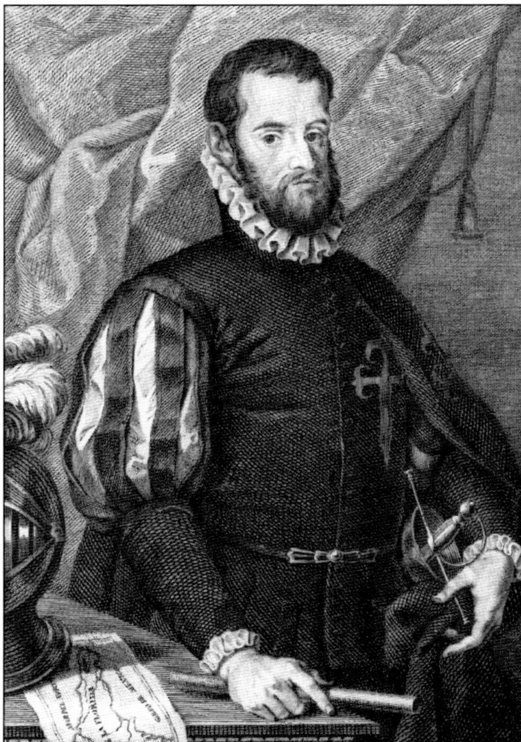

In the 1560s, the Tequesta were engaged by Pedro Menéndez de Avilés, whose attempt to place a mission and fort near the Everglades on the Miami River failed. After that, the Spanish kept their attention focused on North Florida while South Florida's Indigenous people kept to their relative isolation. Over time, however, populations declined. In 1763, the British, allied with more northern Indian tribes, took over. (LOC.)

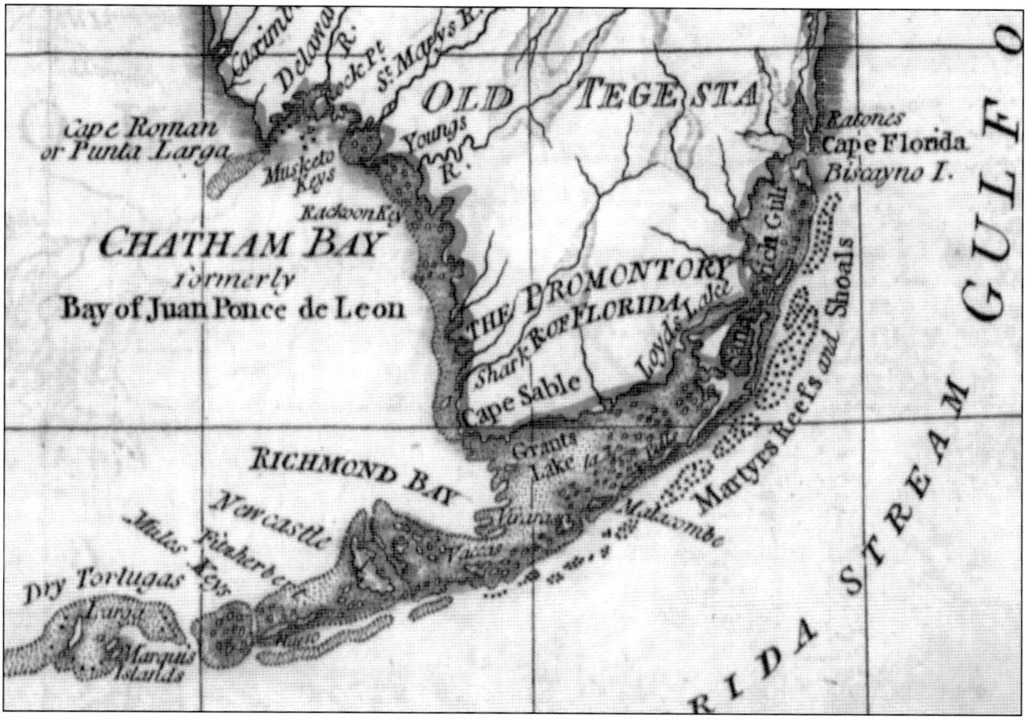

After Spain relinquished Florida to Great Britain, her surveyors were set to work. This 1776 map by Bernard Romans is one result. The surveyors found that there were no people living in South Florida. Evidence of thousands of years of human culture was quickly reclaimed by the environment. Britain and Spain, 20 years later when it regained Florida, encouraged Indian tribes from north of Florida to settle there. (LOC.)

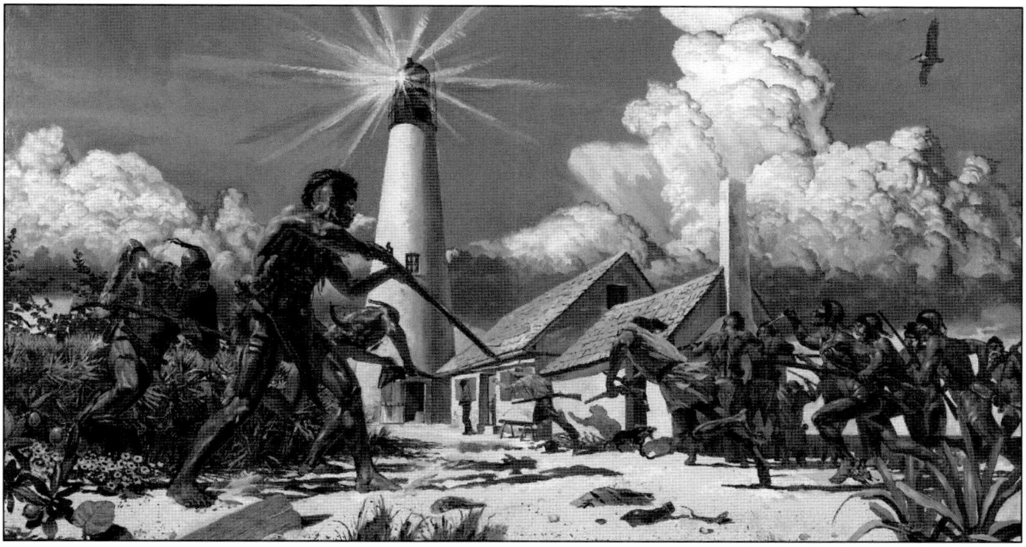

The United States acquired Florida in 1821. For the first time, non-Indigenous people began residing permanently near the Everglades. The American policy of Indian removal and allowing repeated encroachment into treaty lands forced Seminole groups south into the Everglades and Big Cypress. In 1836, Everglades-based Seminoles successfully attacked the nearby symbol of the government's presence near the Everglades, the lighthouse on Key Biscayne. (HM.)

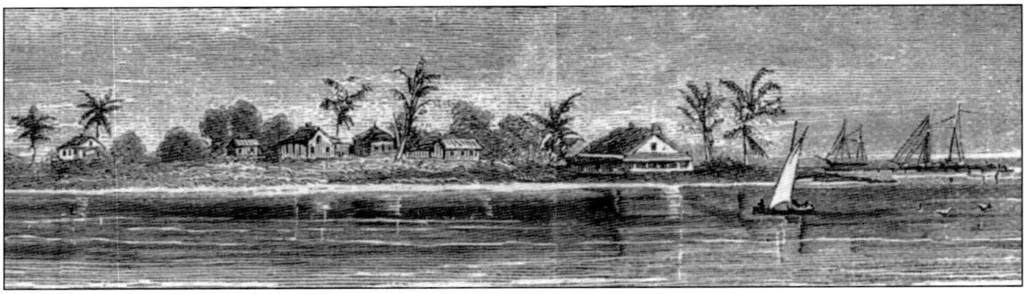

In 1840, war leader Chekika led a raid on the American settlement nearest the Everglades, the wrecker town on Indian Key. Among its results was the death of Henry Perrine, who was waiting for the war's end to insert white American farming settlements on Cape Sable. After the successful attack, the Indians returned to the Everglades. This drawing of Indian Key is from 1872. (MCPL.)

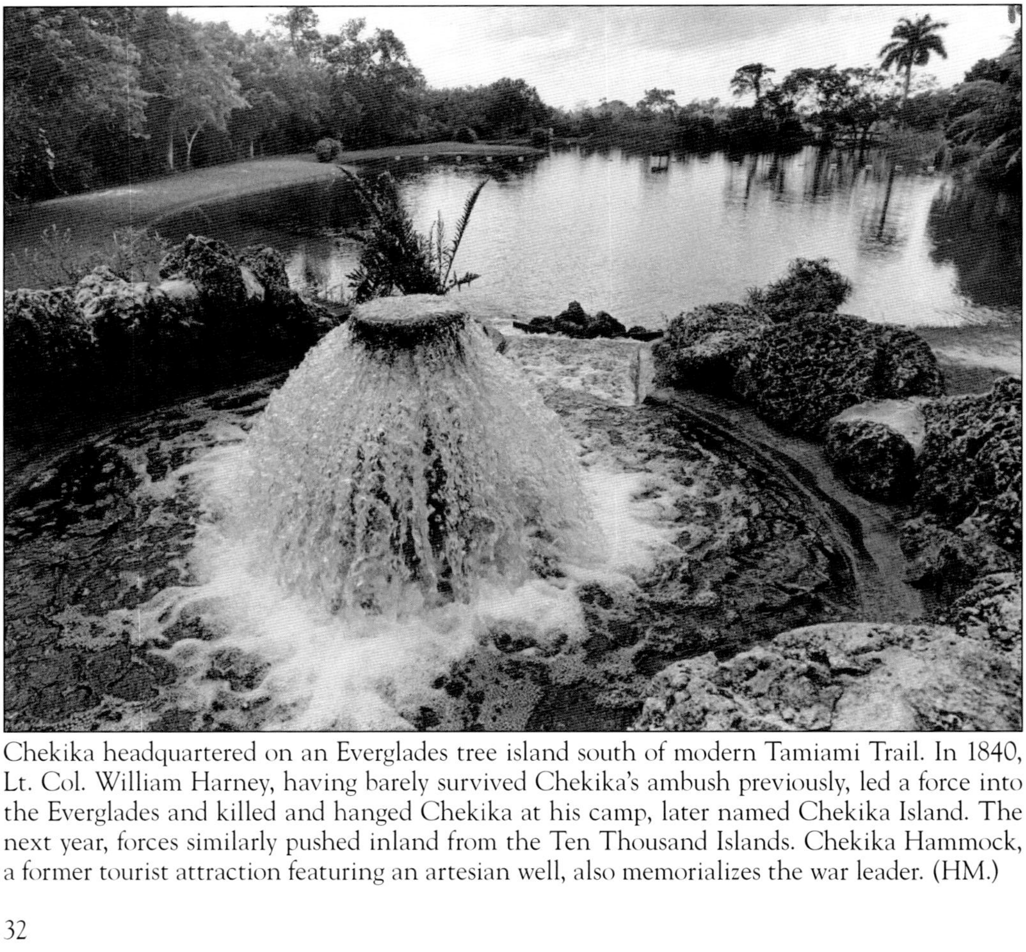

Chekika headquartered on an Everglades tree island south of modern Tamiami Trail. In 1840, Lt. Col. William Harney, having barely survived Chekika's ambush previously, led a force into the Everglades and killed and hanged Chekika at his camp, later named Chekika Island. The next year, forces similarly pushed inland from the Ten Thousand Islands. Chekika Hammock, a former tourist attraction featuring an artesian well, also memorializes the war leader. (HM.)

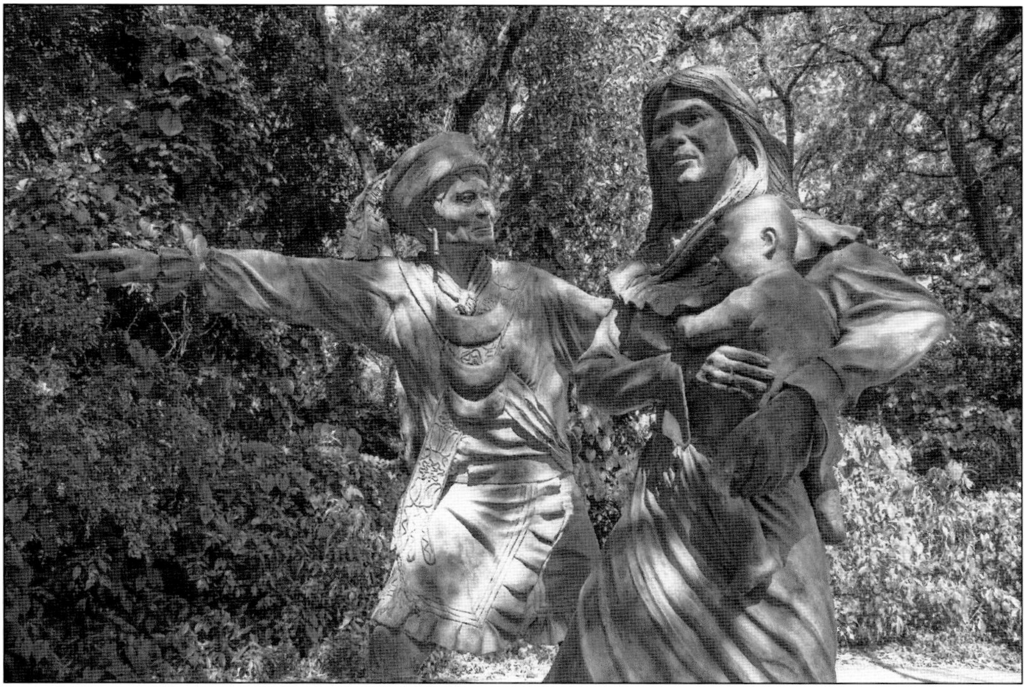

Abiaka (Abiaki, Arpiucki, or Sam Jones) was a respected Seminole spiritual leader. He defeated Zachary Taylor at the Battle of Okeechobee and outwitted Maj. William Lauderdale at the Battle of Pine Island Ridge, Abiaka's Everglades village. Abiaka outlived the wars, defied removal from South Florida, and is credited with saving his people, as depicted by this 1995 statue installed at the site that previously was his Everglades village. (KH.)

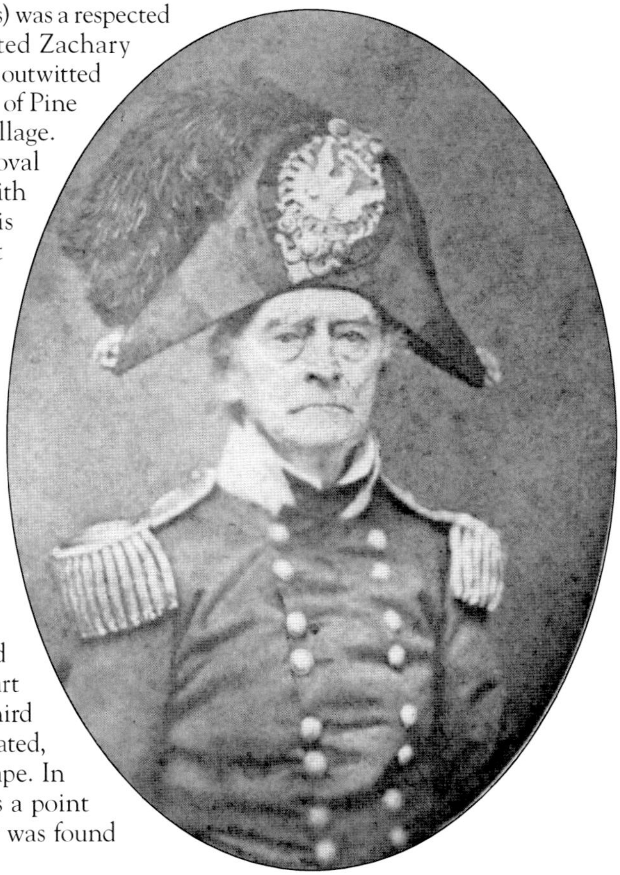

The military built temporary forts. Gen. Thomas Lawson, understanding the military importance of Cape Sable, established Ft. Poinsett, made of sand and sticks, on East Cape in 1838 to thwart Cuban arms smuggling. During the Third Seminole War, Ft. Poinsett was reactivated, and Ft. Cross was built on Middle Cape. In the 1850s, Ft. Poinsett's location was a point for coastal mapping; a survey marker was found in 2007. (USNLM.)

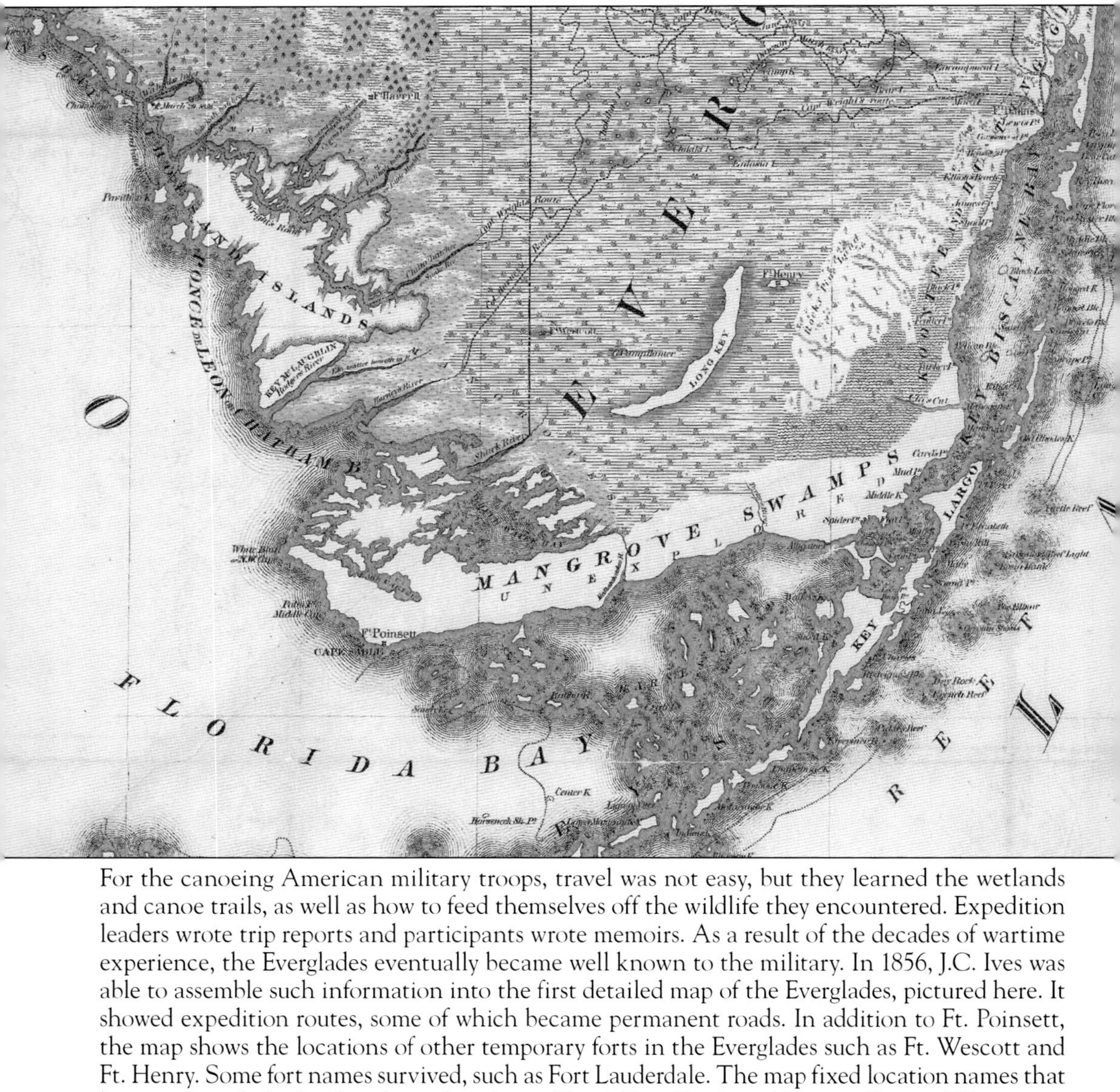

For the canoeing American military troops, travel was not easy, but they learned the wetlands and canoe trails, as well as how to feed themselves off the wildlife they encountered. Expedition leaders wrote trip reports and participants wrote memoirs. As a result of the decades of wartime experience, the Everglades eventually became well known to the military. In 1856, J.C. Ives was able to assemble such information into the first detailed map of the Everglades, pictured here. It showed expedition routes, some of which became permanent roads. In addition to Ft. Poinsett, the map shows the locations of other temporary forts in the Everglades such as Ft. Wescott and Ft. Henry. Some fort names survived, such as Fort Lauderdale. The map fixed location names that became Everglades landmarks such as Long (Pine) Key, Shark and Harney Rivers, Whitewater Bay, Cape Sable, Sandy Key, (Ten) Thousand Islands, Pavilion Key, and Chichiki (Chekika) Island. The Everglades was no longer unknown nor impenetrable. (USNA.)

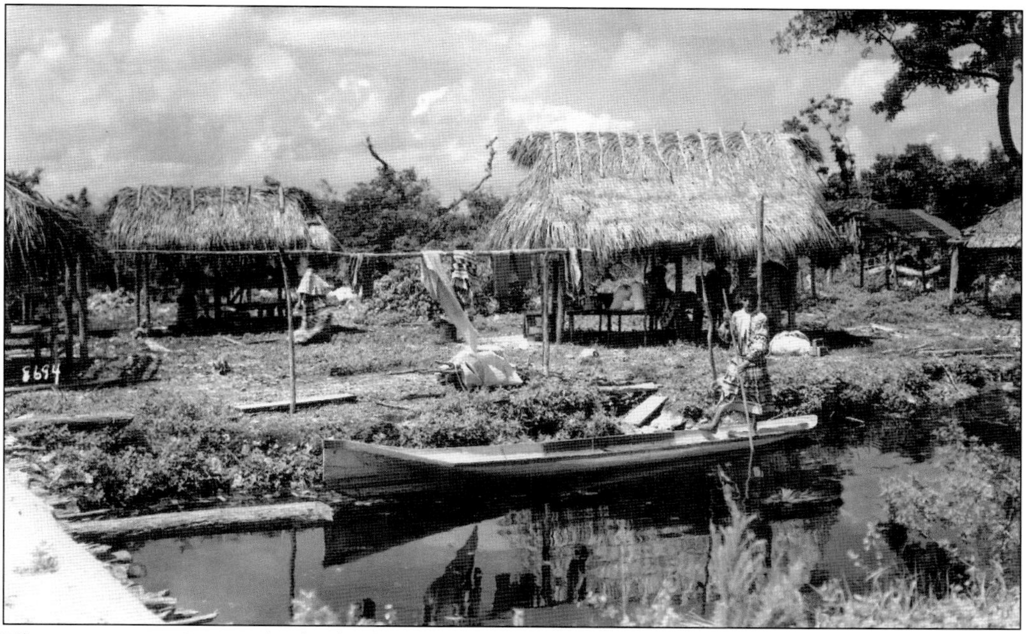

The remaining Seminoles had adapted by living in small independent family-based camps, choosing to keep themselves apart while the Civil War raged and pioneers settled the coast. Such family camps were scattered through the Everglades (above). They fished by bow-and-arrow and spear for gar, catfish, and bass and hunted by bow-and-arrow and gun for deer, alligator, and birds. The image below shows a 1915 hunting party along Shark River. They gathered fruit such as pond apple, cocoplum, and palms, collected medicinal plants, harvested cypress, and grew garden crops such as pumpkin, bananas, and corn. As years passed and the increasing presence of settlers and competition for game made independent subsistence difficult, they engaged with the new economic realities through trading posts established on canoe-navigable waterways as early as the 1870s. (Above, HM; below, MDPLS.)

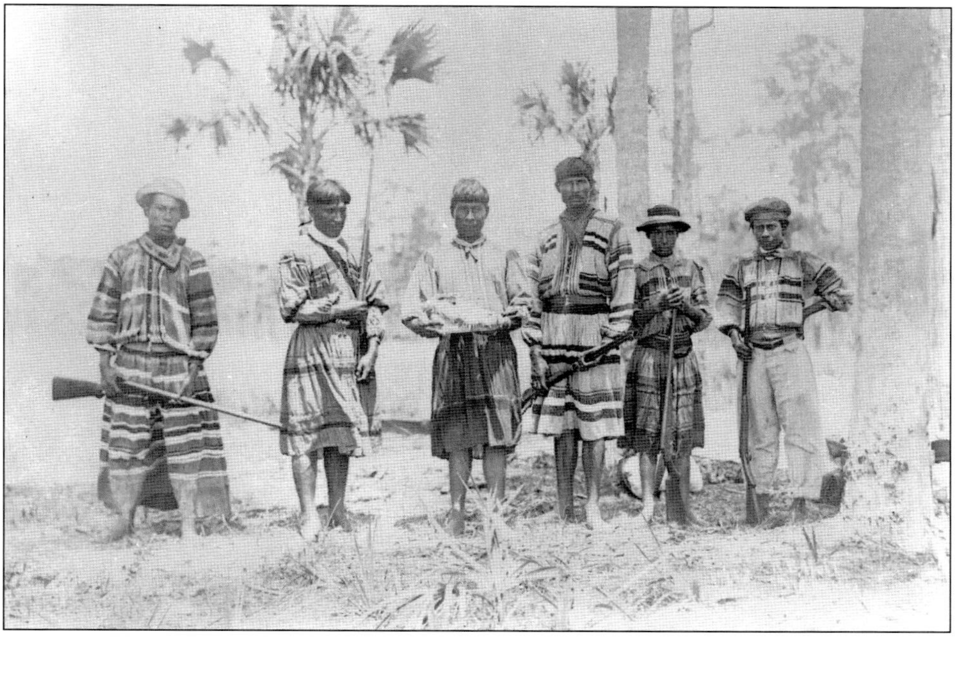

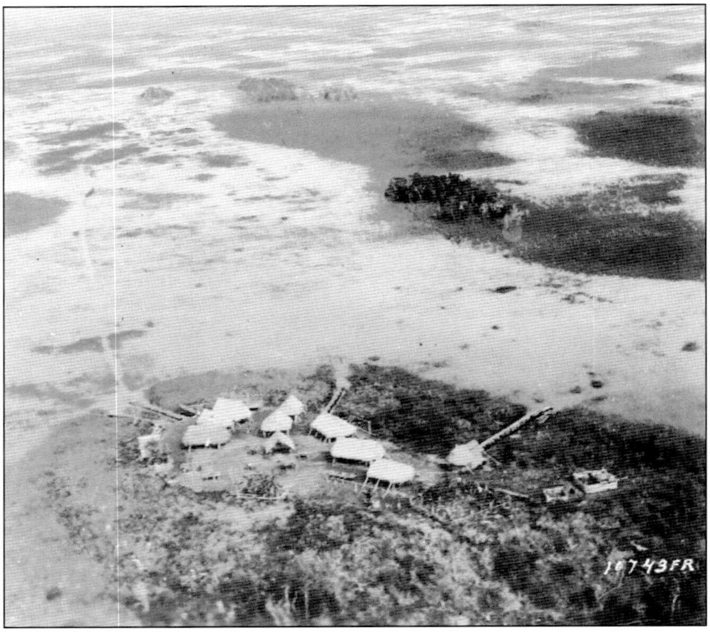

An Everglades camp was a cluster of structures on high ground, generally on a tree island, as shown in this 1929 photograph taken from a blimp. Travel was not easy. Canoes remained the principal wet season transportation for decades, until the development of airboats. The dry season required walking. Homes were open or partially enclosed cypress-framed, palm-thatched structures called "chickees," from the concept of a place where people live. (HM.)

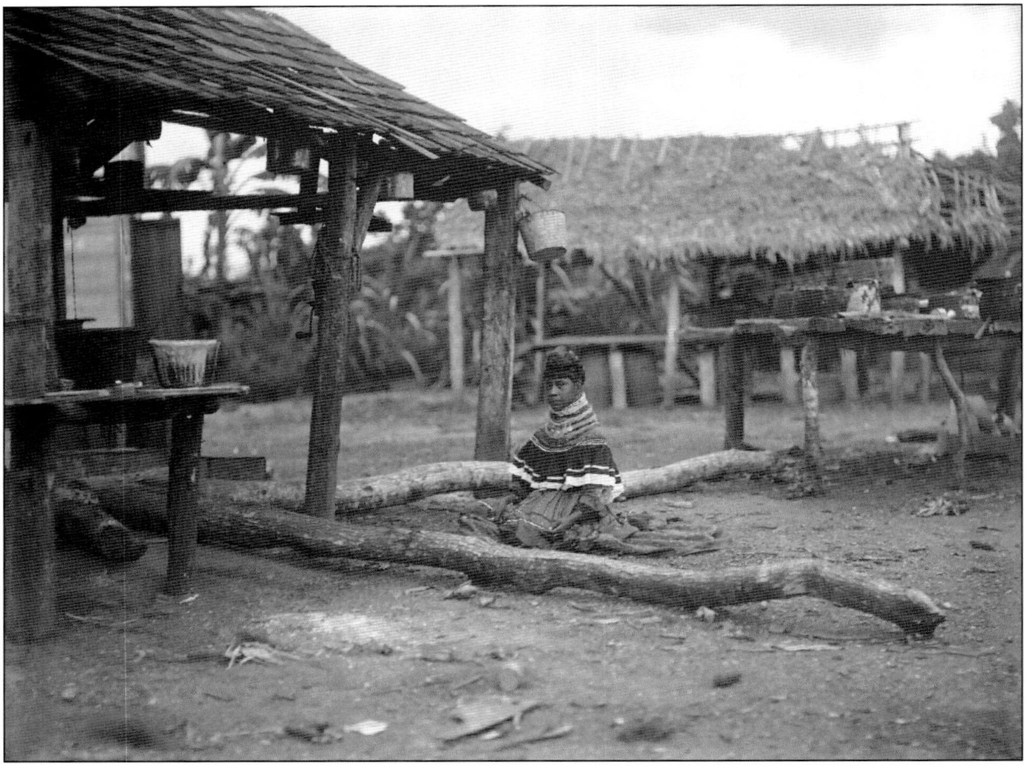

Chickees evolved during the Seminole Wars as quickly built, readily abandoned, air-cooled shelters, and remain iconic examples of Seminole architecture. Sleeping was on a raised floor; supplies were stored in the rafters. Other structures were work areas. A constantly lit fire in the cooking shelter was fed by regularly pushing the burning tips of radiating cypress logs into the fire, as shown here. A kettle of corn-based sofkee was kept warm through the day. (AMNH.)

Indians from camps in the eastern Everglades, who came to be called Miami Seminoles, frequented the Miami River stores of John Ewan, William Brickell, and J.D. Girtman. This 1910 image shows a family heading from the Everglades to Miami. They would stay overnight at a campsite or outside the trading post. In the late 1800s and early 1900s, Seminoles were a regular part of the Miami community. (AMNH.)

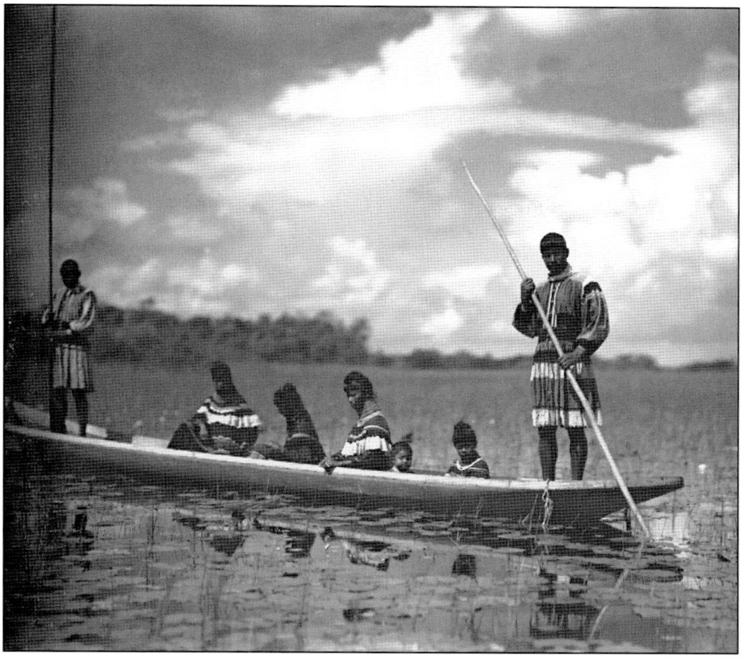

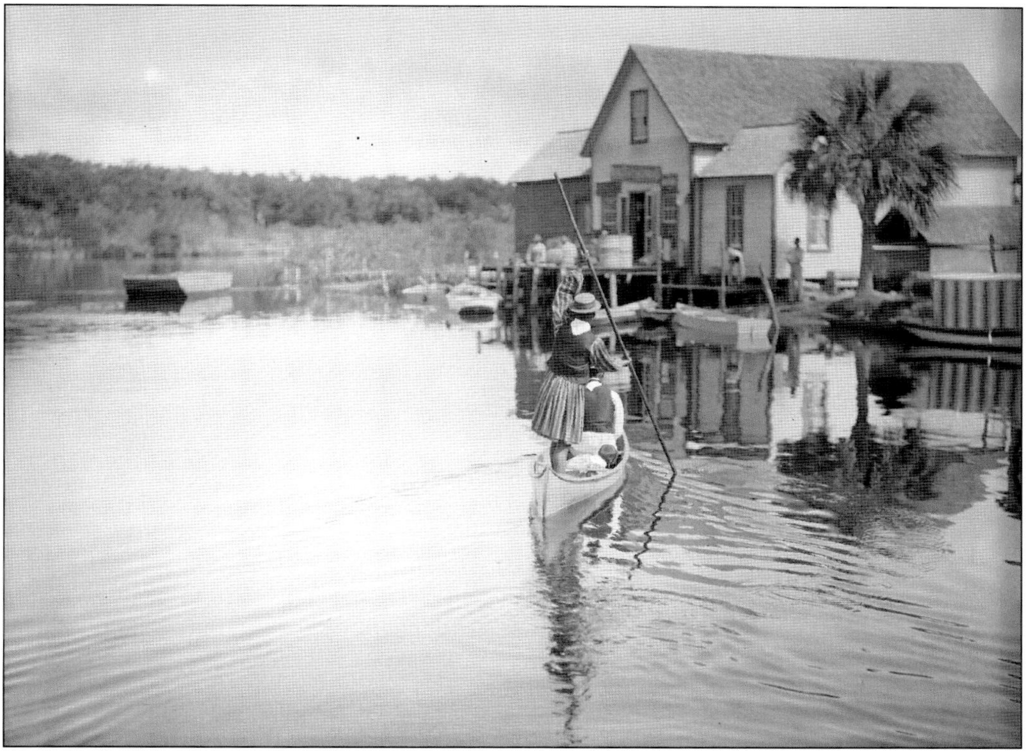

Indians from the western Everglades and southern Big Cypress did business at the Storter post in Everglade and Smallwood post in Chokoloskee. They traded bird feathers, alligator hides and teeth, fur, and meat for food staples, tools, *wyomee* (alcohol), beads, ribbons, and cloth. They also needed ammunition, pots, pans, and sewing machines. This 1906 image shows a Seminole approaching the Storter store at Everglade. (AMNH.)

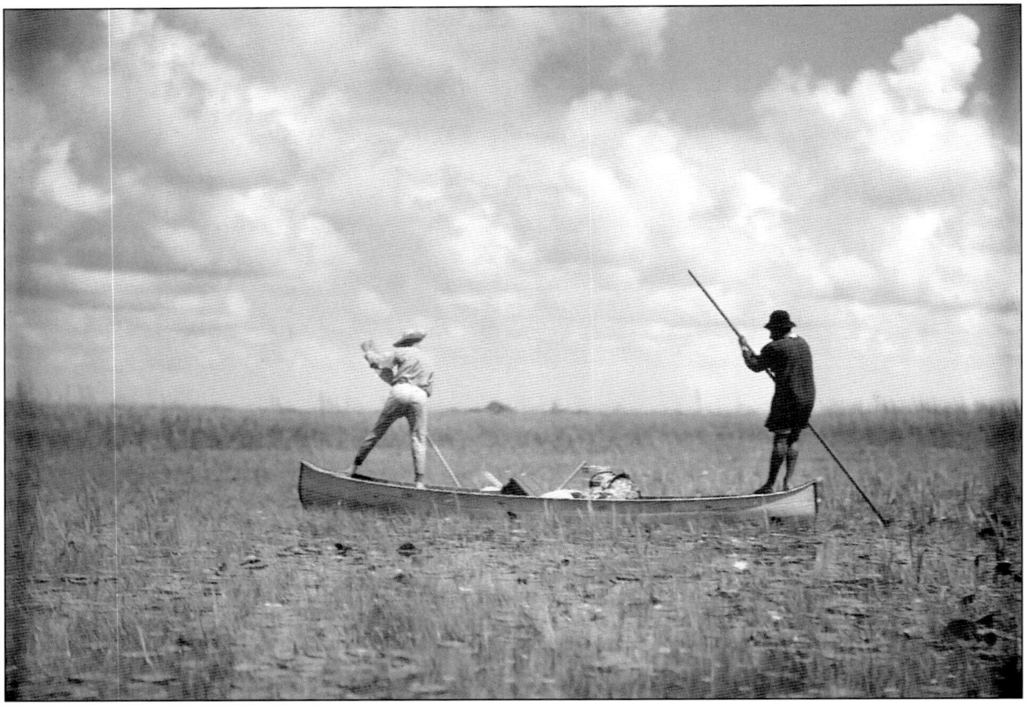

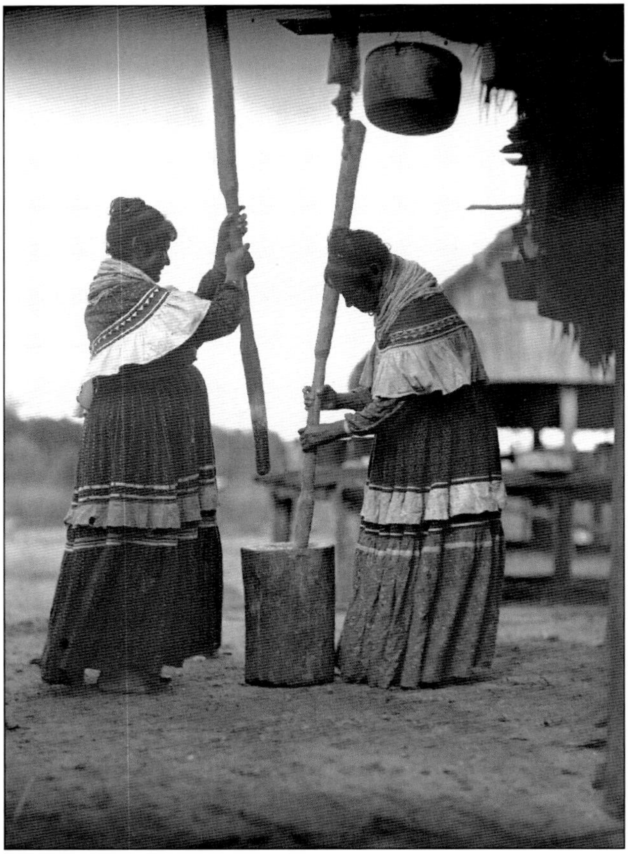

Although most Everglades and Big Cypress Seminoles continued to resist visits by outsiders, some chose to guide for explorers, hunters, and other visitors. One visiting adventurer was author A.W. Dimock, who explored the Ten Thousand Islands, Everglades, and Big Cypress with his photographer son Julian in the early 1900s. Seminoles allowed them access and permission to photograph. Julian later returned with a Smithsonian archeological expedition. The image above shows guide Charley Tommy poling a canoe with A.W. Dimock in 1907. The image at left shows women grinding corn. When questioned, Tommy Osceola told Dimock that an Indian could travel to Miami in three days. When asked about a white man making the trip, Osceola just shook his head. Julian Dimock's photographs preserve an unparalleled chronicle of the people of the Everglades at the time. (Both, AMNH.)

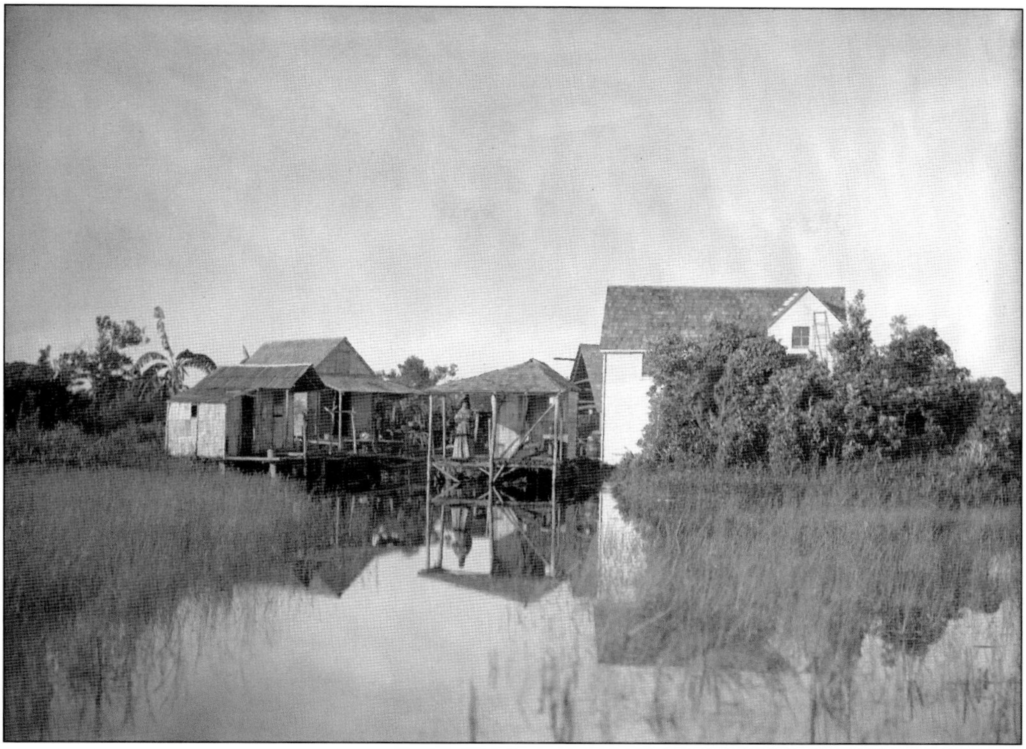

Charlie Tigertail was a particularly enterprising man. He had his own trading post just west of Shark River Slough at what is now called Coconuts Camp. With a leg injury that kept him from hunting, he brought supplies from Miami to build his store and a substantial house (above). At Mr. Charlie Tiger Tail's Store, he traded with Shark Slough Seminoles. He also had a camp and garden on Turner River south of what is now Tamiami Trail and traded in Miami. He and Ted Smallwood of Chokoloskee were friends and business partners. A.W. Dimock featured Tigertail's store in his novel *Dick in the Everglades.* The photograph at right shows Charlie Tigertail in 1914 with US vice president Thomas Marshall. (Above, AMNH; right, SLAF.)

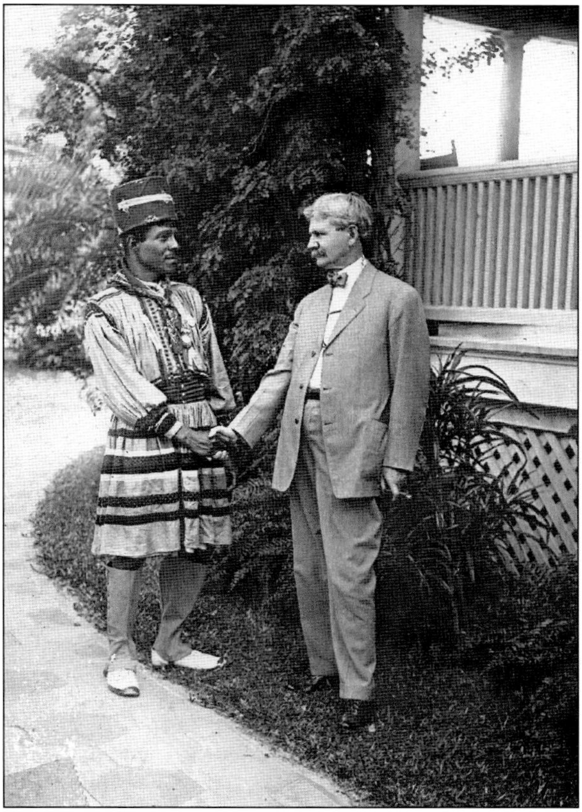

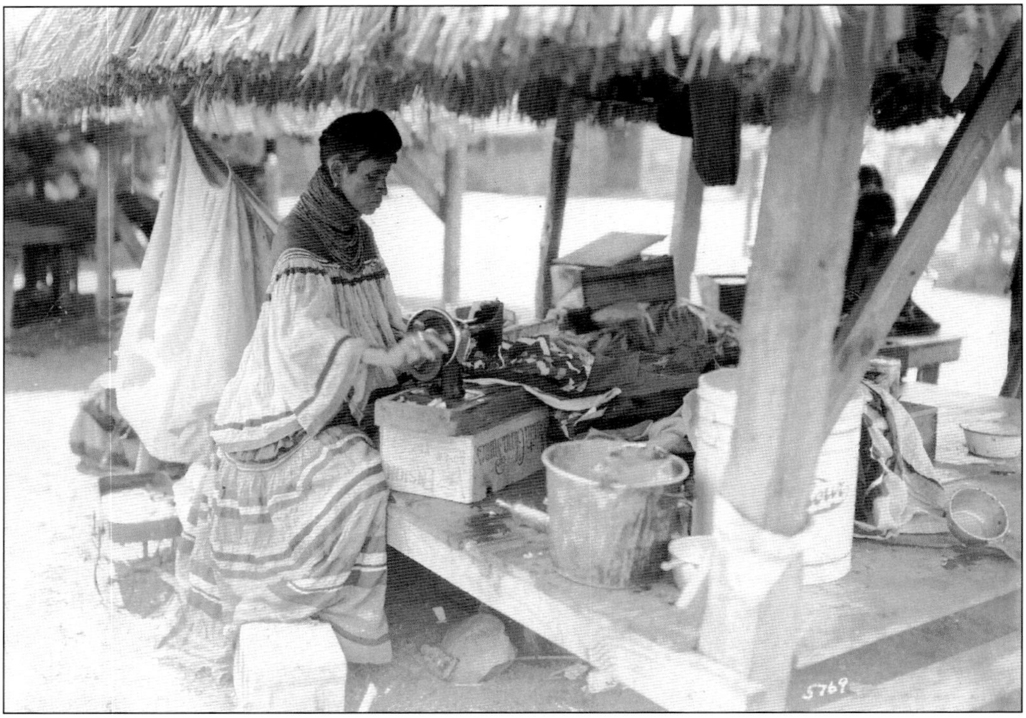

Even prior to their arrival in Florida, the clothing of the future Seminole people was being influenced by European designs and cloth. From the early 1900s, sewing machines allowed further evolution into iconic Seminole styles, composed of strands of ribbon or cloth sewn together horizontally, initially appliqué and later patchwork. Women's long skirts and short, long-sleeved blouses with small capes were accented by ruffles and many-stranded beaded necklaces. (HM.)

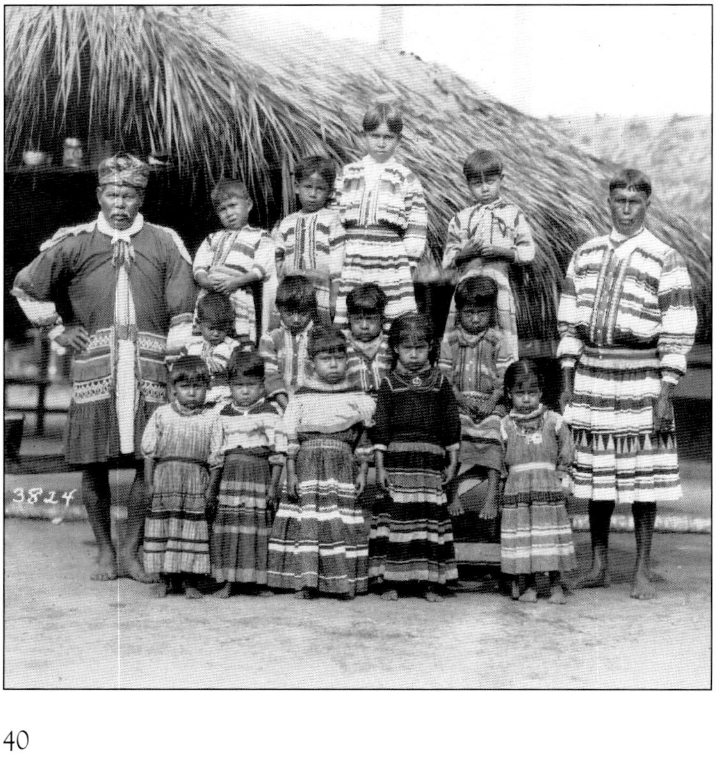

Seminole men's clothing initially included leggings, sashes, and belts. Turbans made of wound cloth evolved into individualized art forms, later replaced by other sorts of decorated hats. Families dressed up to go to town. By the 20th century, the long shirt was being replaced by trousers and evolved into today's characteristic patchwork shirts and jackets. The men and children in this 1923 image are posing for tourists. (HM.)

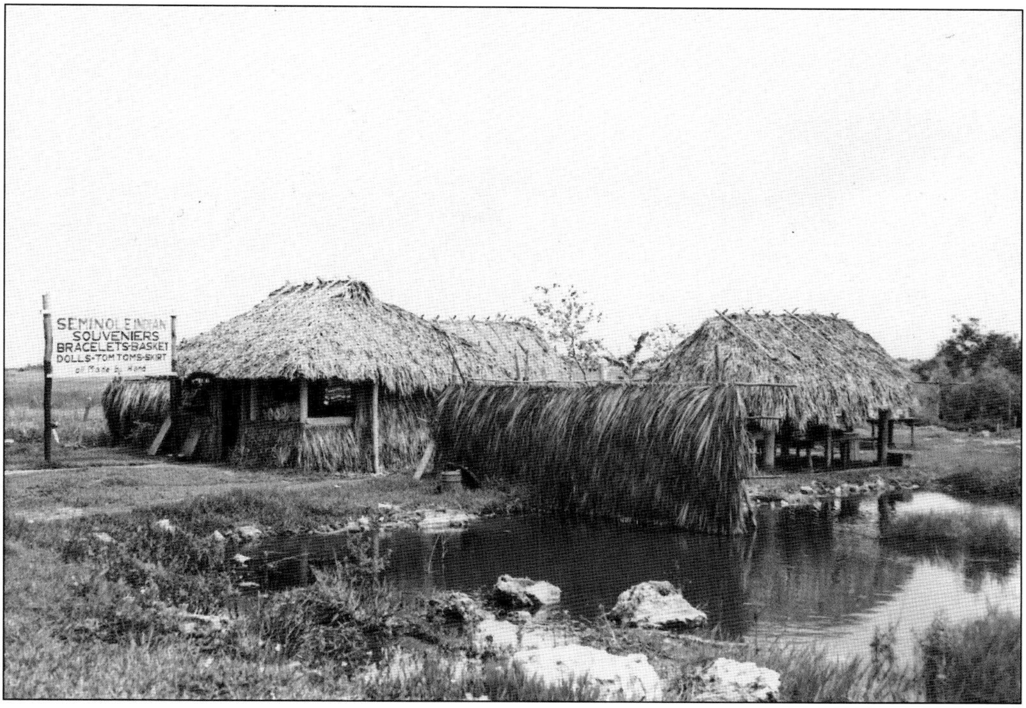

Opening in 1928, Tamiami Trail further upended the lifestyle of Everglades Indians. Although altering water flow, blocking trails, and allowing unimpeded access, it also provided opportunities for families to move their homesites onto the higher ground of the roadbed. Some families developed their camps into tourist attractions, popularly called Indian villages. The villages offered cultural experiences, alligator wrestling, souvenir sales, and later, airboat rides. (NPS.)

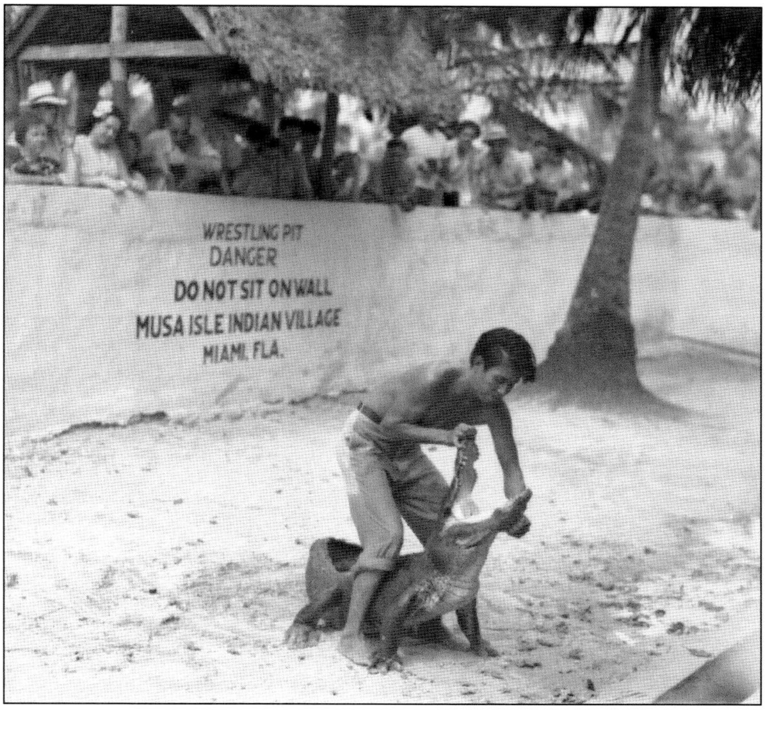

Some Everglades Seminoles chose to engage in the tourist economy by working or living at attractions in Miami. Principal among these were Musa Isle and Coppinger's Tropical Gardens, which opened in 1914 at the site of a preexisting Indian village. This 1947 image shows Bobby Tiger performing in Musa Isle's alligator pit for tourists. In 1952, Musa Isle was the senior author's first introduction to alligators. (MDPLS.)

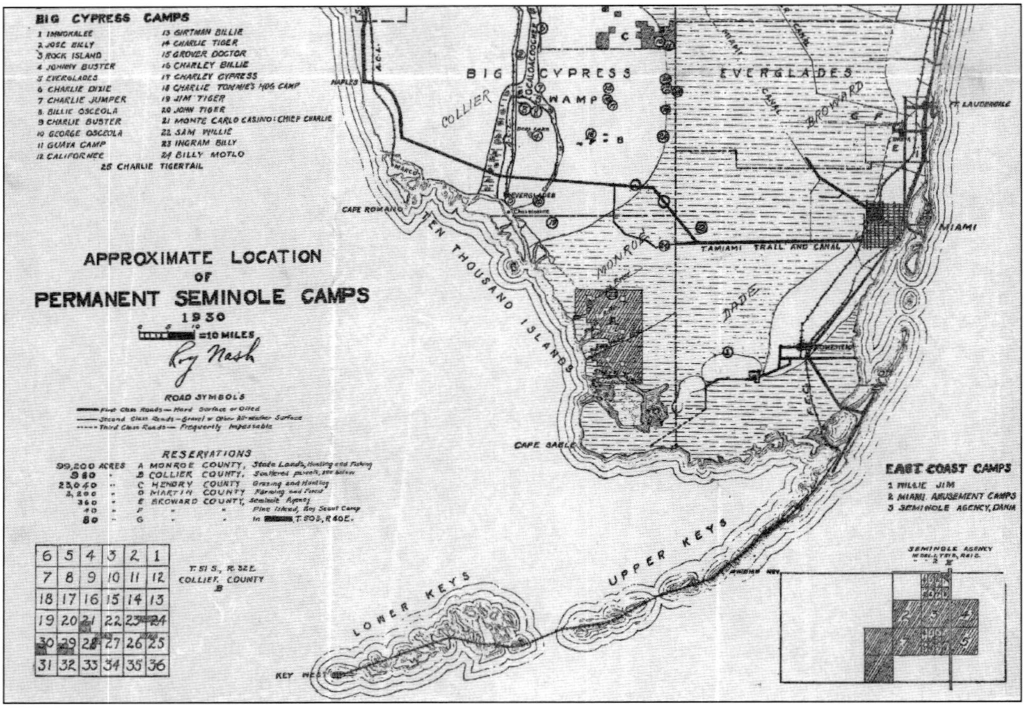

In 1911, with the encouragement of Florida's women's clubs, the state set aside 100,000 acres as a Seminole reservation in the southern Everglades (shown stippled in this 1930 map), encompassing the western part of the southern Everglades and southern Big Cypress. Families had camps on tree islands in this area. In 1935, the state abolished the reservation in preparation for creating the national park. Agreeing to compensation took decades. (SLAF.)

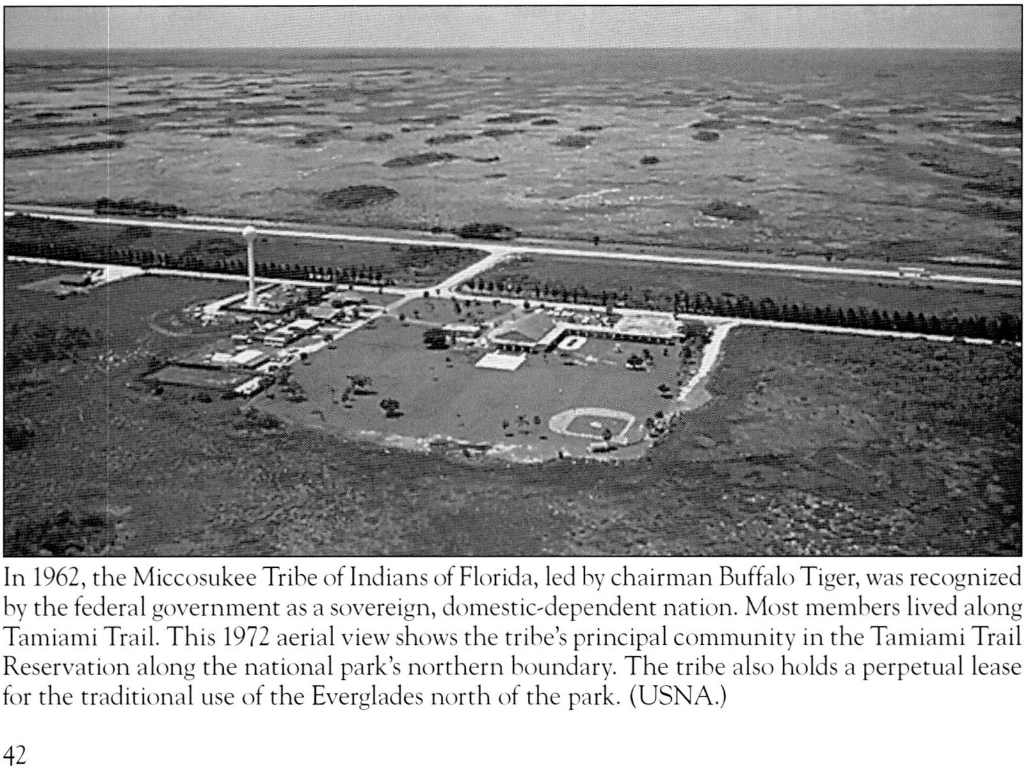

In 1962, the Miccosukee Tribe of Indians of Florida, led by chairman Buffalo Tiger, was recognized by the federal government as a sovereign, domestic-dependent nation. Most members lived along Tamiami Trail. This 1972 aerial view shows the tribe's principal community in the Tamiami Trail Reservation along the national park's northern boundary. The tribe also holds a perpetual lease for the traditional use of the Everglades north of the park. (USNA.)

Three

Settling the Everglades

American settlers arrived and inexorably overran the Everglades. After the Civil War, pioneer settlement began in earnest, starting on the coast. Northerners arrived, families claimed home sites, civilization escapers claimed tree islands, and trading posts claimed trade routes. Communication and transportation remained by boat, mostly along the coast. The only towns were distant Key West and Fort Myers. The Everglades was backcountry, a place to escape the law, recover from misfortune, hunt for food and for market, and make moonshine. It also became a place for the adventurous to explore and write about. After plume laws were enacted and wardens engaged, the bird hunting–based economy faltered, but exploitation of other natural resources continued. Encroachment of swamp drainers and land developers expanded. By the 1870s, pioneer settlements began around the future Everglades National Park at Chokoloskee, Everglade, Flamingo, Cape Sable, and Fort Dallas—the future Miami. Individuals came and went, especially in the remote and minimally policed Ten Thousand Islands and along coastal rivers.

Starting in the late 1890s, railroads shifted the region's economic priorities. Railroads encouraged land sales and agriculture, brought money and the moneyed, enticed tourists, built fancy seasonal hotels, attracted new residents and developments to house them, and set up the new city of Miami on the very edge of the Everglades. It also fueled demand for continued drainage, eventually consuming the Everglades' eastern half. Another game-changer for the southern Everglades was the opening of the Tamiami Trail in 1928, later to mark Everglades National Park's northern boundary. Other than drainage itself, until the 1960s, there was no greater insult to the southern Everglades environment than the imposition of the Tamiami Trail. The highway could have gone elsewhere; a proposed Cross State Highway would have passed through already drained land south of Lake Okeechobee. But coastal city interests made sure a direct southern route won out. The flow-blocking road ended millennia-old impediments to crossing the Everglades. What just a few years before required a canoe, local knowledge, balance, back strength, persistence, and several days, was now open to Sunday picnickers in their Model A Fords.

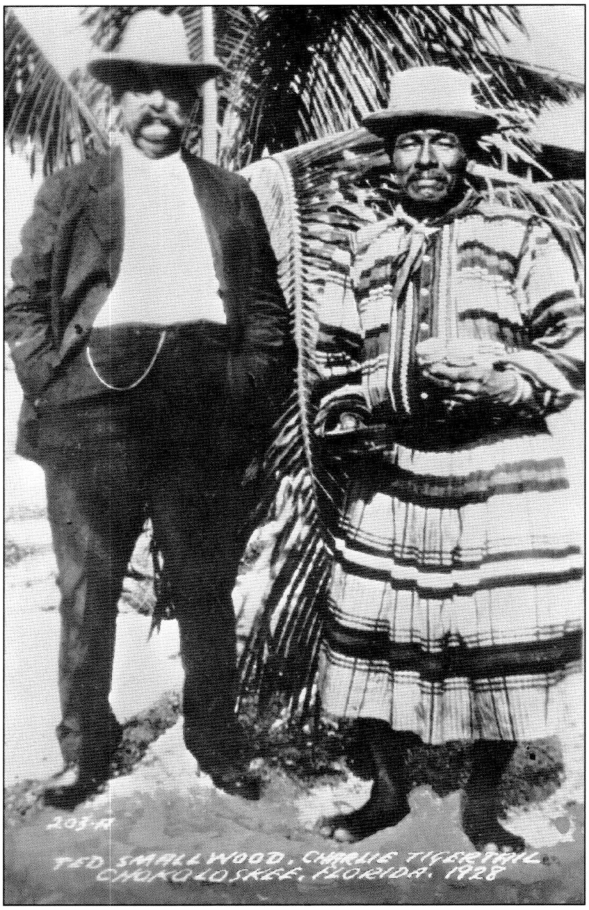

Chokoloskee Island (pronounced "Chuckaluskee," meaning "old house") is Ten Thousand Islands' highest elevation. Initially named Comfort in 1891, the settlement remained isolated until 1956 when a causeway was built. John Weeks held the first claim, followed by the Santini family for 25 years. First postmaster C.G. McKinney became a popular pioneer-life writer. Chokoloskee's story is greatly intertwined with that of Charles Sherod "Ted" Smallwood (left), shown with Charlie Tigertail. (SLAF.)

Smallwood came to Chokoloskee in 1891. He and his father bought the Santini claim in 1896. He established his first store in 1906 to service settlers and southern Everglades and Big Cypress Seminoles. Chokoloskee was the only ground in the Ten Thousand Islands not to submerge in the 1910 hurricane; after the 1924 hurricane, he raised his store on piles. This image shows Smallwood and his elevated store. (SLAF.)

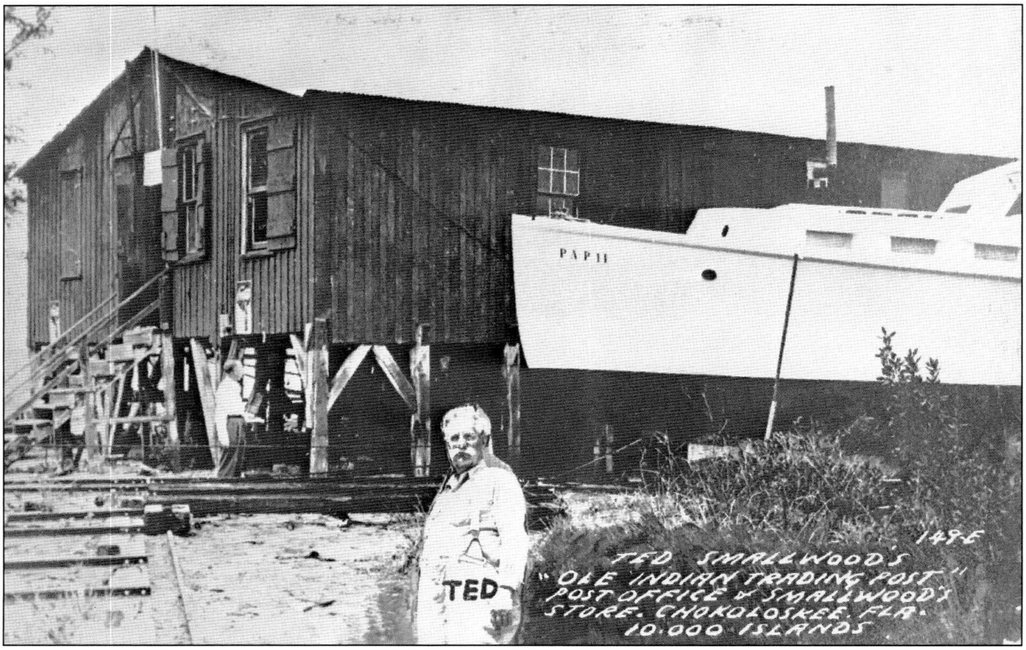

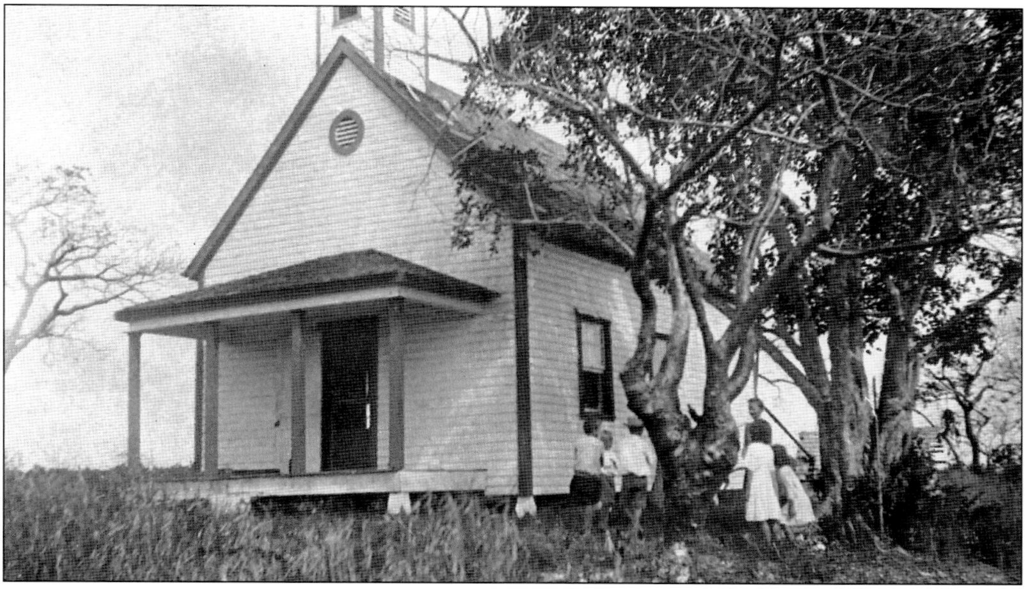

Settlers hunted for food and for trade, fished, made charcoal, and tended crops. Farming was a successful enterprise. Sugarcane syrup and vegetables were sold in Key West and Fort Myers. By 1898, Chokoloskee had grown sufficiently to need a school. So the residents built one, shown in this 1918 image. The hurricane of 1910 forced many outlying residents to abandon their homes and farms. (SLAF.)

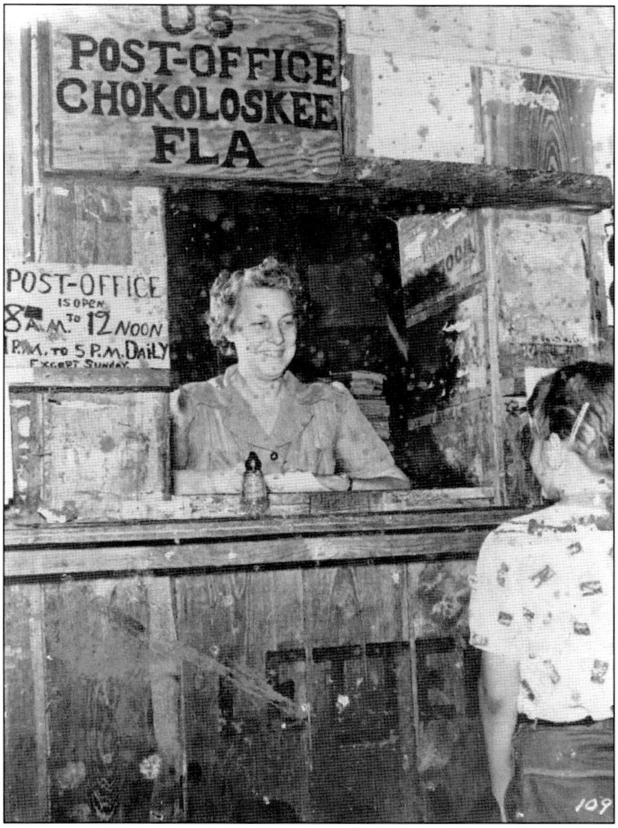

Ted and Mamie Smallwood and their trading post figured heavily in the evolving history of Chokoloksee and the Ten Thousand Islands into the 1950s. Beyond being a store, it was the town's center—a meeting place, local news exchange, and post office. This image shows Mamie at the post office window. The elevated building persists today as a family-run museum. (SLAF.)

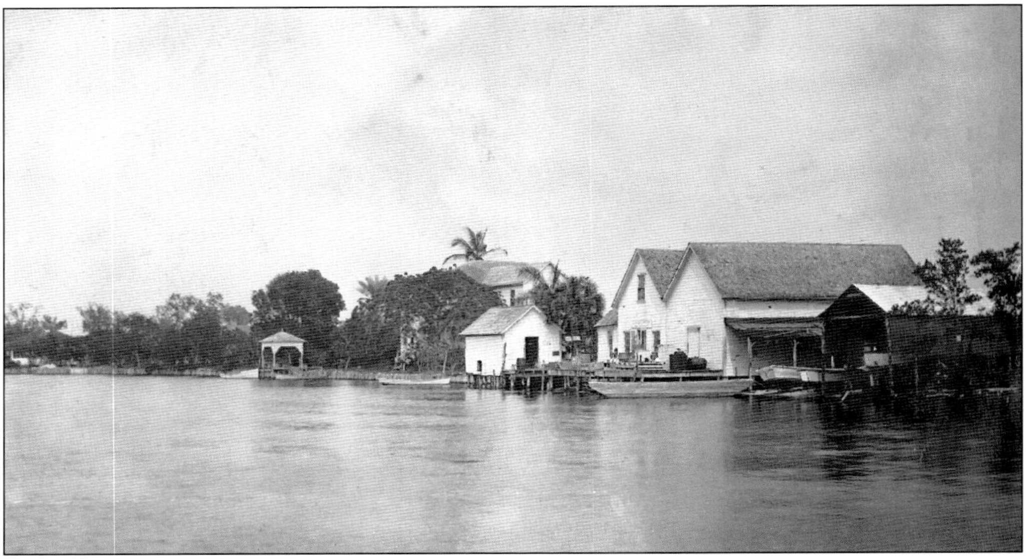

A similar history played out four miles north. In 1873, William Smith Allen moved from Key West to the mouth of what became the Allen River, becoming the first resident of the future Everglades City. The settlement was initially named Everglade after the post office rejected its application as Chokoloskee. In 1883, George W. Storter Jr. and his father joined the farming community, purchasing Allen's claim in 1889. Nearby, settlements developed at Sand Fly Pass and Half-Way Creek. Storter Jr. farmed sugarcane with notable success, and in 1892, established a trading post (shown in 1917). He enlarged the Allen house as a gathering and dining place. By 1910, the Everglade and Chokoloskee area's population was 144. Both towns were accessible only by boat. (Both, SLAF.)

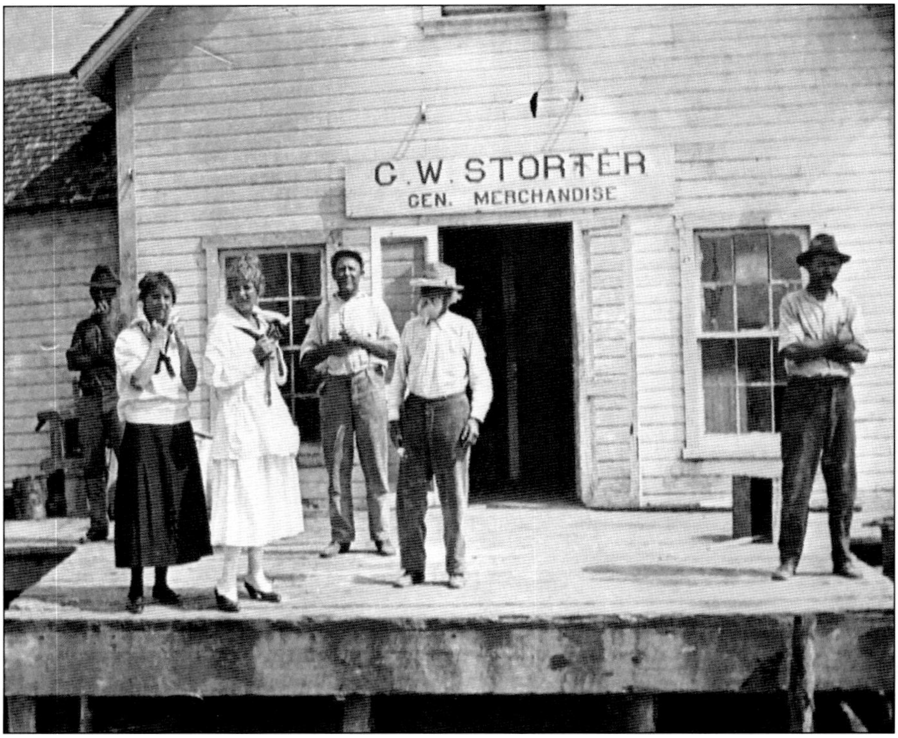

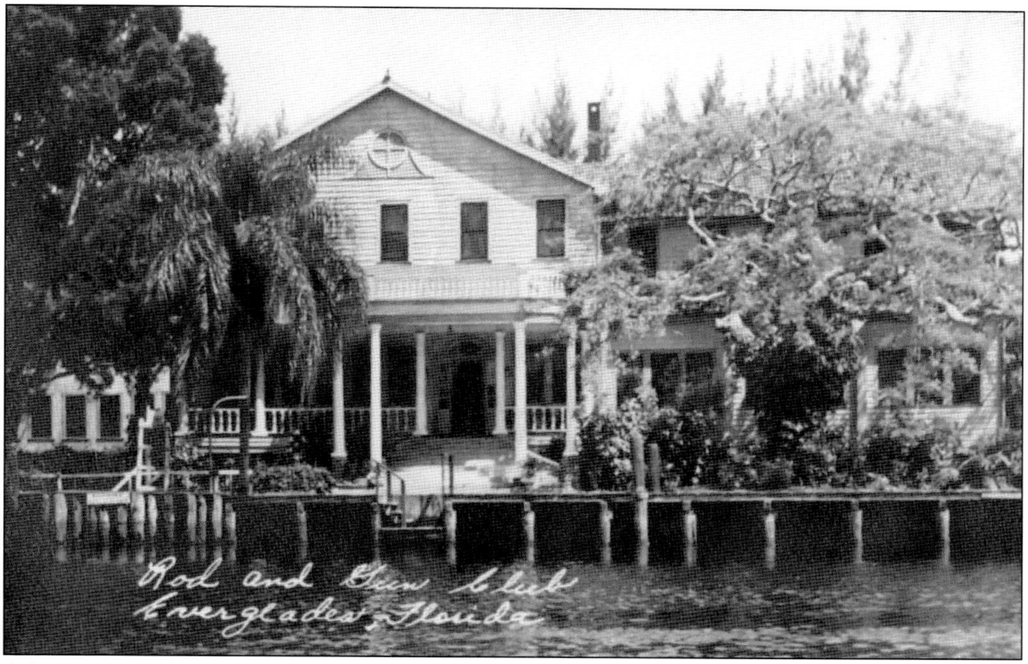

Advertising executive Barron Gift Collier Sr. first visited the region in 1911, buying Useppa Island for a resort and eventually becoming the largest landowner in Florida. His over 1.3 million acres included the town of Everglade, renamed Everglades in 1923, and Everglades City in 1965. Collier dredged the harbor and the Allen River, renamed Barron River. He turned the Storter home into the still-extant Rod and Gun Club (above). A bit north, he built the industrial Port DuPont. He bought the grapefruit grove at Deep Lake and its narrow-gauge Deep Lake Railroad, which transported citrus to Everglade and tourists to Deep Lake (below). Its route became State Road 29. He sold the line to the Atlantic Coast Line Railroad, which in 1928 ran its Haines City Branch to Everglades and remained in service until 1958. (Above, HM; below, SLAF.)

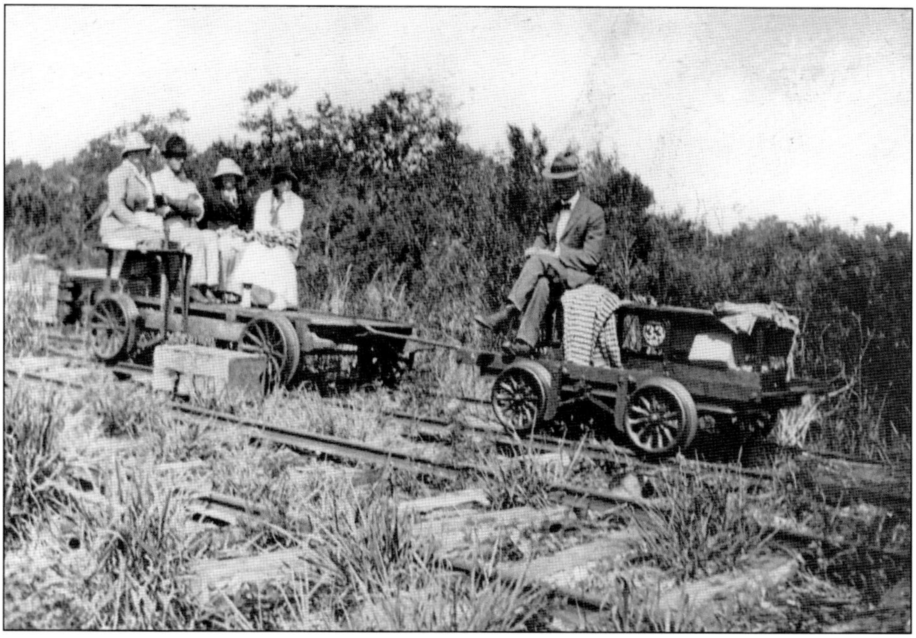

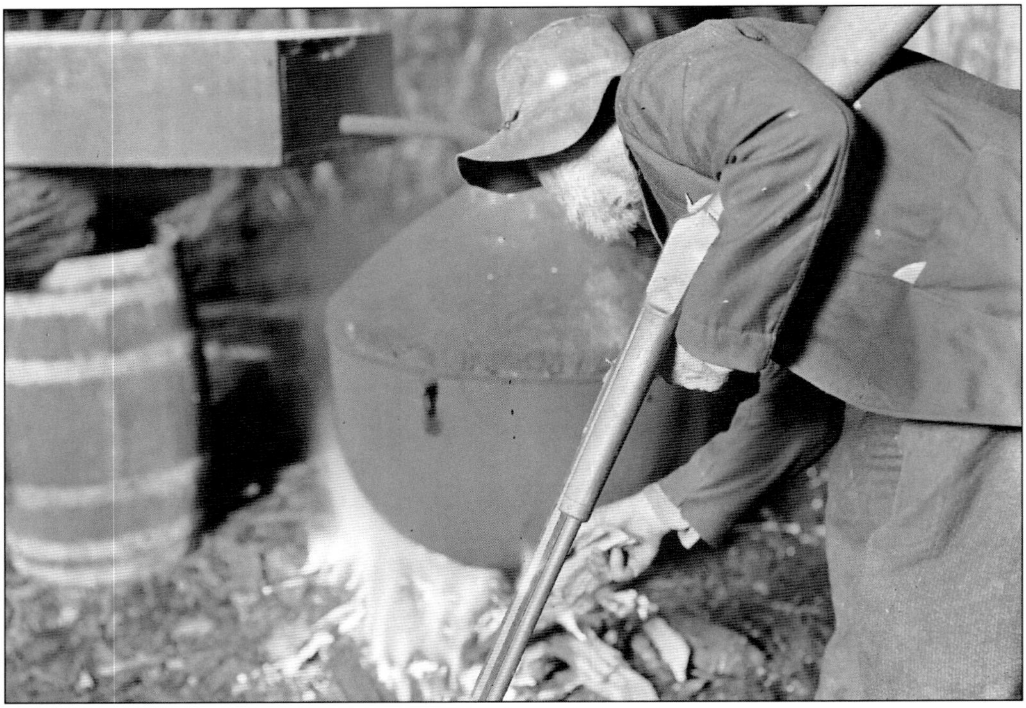

The higher spots in the Ten Thousand Islands, including the ancient mounds of indigenous inhabitants, were occupied by a succession of settlers who mostly sought isolation in a place inconvenient to law enforcement where they could fish, hunt, farm, and distill. The above 1906 image shows moonshine-making in a hammock. Historically notable homesites include Sandfly Pass, Turner River, Lopez River, Chatham Bend, Possum Key, and Onion Key. The persistently most famous Ten Thousand Islands resident was Edgar Watson, who built a substantial house at Chatham Bend (below) and farmed 35 acres, making well-appreciated Island Pride cane syrup. He also developed a reputation that neighbors came to fear, so they shot him dead as he landed at the Smallwood store after the 1910 hurricane. Peter Matthiessen tells a fictionalized version of the Watson legend in *Shadow Country*. (Both, AMNH.)

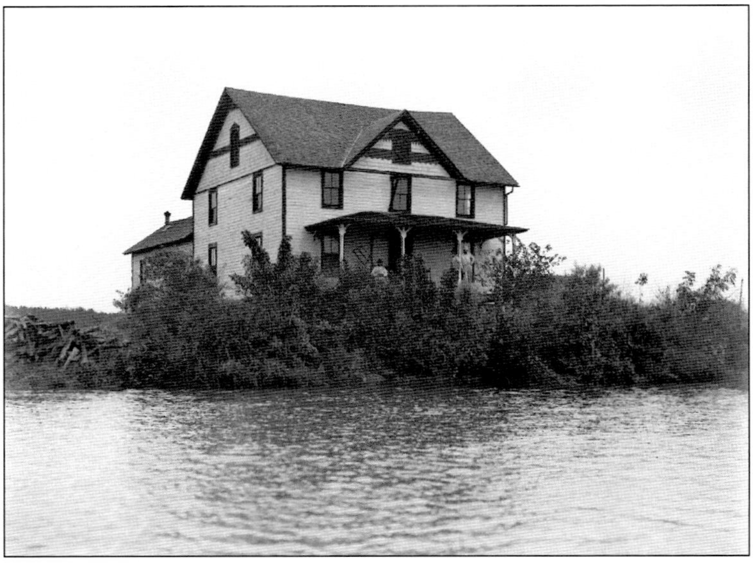

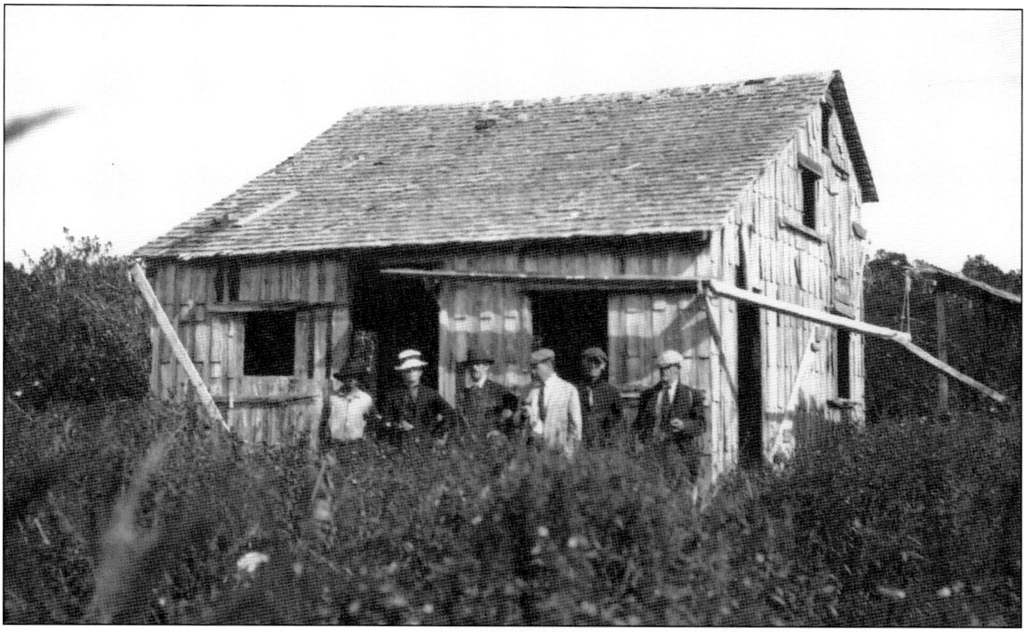

Other pioneers included Spaniard Gregorio Lopez on Lopez River and French-speaking Jean Chevelier on Possum Key. Cistern walls remain at the Lopez homestead; Chevelier's house is pictured in 1924. Nicknamed the Old Frenchman, Chevelier sold plumes directly to Paris and was memorialized in the book *The Cruise of the Bonton*. Chevelier Bay is named for him, as were James Franklin Jaudon's 1920s development company and his never-to-materialize town. (HM.)

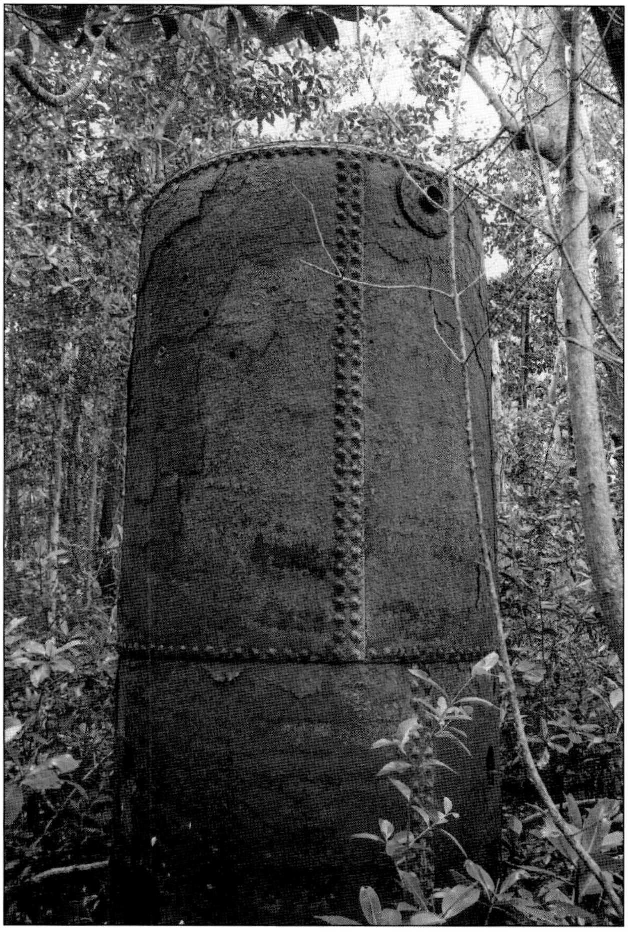

The Harney and Shark Rivers had few high ground sites. The indigenous history of one site, Canepatch, goes back two millennia. It is now a park campsite. In 1904, the Manetta Company began moving its tannin factory from Miami to Shark River to harvest its red mangroves. Destroyed by the 1910 hurricane, its operations resumed during World War I. Remnants were uncovered by Hurricane Donna in 1960. (KB.)

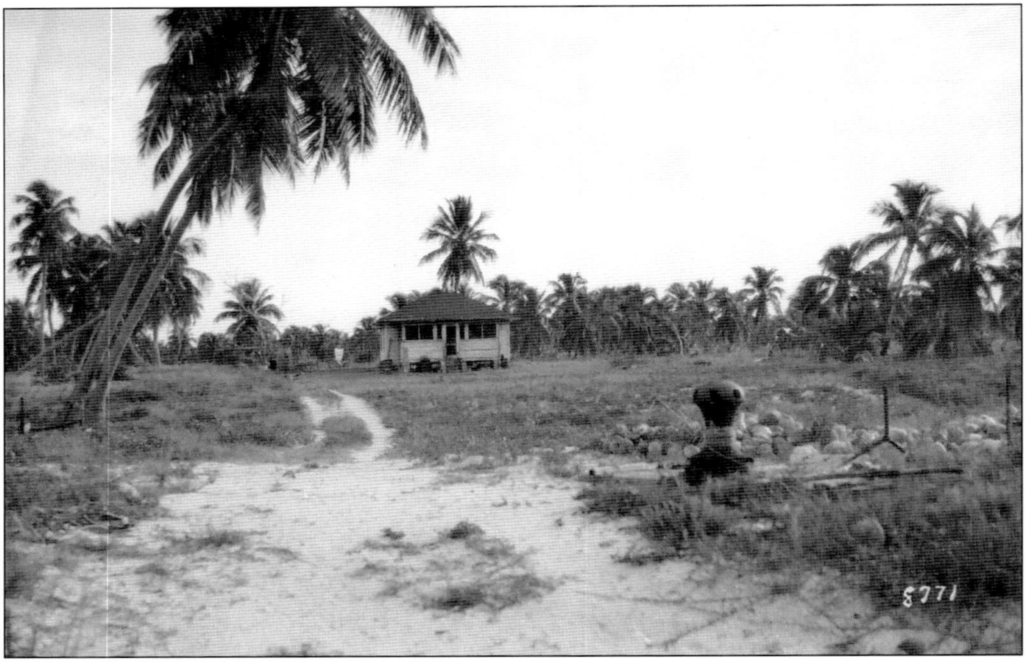

South of Shark River, Cape Sable was a charted coastal landmark for centuries. Its use by Indigenous people is undetermined, but in the 1700s, Bernard Romans saw evidence of prior farming. Later, coastal prairies supported pioneer homes and farms. During the Civil War, farming there fed the union-held town of Key West. In 1884, Canadian James A. Waddell planted a coconut plantation on the cape and engaged caretakers who lived in a cottage. The image above shows the Waddell grove in 1929; below are Cape Sable coconuts stacked on the Middle Cape beach. By 1904, Cape Sable had its own post office. At nearby Sawfish Hole, a community made buttonwood charcoal. Land "down at the cape," much of it coming to be owned by the Model Land Company, was viewed as a potential new Miami Beach. (Above, HM; below, NPS.)

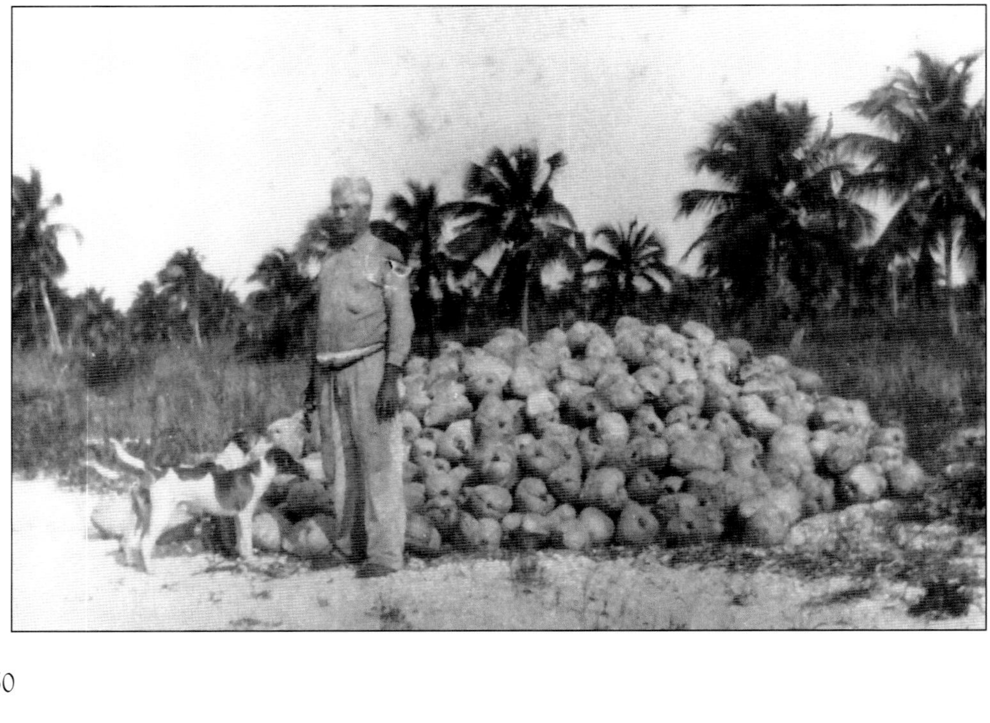

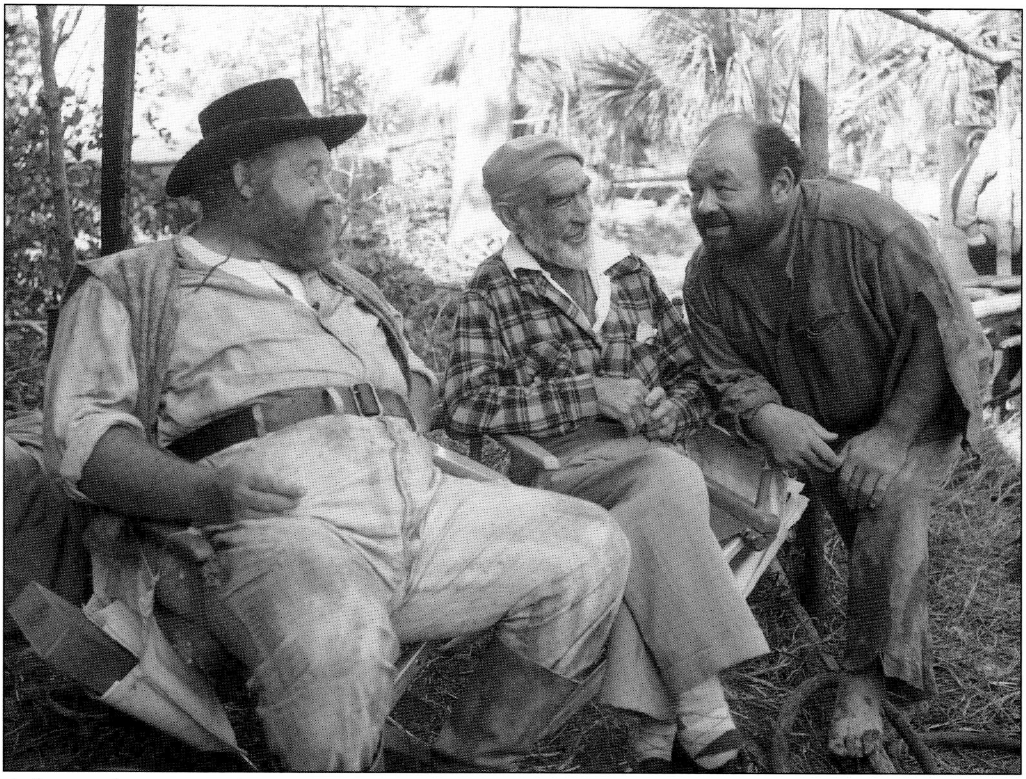

A fictional account of pioneer life along the coast was offered by the 1958 movie *Wind Across the Everglades.* The movie sensationalized a conflict between a plume hunter, Cottonmouth (played by Burl Ives, left), and an honorable game warden (Christopher Plummer). In the center of this photograph is a real Ten Thousand Islander, Pelican Key resident Roy Ozmer. (SLAF.)

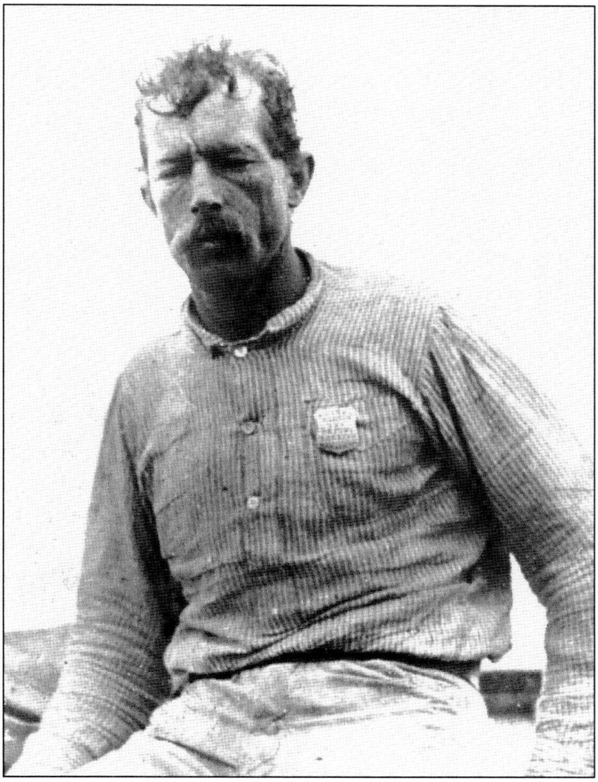

A true warden story is that of Guy Bradley. His father, Edwin, previously a "barefoot mailman" and Dade County school superintendent, bought a quarter-mile of Flamingo area bayfront and served as a land agent. Guy was deputized as a warden, and in 1905, while engaging local plume hunters in Florida Bay, he was shot and killed. The known perpetrators were freed. Bradley's murder galvanized the anti-plume crusade nationally. (NPS.)

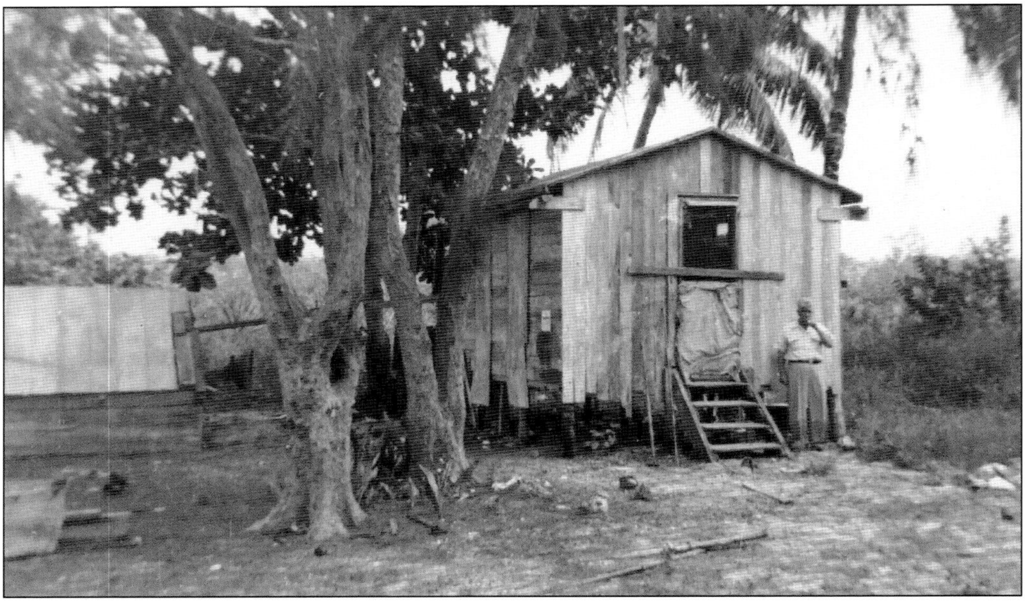

The first claim to the Flamingo area was by charcoal hauler Duncan Brady. Others settled on high ground at Madeira Bay, Cape Sable, and the Florida Bay keys. The name Flamingo was chosen so as to get a post office. Settlers hunted, plumed, fished, made charcoal, and farmed cane and vegetables for Key West. Residents were rough, tough, independent, and mosquito tolerant. Pictured here is Leon Hamilton's house. (NPS.)

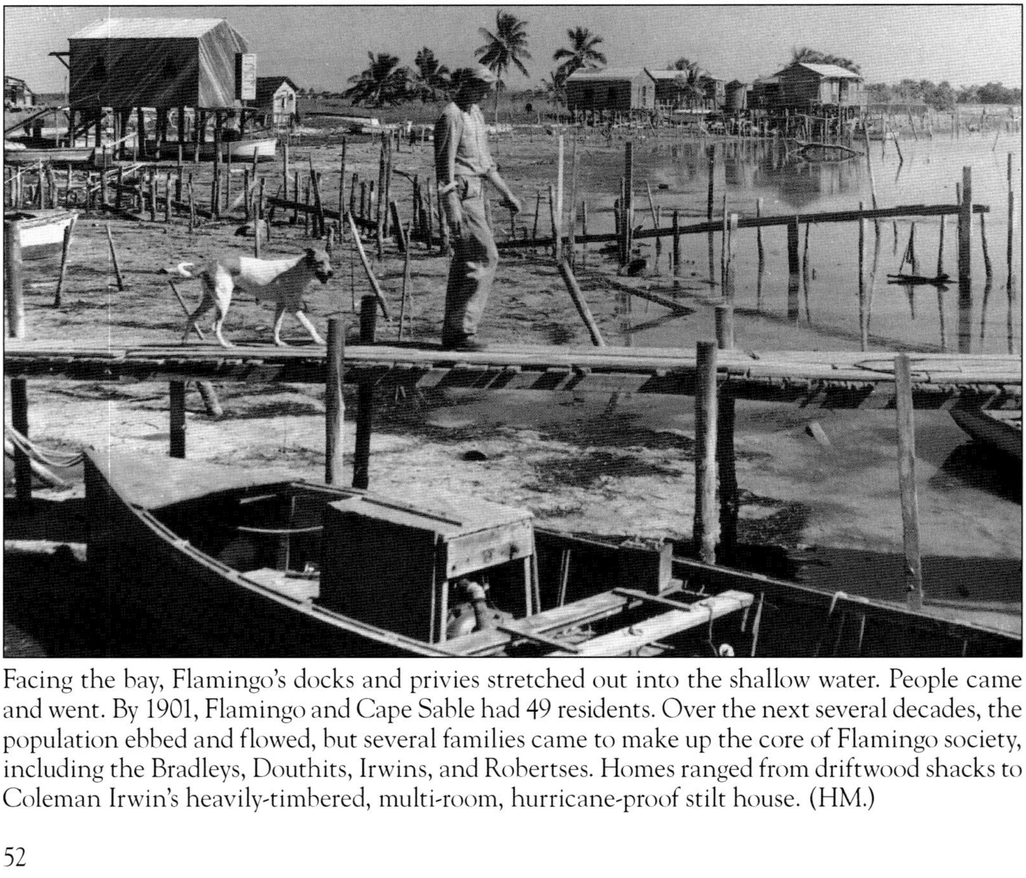

Facing the bay, Flamingo's docks and privies stretched out into the shallow water. People came and went. By 1901, Flamingo and Cape Sable had 49 residents. Over the next several decades, the population ebbed and flowed, but several families came to make up the core of Flamingo society, including the Bradleys, Douthits, Irwins, and Robertses. Homes ranged from driftwood shacks to Coleman Irwin's heavily-timbered, multi-room, hurricane-proof stilt house. (HM.)

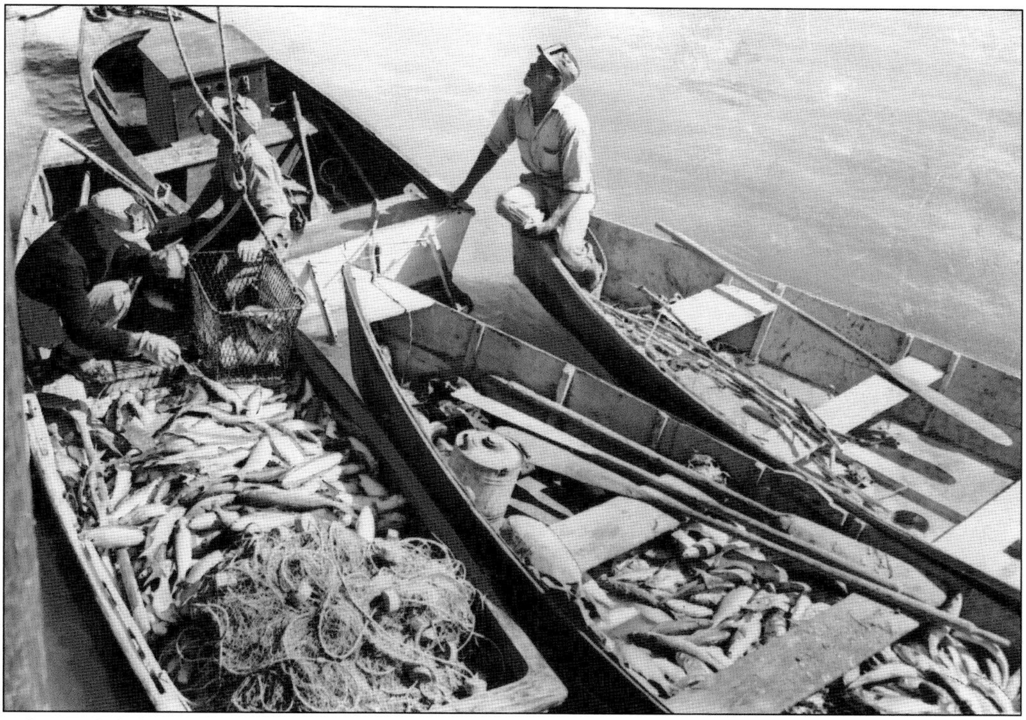

After a fish house was built in 1908 (and the plume trade throttled), commercial net-fishing became Flamingo's primary occupation. Fish houses processed the catch for boat transport to the Florida Keys. After the road's arrival in 1922, the fish were trucked to Homestead, so long as it did not rain too much. Other businesses included Brown's Fishing Camp and Szadyville Cafe. Flamingo waited for development to arrive; it never did. (HM.)

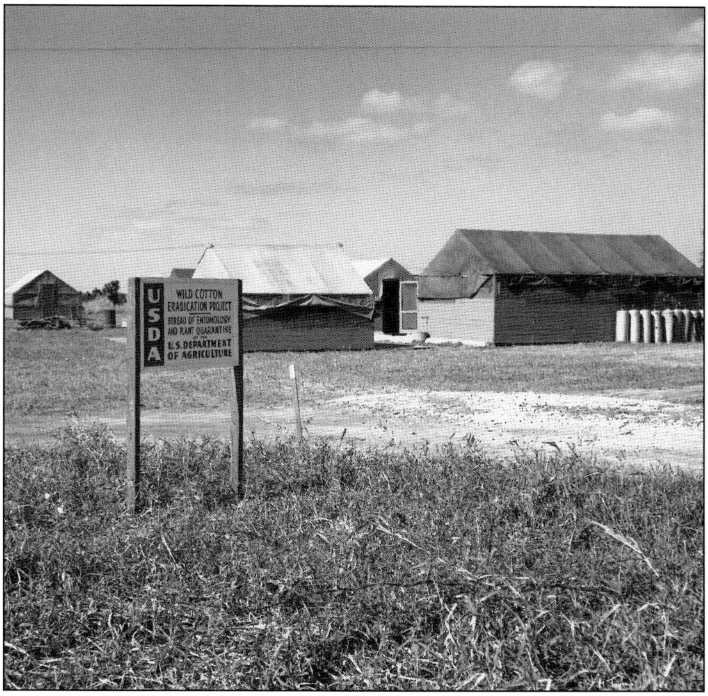

In 1932, the US Department of Agriculture established a camp at Flamingo to eradicate native cotton; its pink bollworm was considered a threat to commercial cotton, even though over 250 miles distant. The USDA also constructed coastal trails and removable bridges. In 1933, the Civilian Conservation Corps posted an African American company; thereafter, local black workers were hired seasonally. Continuing until 1972, the program somehow never managed to eradicate cotton. (SLAF.)

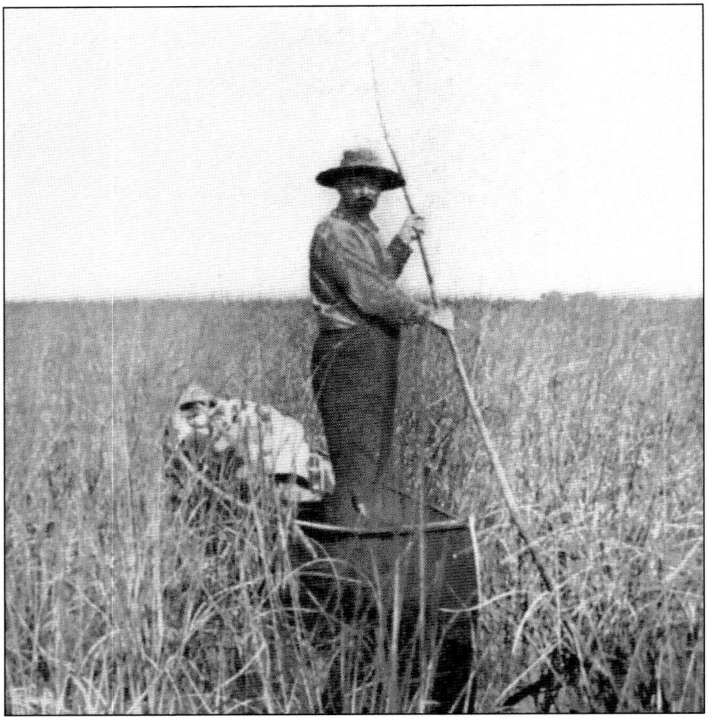

As at Flamingo and the Ten Thousand Islands, limited law enforcement made the Everglades itself attractive to civilization-escaping people. One such was Ed Brewer (pictured), considered a bootlegging undesirable in Miami, who lived a bit away from town at Paradise Key in the 1890s. On the Gulf Coast, he and Jean Chevalier's run-in with Chevalier's neighbor Edgar Watson became part of the Watson legend. (KH.)

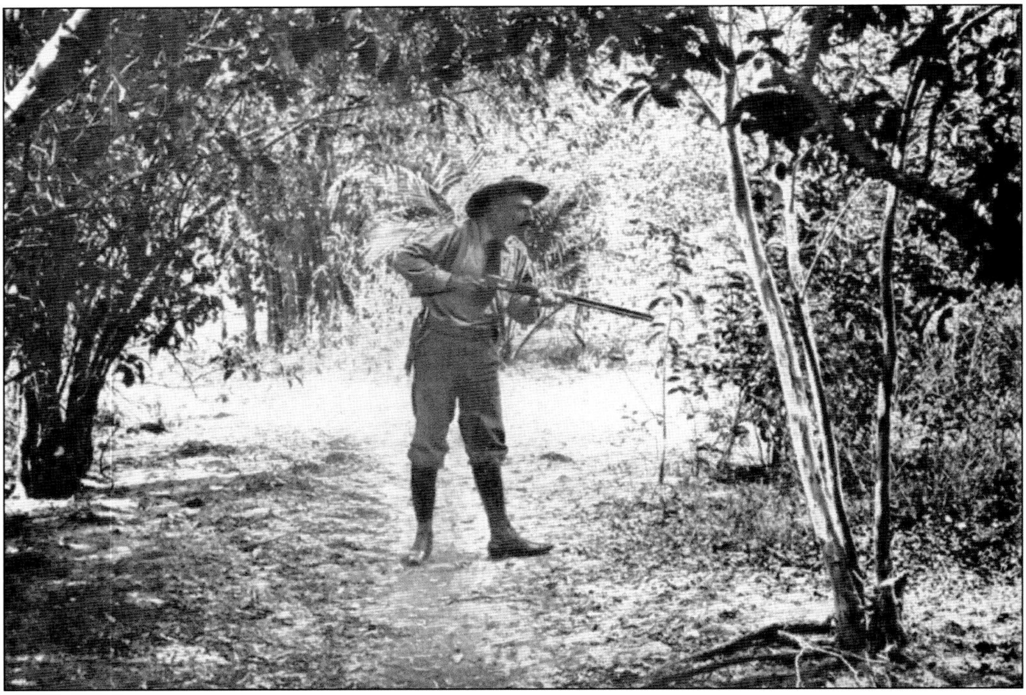

In the late 1800s, gentlemen-sportsmen were attracted to the Everglades for adventure and stories to sell. Few actually penetrated the Everglades. One who did was Hugh Willoughby. In 1896, he hired Ed Brewer to take him from Shark River to Miami. Brewer paddled. Willoughby recorded his course, made observations, photographed himself in self-aggrandizing poses, as shown here, and later promoted himself as a brave pioneer in crossing the Everglades. (KH.)

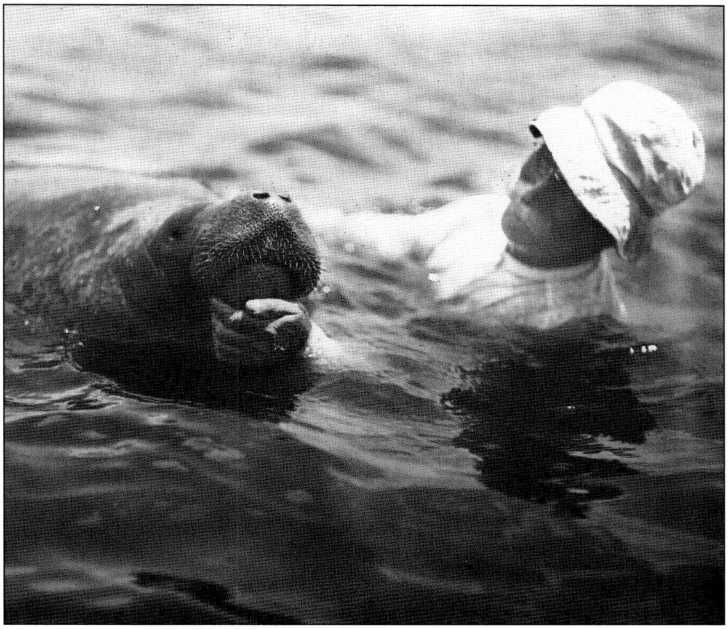

Author A.W. Dimock, mentioned earlier, was a different sort of sportsman. Following diverse business interests, he took up adventure writing and explored the southwest coast by houseboat and skiff. In 1906, he started at Storter's store in Everglade, traversed the Gulf Coast, went upriver, and crossed the Everglades to Miami. Unlike Willoughby's tale of hardships, Dimock called his expedition a picnic. This image shows Dimock swimming with a manatee. (SLAF.)

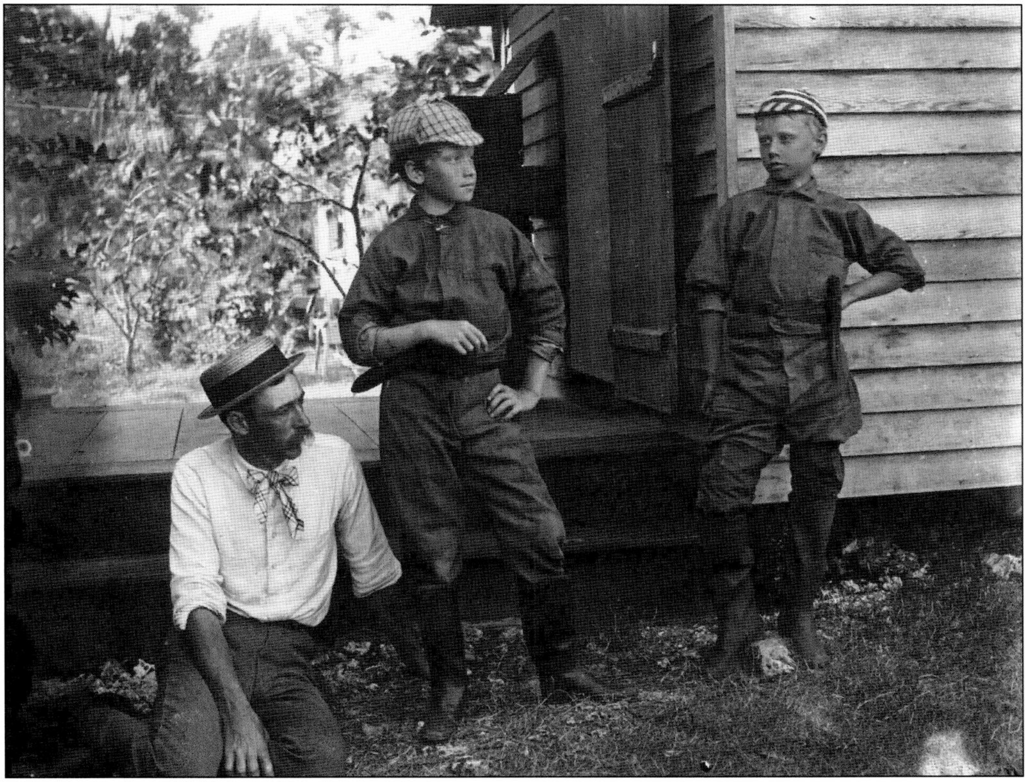

Another adventurer, Kirk Munroe, moved to Coconut Grove in 1886, becoming a nationally famous writer of boy's adventure stories. Shown at left in this 1890 image, he explored the Everglades by canoe, preparing for such stories as *Canoemates: A Story of the Florida Reef and Everglades* and was among the first settlers to see Paradise Key. He and his wife, Mary, were later instrumental in Royal Palm Hammock becoming a park. (HM.)

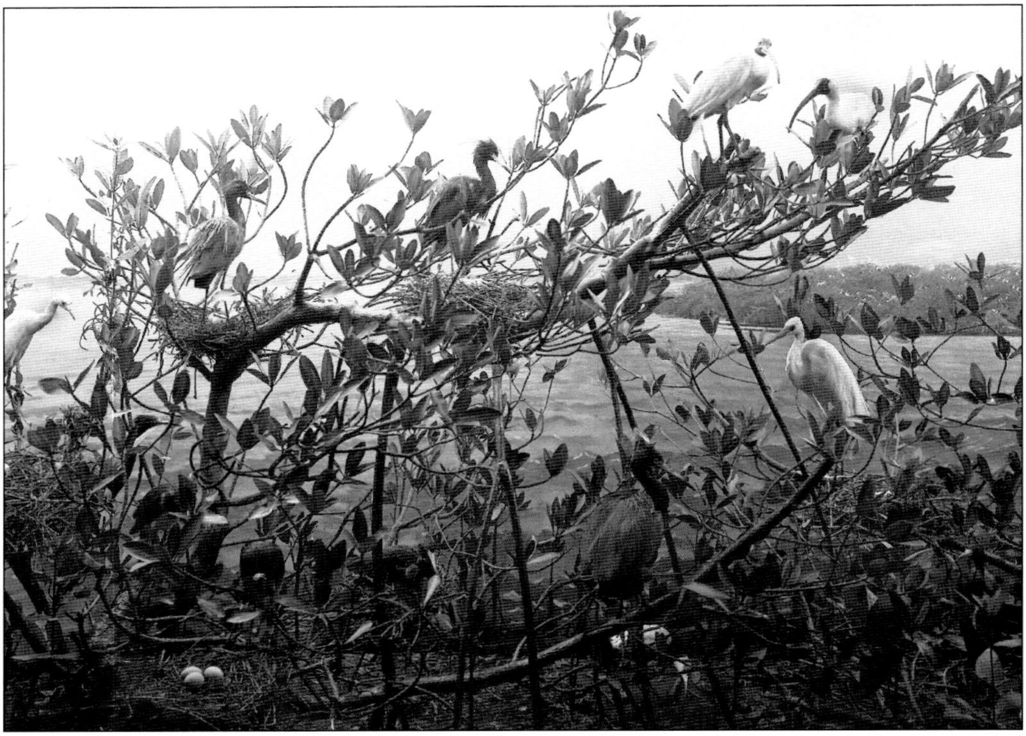

The Everglades also attracted scientists. Ornithologist conservationist Frank Chapman succeeded in visiting the Cuthbert colony only four years after Guy Bradley's murder, whom he had hired as warden. Guided by Guy's brother Luis, he and artist Louis Agassiz Fuertes used the experience to create the Cuthbert Rookery Diorama at the American Museum of Natural History, illustrating his anti-pluming conservation message. Shown in this 1909 image, it remains on display. (AMNH.)

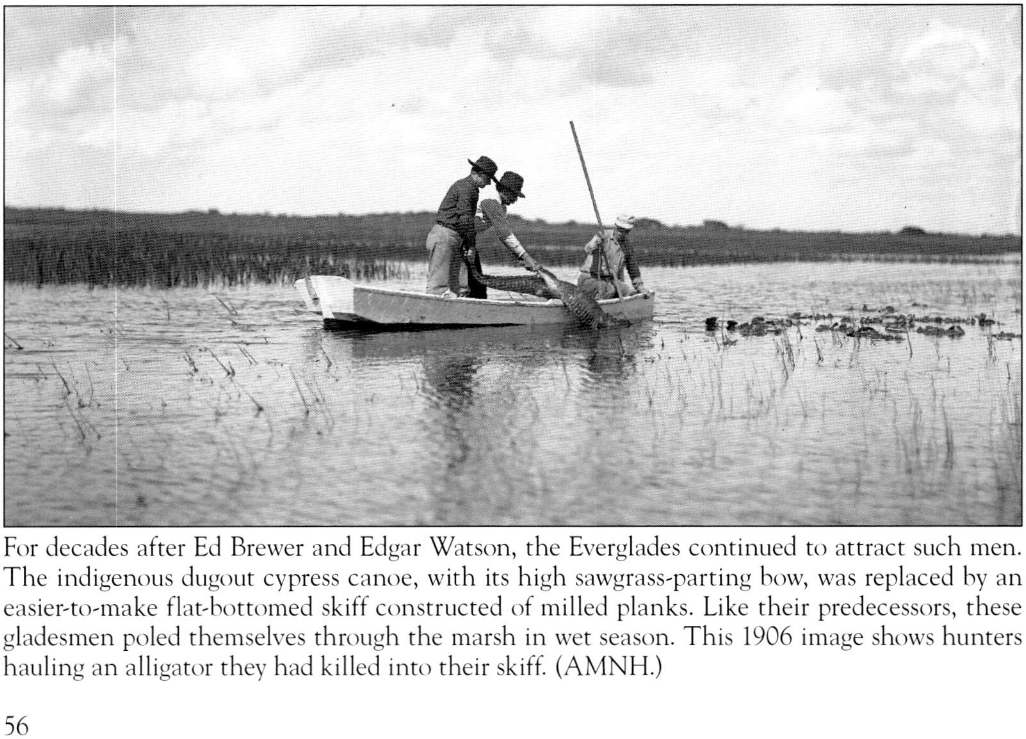

For decades after Ed Brewer and Edgar Watson, the Everglades continued to attract such men. The indigenous dugout cypress canoe, with its high sawgrass-parting bow, was replaced by an easier-to-make flat-bottomed skiff constructed of milled planks. Like their predecessors, these gladesmen poled themselves through the marsh in wet season. This 1906 image shows hunters hauling an alligator they had killed into their skiff. (AMNH.)

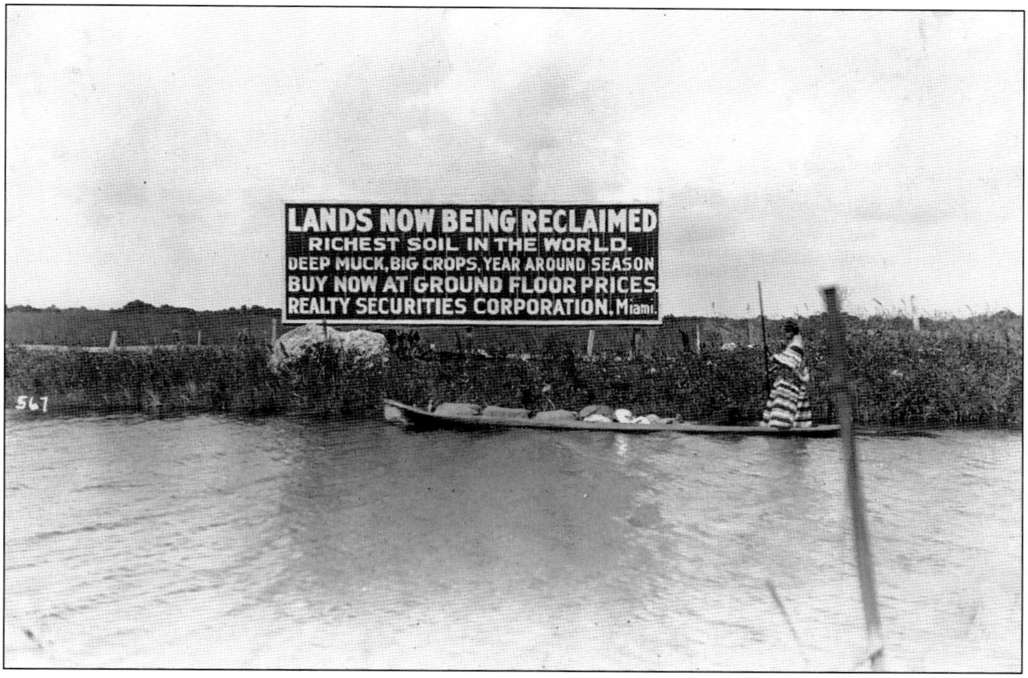

While Seminoles and some backwoodsmen were eking out livings in the Everglades, these same Everglades were being offered for sale. With the uplands having been claimed and further drainage promised, land agents, such as the Everglade Land Sales Company and the Realty Securities Corporation (pictured), touted the land's potential for profit. Fraud in sales of the flooded lands became a national controversy. (HM.)

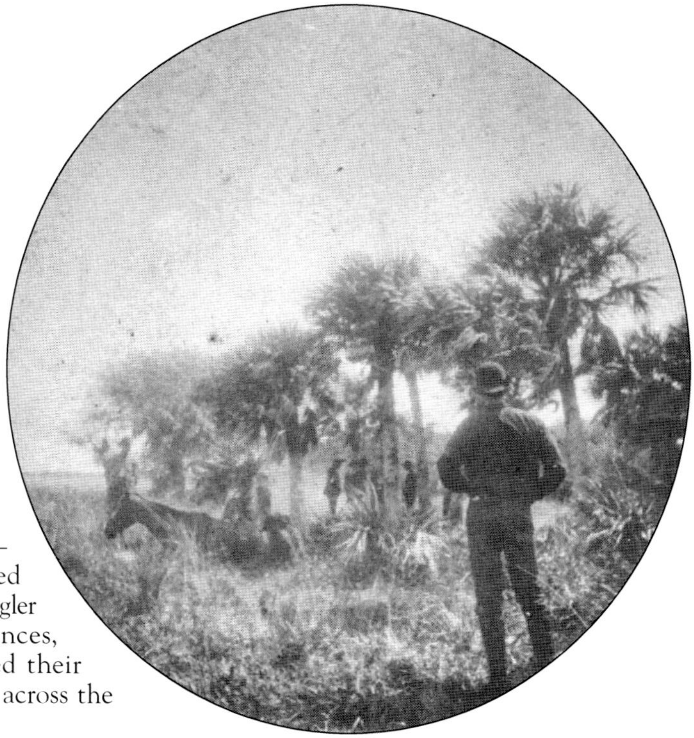

Surveyors were crucial in Everglades history, beginning with John Jackson in the late 1800s. In 1892, James Ingraham crossed the glades for the Plant railroad interests, although he gave up surveying partway in favor of survival. This rare image shows one of their campsites. In 1902–1903, William Krome surveyed Homestead to Cape Sable for Flagler interests. From their experiences, both successfully discouraged their bosses from putting railroads across the Everglades. (NPS.)

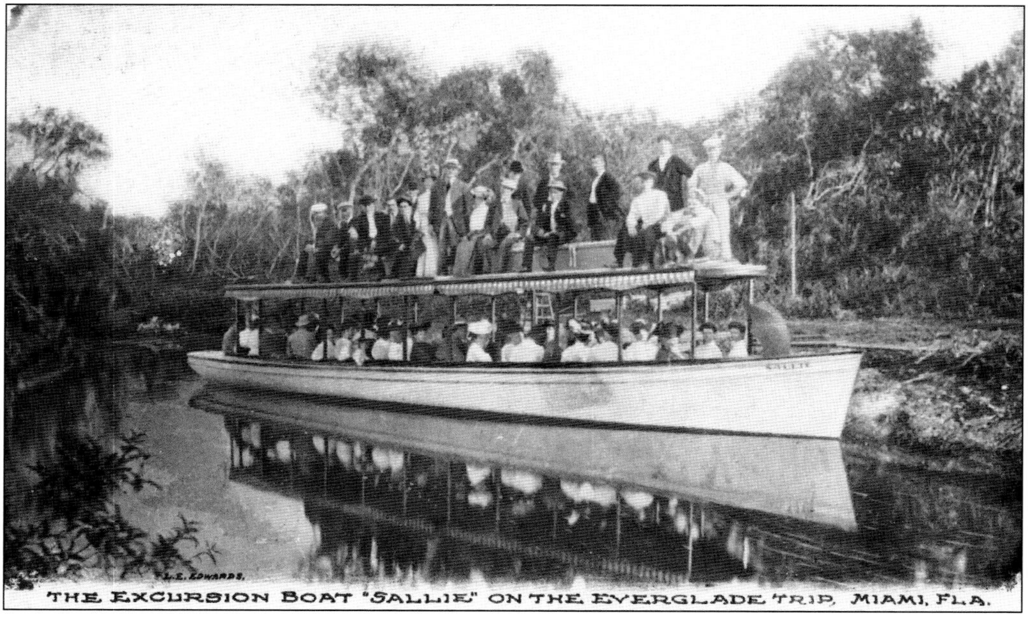

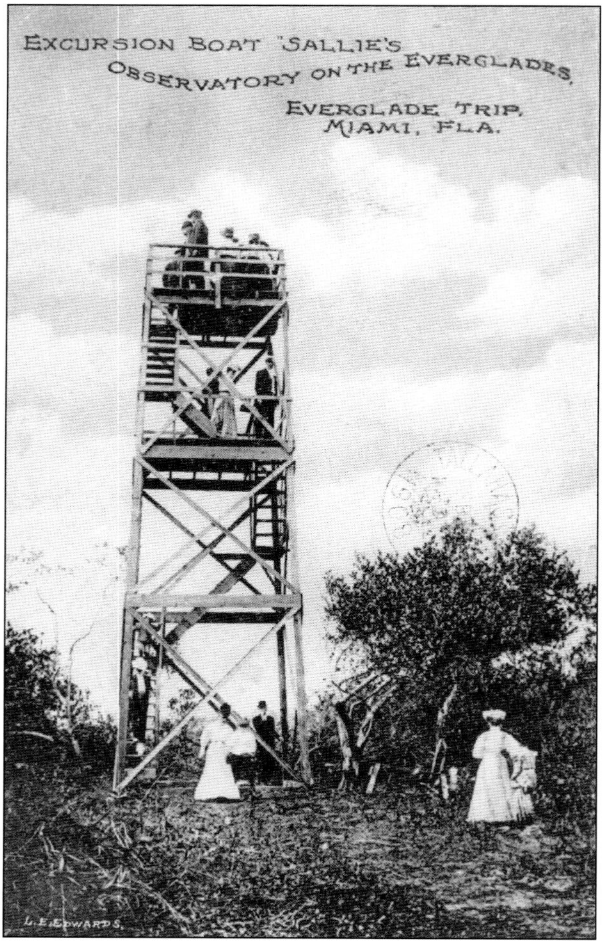

It was the railroad coming to Fort Dallas, soon to be named Miami, in 1896 that opened the way for less-than-adventurous Everglades tourists. The ultra-luxurious Royal Palm Hotel was up and running at the Miami River's mouth, and boat excursions went upriver to allow gazing upon the Everglades. The image above shows the *Sallie* headed to the rapids at the headwaters of the north fork. On arrival, the finely dressed passengers rode a mule-drawn rail tram to the 40-foot Sallie's Observatory (left). Later, a taller Car Dale Tower was built near the Richardson Groves' Musa Isle attraction a bit downriver. The Everglades beyond the tower remained a sea of sawgrass punctuated by tree islands, as it had been since first described in the 1700s. Today, the westward view from a similarly-placed Sallie's Observatory would be of Miami International Airport. (Both, SLAF.)

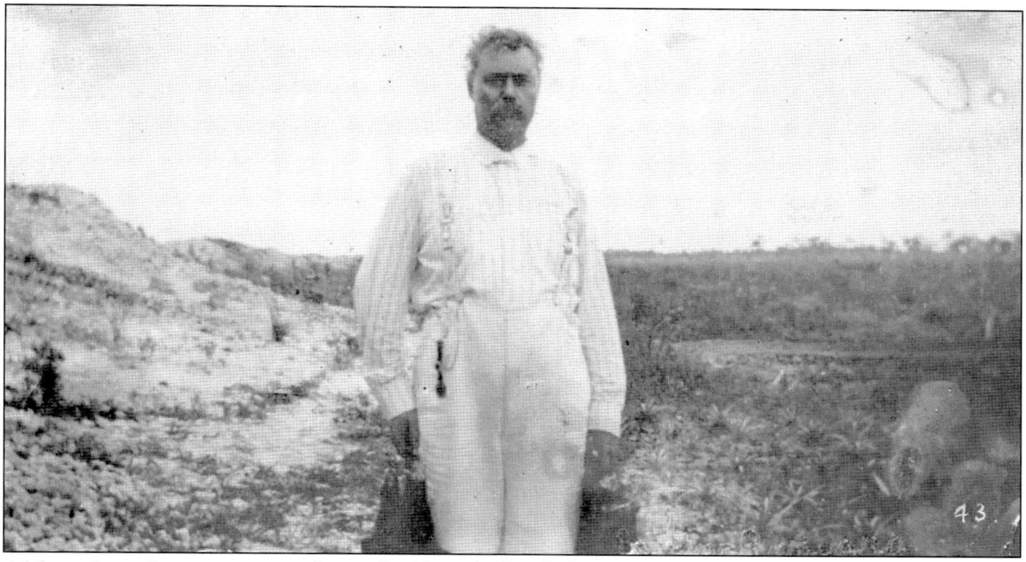

Although early attempts to drain the Everglades, led personally by Gov. Napoleon Bonaparte Broward (above), had little effect on the southern Everglades, digging the Miami and New River Canals from Lake Okeechobee to tidewater certainly did. Dredging to create the Miami Canal started in 1909. The rapids had been blown up the previous year, and the canal fed into the dredged Miami River. Opened in 1912, the Miami Canal increased the river's discharge and sediment load, lowering water levels in the nearby Everglades. Carried by larger tour boats, such as the steamer *Lady Lou*, tourists now could boat into the Everglades itself, although mostly viewing piles of dredging spoils. The Miami Canal, Miami River, and Everglades beyond are shown in the aerial photograph below from 1912. This is now NW Twenty-Seventh Avenue in Miami. (Above, UFTEW; below, LOC.)

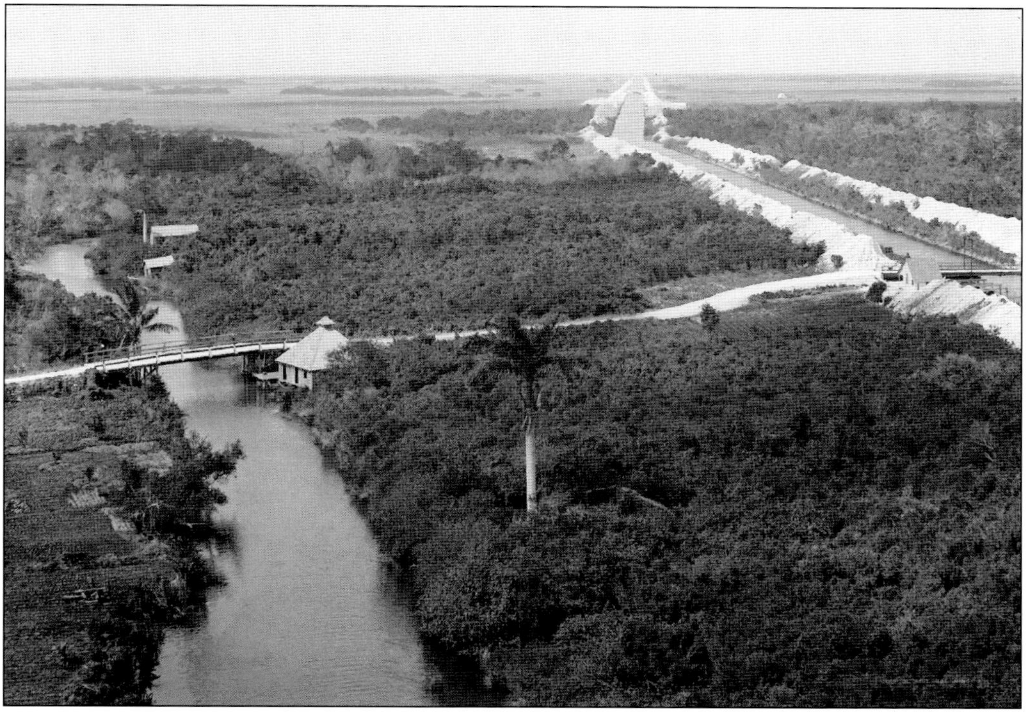

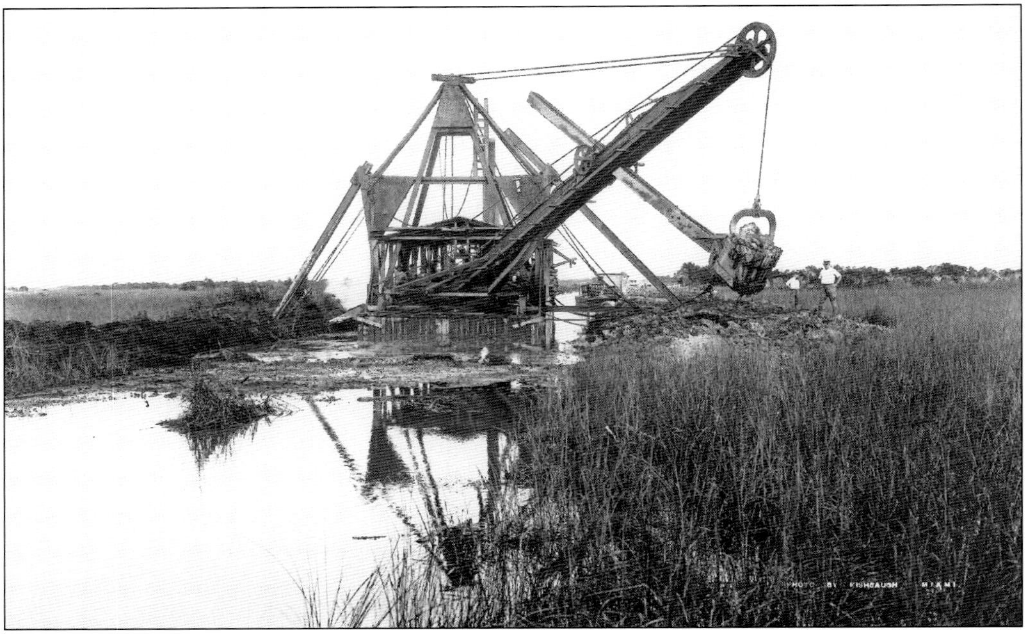

Tamiami Trail construction began in 1915. Surveyors set out from Miami, and others from Tampa. Interrupted funding, politics, war, and the land bust slowed progress. Dredging for road fill was something of a developing art; some dredges floated (above), while others "walked." Crews lived on barges (below). Excavating Everglades peat and soft limestone went faster than through the harder Big Cypress limestone. At the Everglades' western edge, Miami's Chevelier Corporation routed the road through its property. But when Lee County ran out of money, Barron Collier had a new Collier County created, passed bonds, and forced the road back north toward his land. The abandoned Chevelier road became Loop Road, now in Big Cypress National Preserve. Requiring a new county, 13 years, $13 million (over $200 million today), and 2.6 million dynamite sticks, the Tamiami Trail was completed in 1928. (Both, SLAF.)

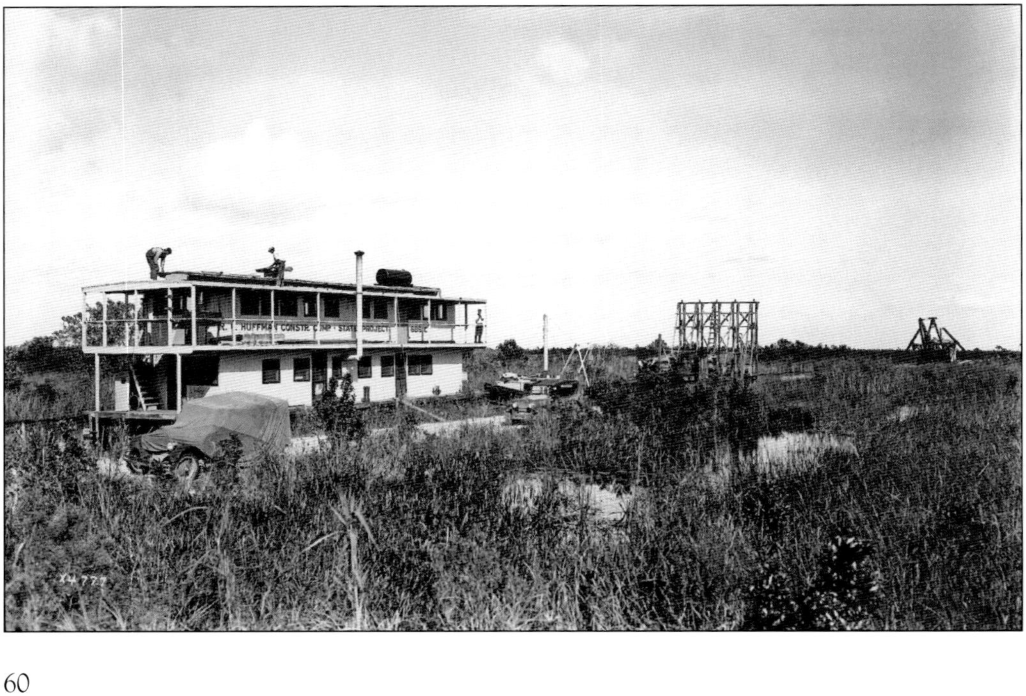

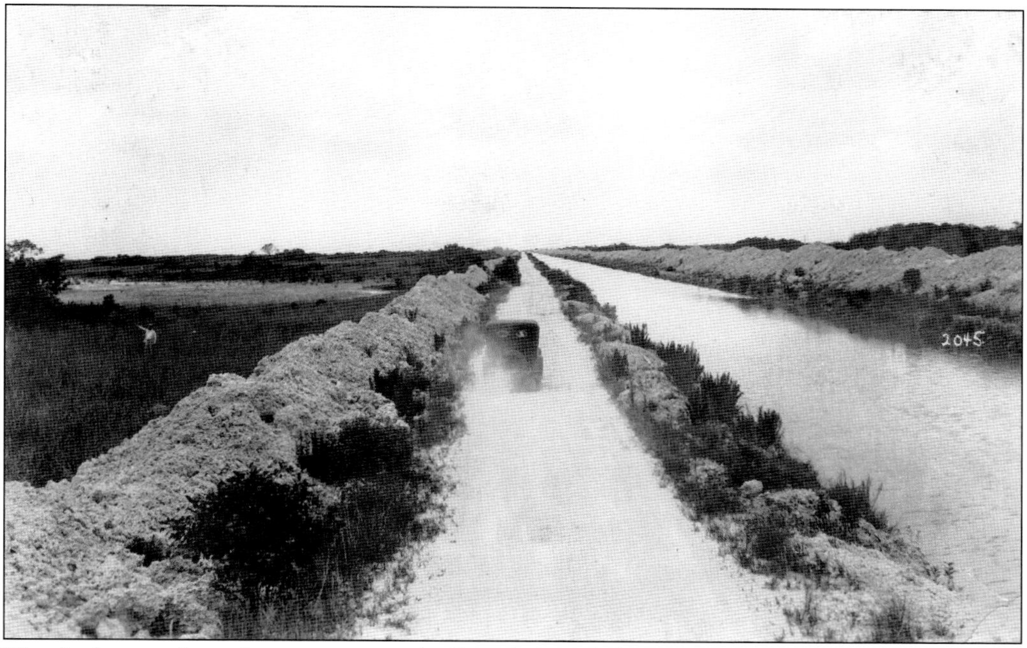

The dredges working their way across the Everglades piled up peat and rock to be flattened into a roadbed (above). High and wide but with inadequate culverts, the roadbed led to multiple environmental and cultural impacts. Too little thought seems to have been given to how much it would block water flow in the wet season, as suggested by the 1921 photograph of water flowing over the road below. Later, non-native Australian pine trees were planted to hold the roadbed together. The road, located about where Willoughby's canoe trip had been blocked by impenetrable sawgrass, allowed easy access to the Everglades by anyone with a vehicle. It facilitated land sales, which encouraged further drainage and the development that followed. The southern Everglades and its people would never be the same. (Both, HM.)

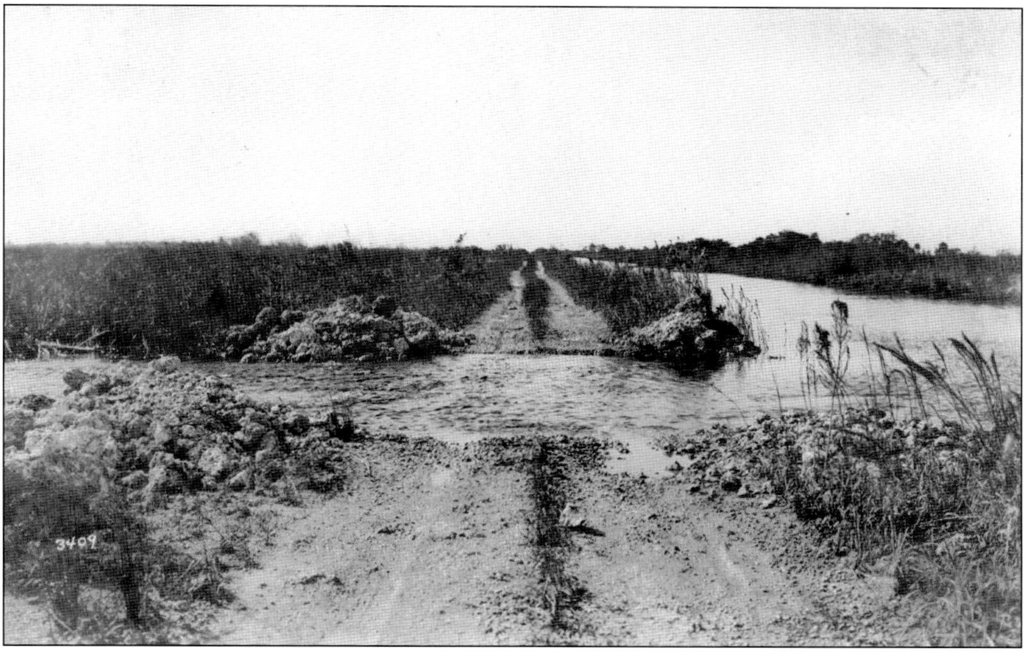

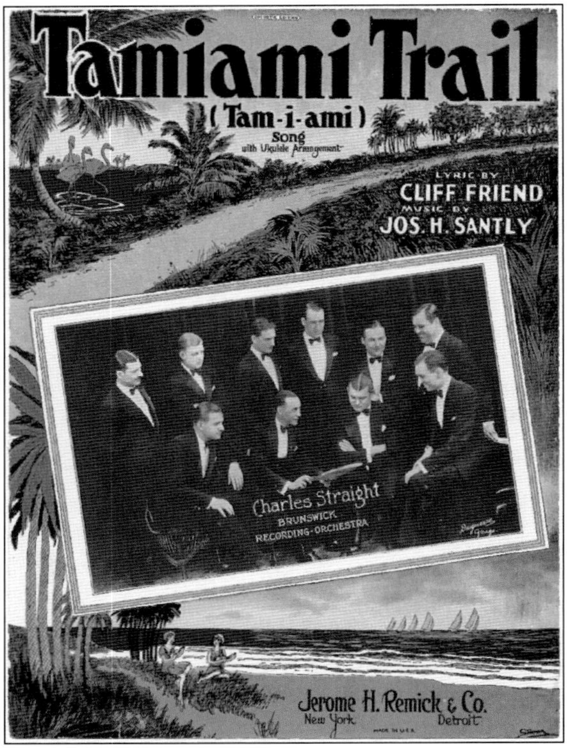

The anticipated Tamiami Trail took on a mystique. It was publicized through articles, postcards, poems, and songs, such as the tune at left. To encourage the project in 1923, ten cars set out from Fort Myers with national attention to cross the Everglades on their own wheels (below). It turns out that the off-road part was not through the Everglades but the Big Cypress—in the dry season, led by Seminole guides from Indian camp to camp through dry prairies and pinelands. They were resupplied by airplanes, had dinner at Collier's fancy Rod and Gun Club, abandoned cars along the way, and were pulled by an undisclosed tractor. The Everglades itself was crossed using the already-built road. Their celebratory arrival in Miami, however, was huge and thoroughly publicized. (Both, SLAF.)

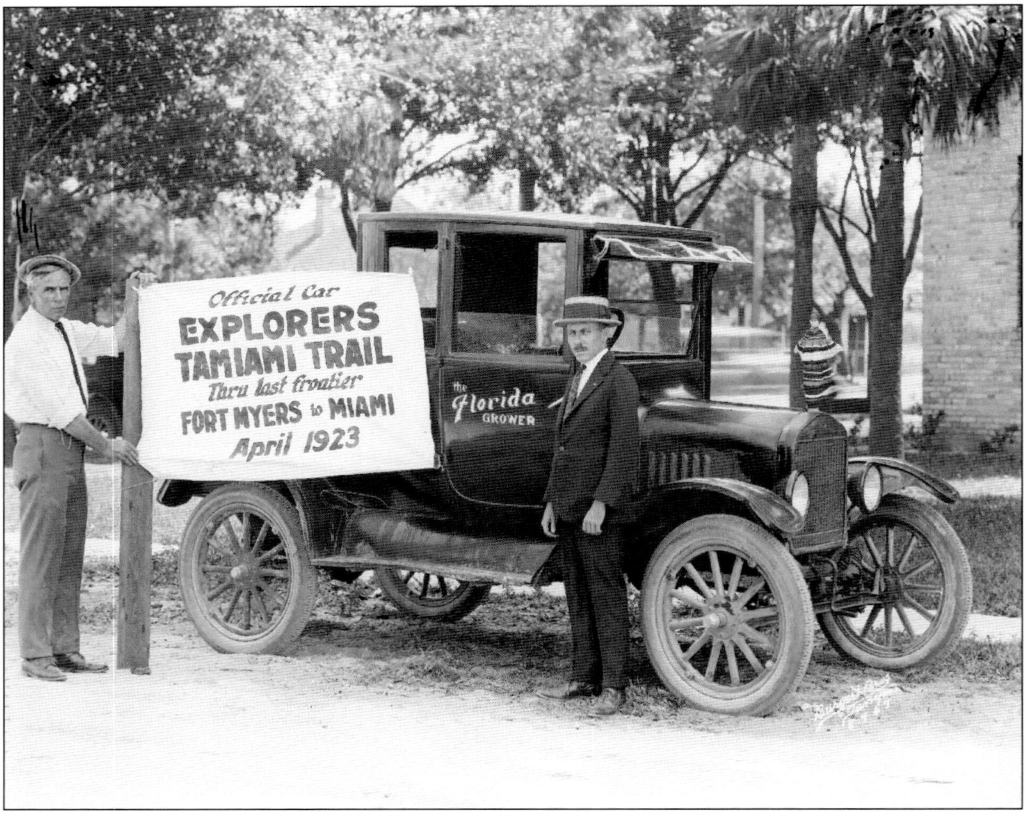

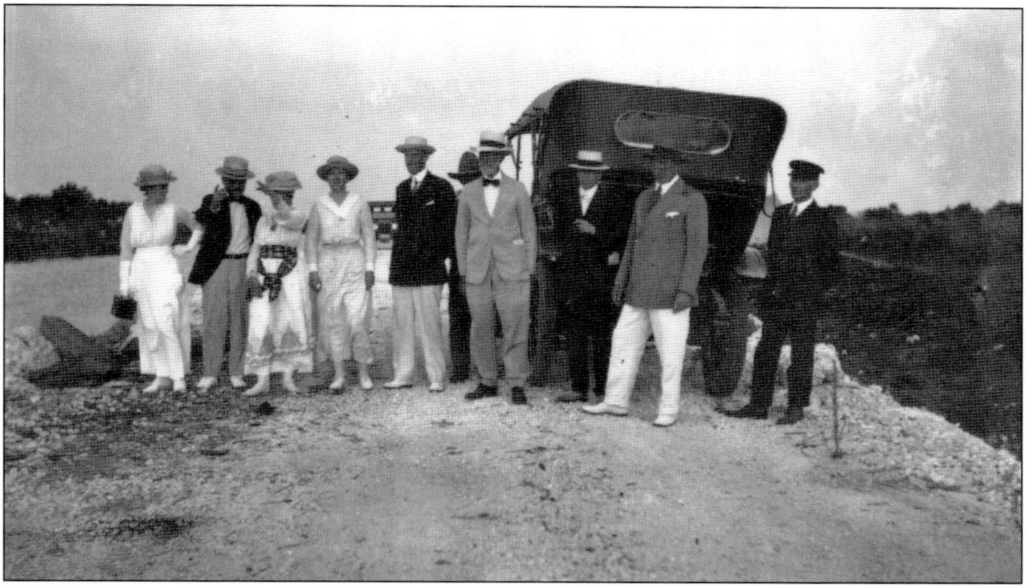

People from Miami began exploring the trail. Even unfinished, the road allowed the car-owning public to experience the wonders of dredging and the birds, alligators, sawgrass prairies, and tree islands that were once but a view from Miami River tourist towers. Sunday drivers headed to the end of the road to see the sights (above) and maybe picnic. Others came looking to buy swampland. On April 28, 1928, only three decades after Willoughby's canoe trip, Tamiami Trail was officially opened, attended by carloads of people. The image below shows cars from Miami heading to the opening ceremonies in the town of Everglades. The road, a lifeline to Collier County development, connected South Florida coasts for the first time by land. The trail was the culmination of a seemingly impossible dream, to travel unimpeded straight across the Everglades. (Both, HM.)

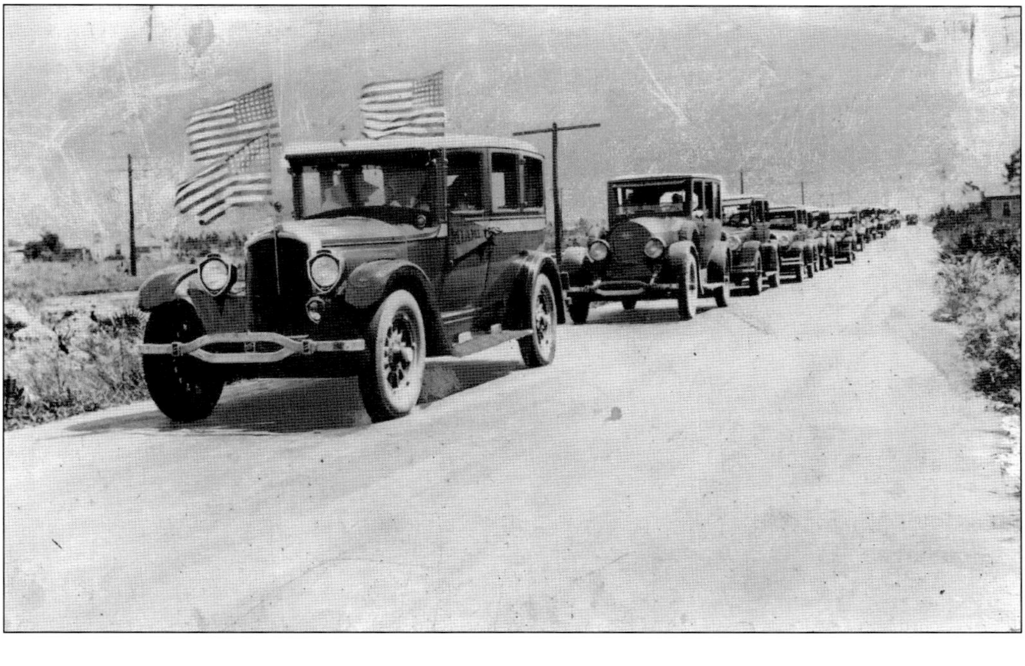

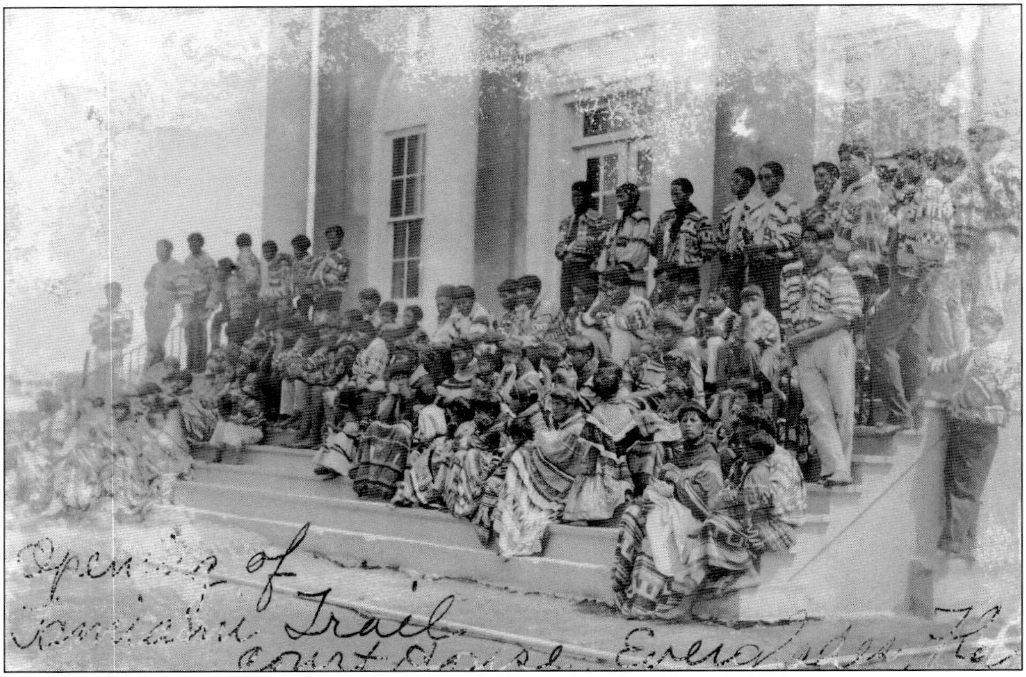

Tamiami Trail changed everything in the southern glades. The age of self-isolating Seminoles, furtive pioneers, and hardy settlers was soon gone. The eastern Everglades was being drained, and development was marching inward. The trail blocked and rearranged the Everglades' natural flow of water and gave Miami hunters ready access to Everglades wildlife. Seminole representatives attended the trail's opening ceremonies on the courthouse steps (above). Along the elevated roadbed, some Everglades Seminoles opened their campsites to tourists. The image below shows a village and a Trailways bus, a company founded by Barron Collier as Tamiami Trail Tours that initially ran among Tamiami Trail's villages and between coastal cities. Tamiami Trail became South Florida's east-west route, cutting like a knife through the Everglades. (Both, SLAF.)

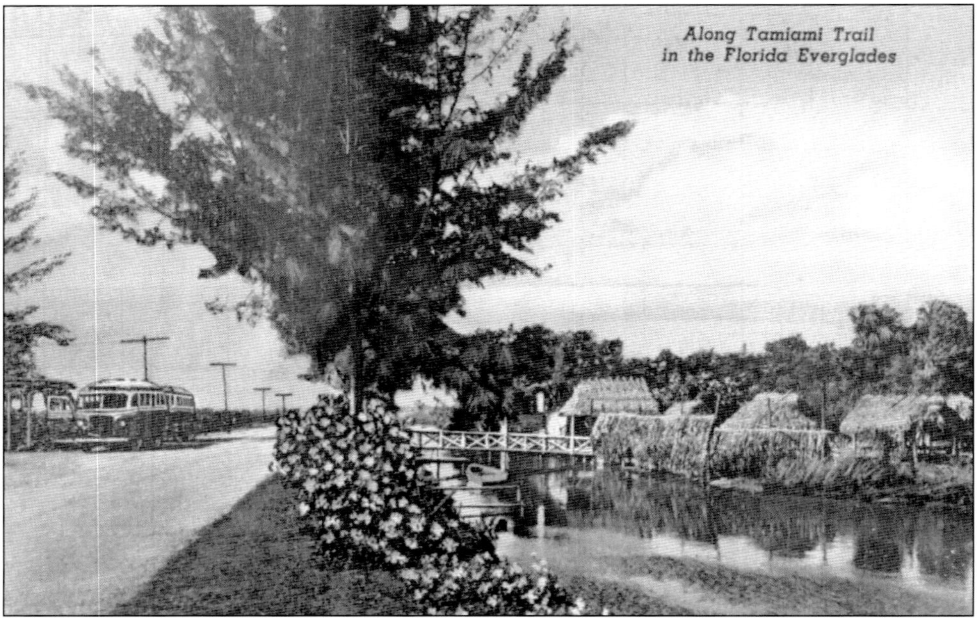

Four

Making of the National Park

The idea of a park in the Everglades was inspired by two interwoven movements of the early 1900s, protecting plume-bearing birds from ladies' hats and reserving areas for the edification of people. The slaughter of egrets brought national attention to the Everglades, and protective legislation followed. Creating a park in the Everglades focused on a patch of tropical forest, Palm Hammock, situated on Paradise Key. Led by the Florida Federation of Women's Clubs, the hammock and over 900 acres became Royal Palm State Park in 1916, the same year that the National Park Service was established. Initially lacking state operating funds, the women's clubs undertook the difficult task of finding money and managing the park, which they did for several decades. By 1921, the state park had been enlarged by 2,000 acres.

As drainage schemes proceeded, the higher edges of the Everglades were opened to agriculture and settlement; the deep interior wetland was another matter. Hurricanes in 1926 and 1928 flooded agricultural land occupying former Everglades just south of Lake Okeechobee. The 1928 storm killed an estimated 2,500 people, leading Congress to authorize ringing the lake with levees. The storm's flooding also suggested that much of the Everglades was in fact undevelopable. As the idea of a larger park in the Everglades gained traction, in 1929, the state and federal governments began studying its feasibility.

Associations, committees, commissions, politicians, activists, and federal officials evaluated, studied, advocated, and negotiated for a tropical Everglades park. A leader was New England landscape architect turned Coconut Grove conservationist Ernest F. Coe. Legislation was introduced, testimony was taken, reports were written, and tours arranged, including by blimp. Congress authorized the park in 1934, although with restrictions on funding, land acquisition, and timing. The first park boundaries, avoiding parcels having any suggestion of development potential, were not what many park advocates had suggested, which would have encompassed much of South Florida's biodiversity. But compromises were considered necessary. In December 1947, Pres. Harry S. Truman arrived at the town of Everglades to dedicate Everglades National Park.

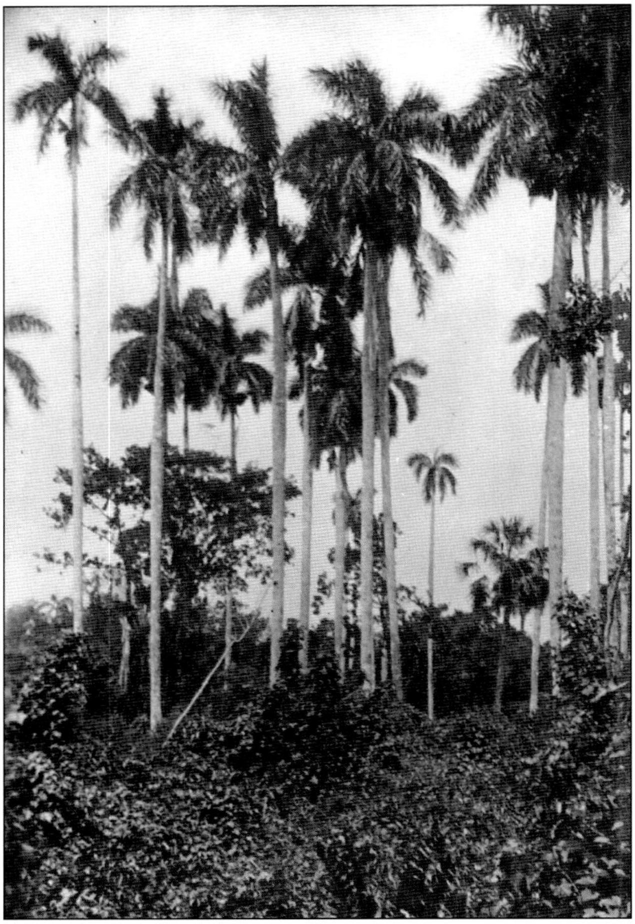

The distinctive patch of forest on an Everglades island, enticingly named Paradise Key, was first visited by pioneer nurserymen in 1893; the trip took three days from Little River. Other expeditions followed. Naturalists praised the hammock's diversity of tropical trees, ferns, orchids, and especially its 100-foot-tall royal palms. Outside of South Florida, royal palms occur only in Cuba. It came to be known as Palm Hammock. (HM.)

Previously, knowledge of Palm Hammock by non-Seminoles had been limited due to its isolation west of the seasonally deep waters of Taylor Slough. The earliest botanical explorers had to canoe, walk, and wade for miles to get there. This 1925 image shows an early vehicular attempt to cross the slough, the deep water of which had protected the hammock from fire by keeping its soil moist through the dry season. (HM.)

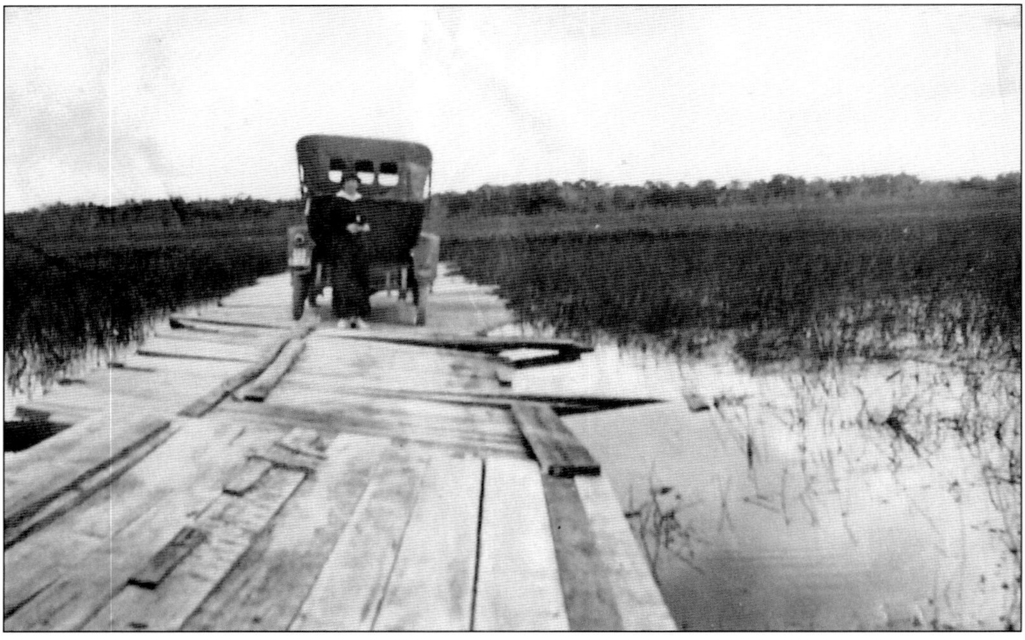

It was a road to cross Taylor Slough that inspired the movement to protect Palm Hammock. Early Everglades surveyor James Ingraham, heading Flagler's Model Land Company, intended to build a road to open for sale lands it received for building the railroad to Key West. The road would bisect the hammock. Mary Munroe, hearing about this, went to Ingraham, who was not opposed to the park idea. Begun in 1915, the image at right shows the road passing through Palm Hammock in 1916. The road later was extended south of Long Pine Key and then to Flamingo and East Cape Sable in 1922. The 1922 image below shows its 200-foot right-of-way being cut through mangroves, a story told by Lawrence E. Will in *A Dredgeman of Cape Sable*. The Ingraham Highway is often mentioned in this book. (Right, UFMMJ; below, SLAF.)

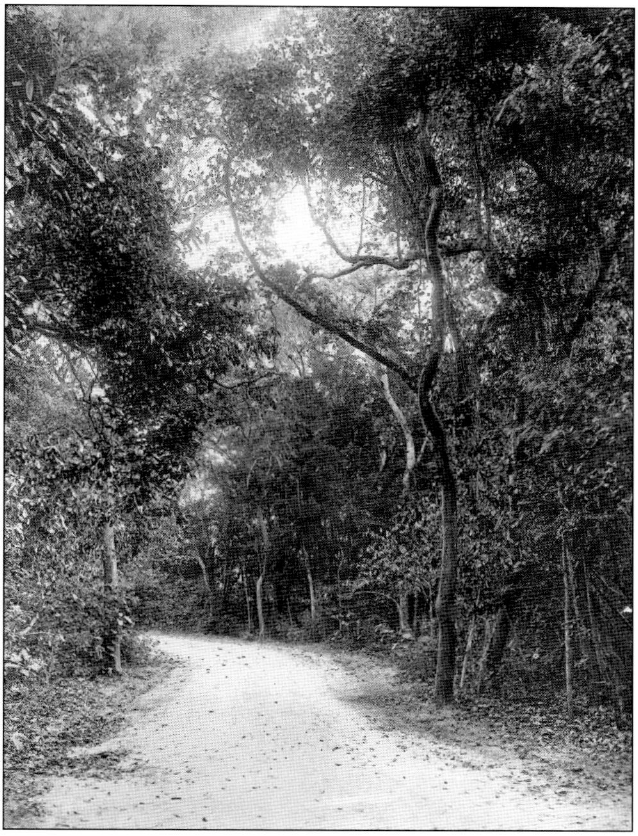

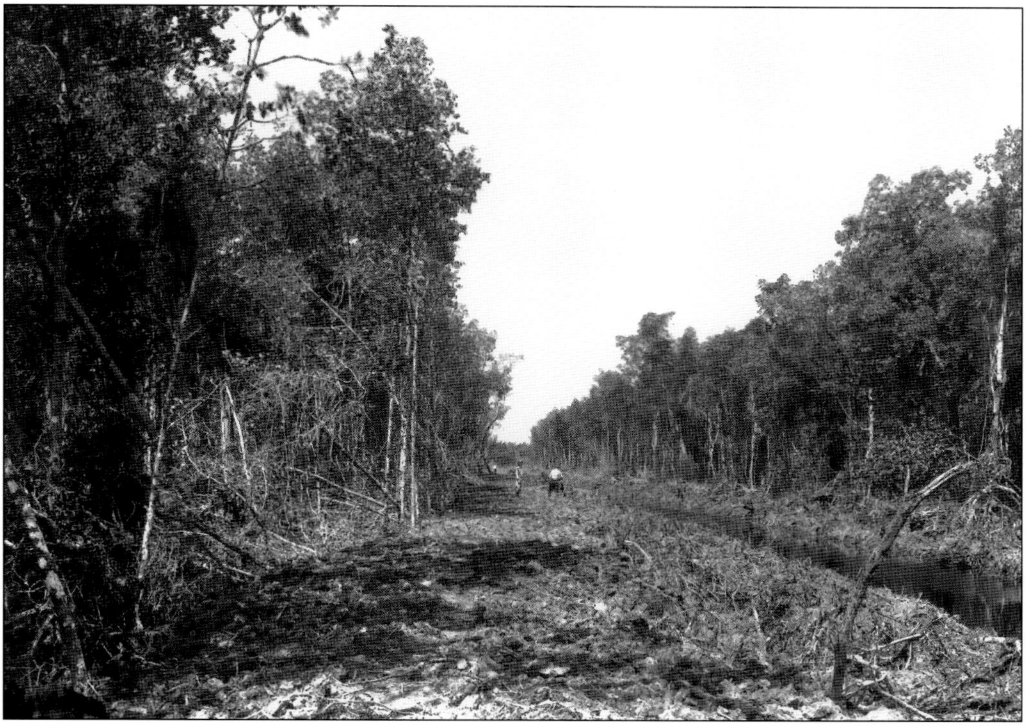

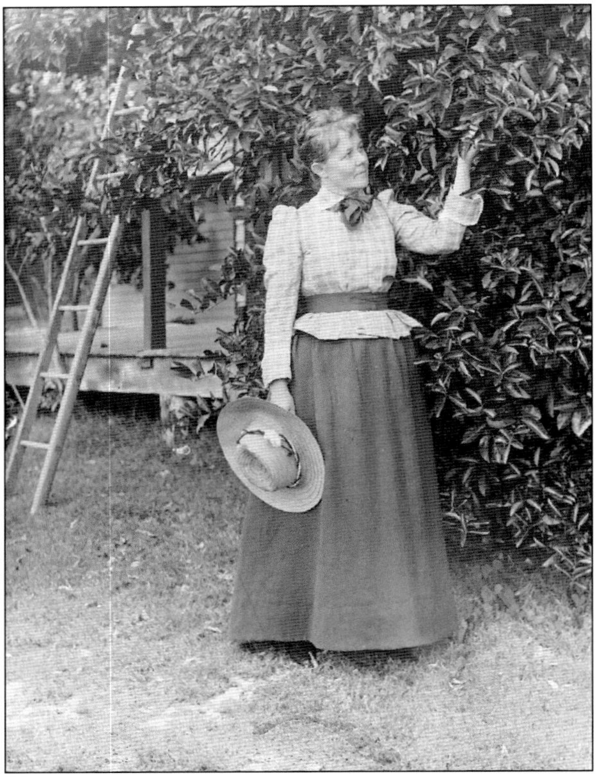

Mary Barr Munroe learned about the hammock from local botanists, and in 1905, she brought the park idea to the Florida Federation of Women's Clubs. Munroe's successful advocacies also included protecting plume-birds and manatees, making it the first animal legally protected in Florida. She created local Audubon societies, the library in Coconut Grove, and conservation-oriented youth organizations. Mary Barr Munroe founded conservation action in South Florida. (HM.)

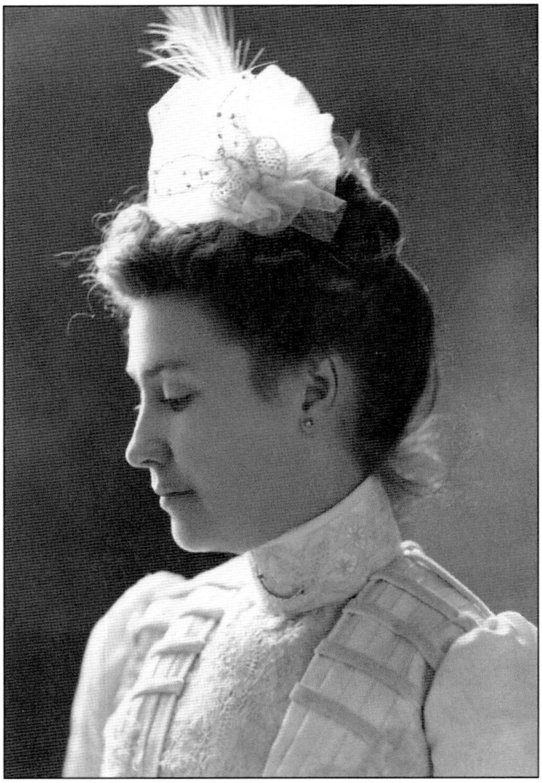

May Mann Jennings took up the cause. Shown in 1901, a bit ironically wearing an egret plume, she was married to William Sherman Jennings, Florida governor from 1901 to 1905. May was a skilled politician in her own right and an influential activist in progressive social causes of the day. Encouraged by her and Mary Barr Munroe, the women's clubs of Florida pushed the legislature to create Royal Palm State Park. (SLAF.)

May and William Jennings, who as governor first enabled Everglades drainage, lobbied for the park, succeeding during the 1915 legislative session, at the last minute, as this telegram shows. The Florida Federation of Women's Clubs became custodian of Florida's first state park. It happened to be near former governor Jennings's landholdings and those of Henry Flagler's widow, Mary Lily Flagler, who crucially donated acreage to provide income for the park. (UFMMJ.)

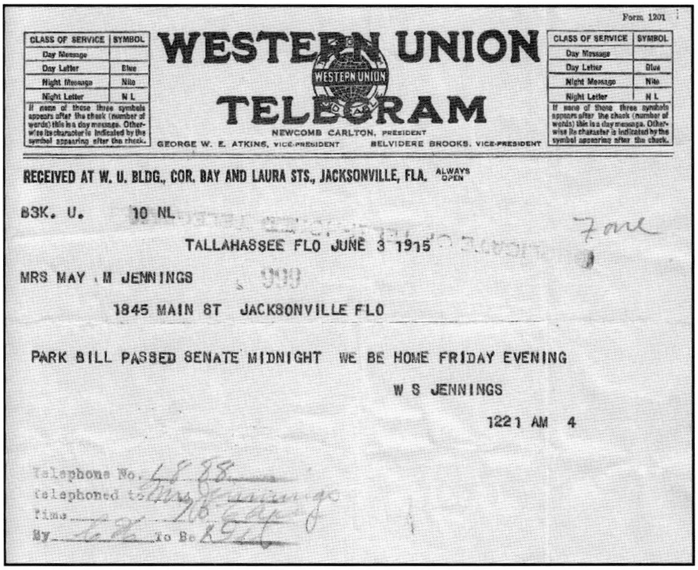
Form 1201

WESTERN UNION TELEGRAM

NEWCOMB CARLTON, PRESIDENT

GEORGE W. E. ATKINS, VICE-PRESIDENT BELVIDERE BROOKS, VICE-PRESIDENT

CLASS OF SERVICE	SYMBOL
Day Message	
Day Letter	Blue
Night Message	Nite
Night Letter	N L

If none of these three symbols appears after the check (number of words) this is a day message. Otherwise its character is indicated by the symbol appearing after the check.

RECEIVED AT W. U. BLDG., COR. BAY AND LAURA STS., JACKSONVILLE, FLA. ALWAYS OPEN

83K. U. 10 NL

TALLAHASSEE FLO JUNE 3 1915

MRS MAY M JENNINGS

1845 MAIN ST JACKSONVILLE FLO

PARK BILL PASSED SENATE MIDNIGHT WE BE HOME FRIDAY EVENING

W S JENNINGS

1221 AM 4

Telephone No.

Telephoned to

Time

By To Be

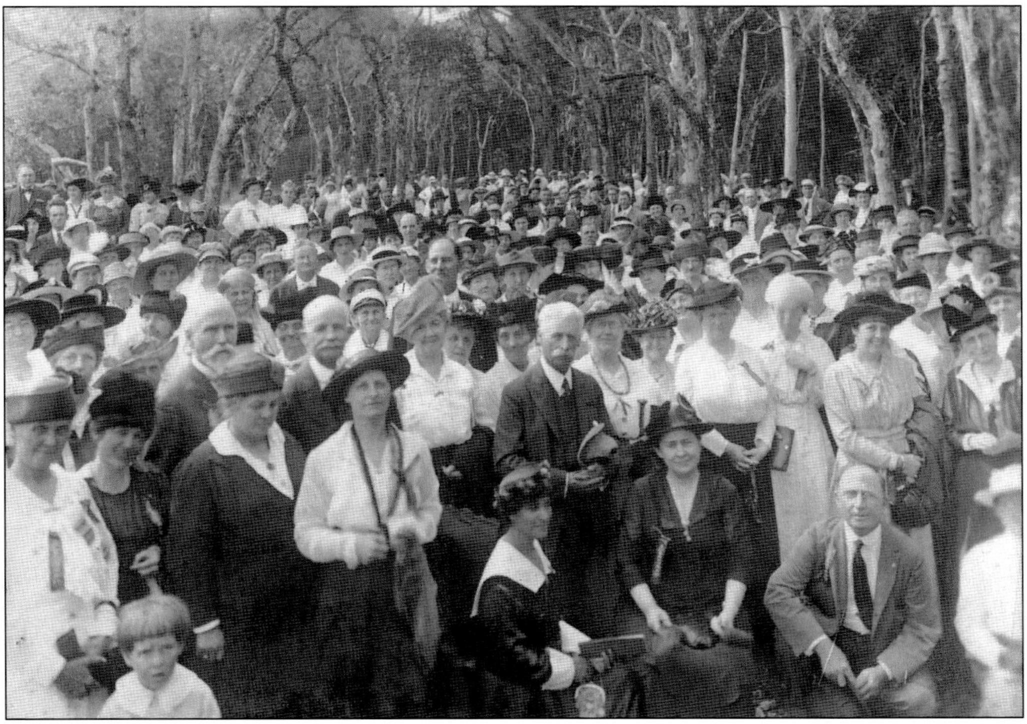

Royal Palm State Park was dedicated on November 23, 1916. This image shows the impressive crowd at the dedication ceremony as the Florida Federation of Women's Clubs took over management of the state park. At the same ceremony, somewhat ironically, the road that had threatened the hammock also was dedicated as the Ingraham Highway. In 1917, the federation celebrated the new park by having its annual meeting there. (UFMMJ.)

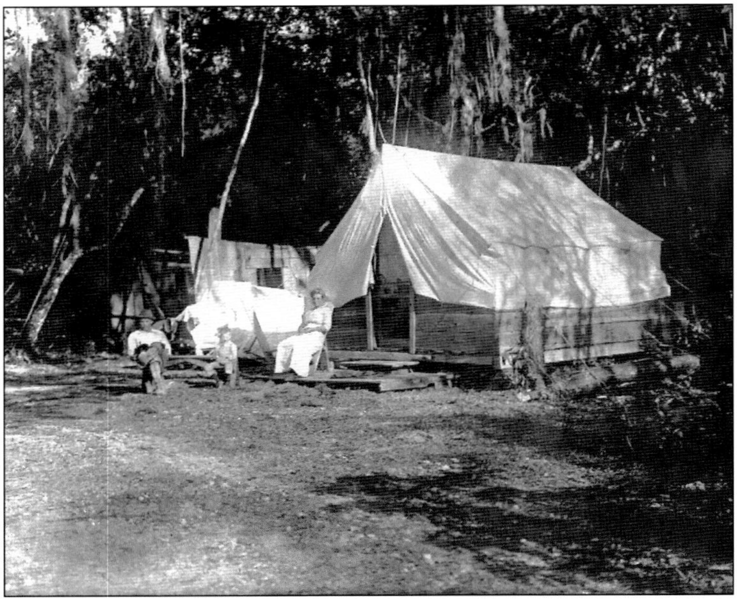

The federation appointed Charles A. Mosier park warden. An accomplished botanist, Mosier and his family initially lived in the tent shown here. A trail, hammock, and several plants are named for him. Without state money, Florida's women's clubs were mobilized to donate coins: "A Mile of Dimes for Royal Palm State Park." Mosier grew royal palms to sell and in 1925, 24,000 postcards were printed to sell. (SLAF.)

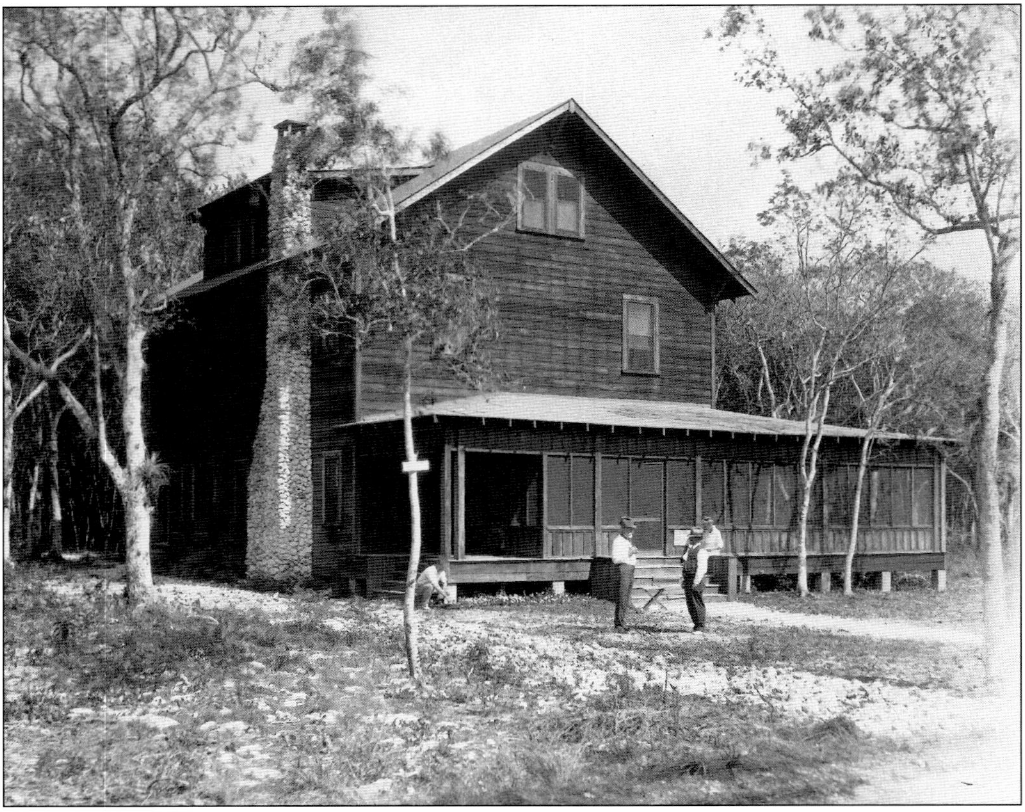

The Florida Federation of Women's Clubs borrowed money to engage Homestead builder John F. Umphrey to construct its headquarters. The Arts and Crafts–style Royal Palm Lodge was built in 1917, shown that year. It was home for the warden-caretaker, visitor contact center, offered accommodations for a few, lunch by the caretaker's wife, and escape from mosquitoes on the screened porch. Royal Palm State Park immediately landed on recommended tourist routes. (SLAF.)

In 1933, a company of the Civilian Conservation Corps was posted to the park for six months. The photograph to the right shows the entrance to their 200-man camp. The crew was led by landscape architect William Lyman Phillips, who also undertook similar projects around Miami, including Matheson Hammock and Greynolds Parks. His crews made substantial changes to the state park, which were welcomed by the federation. He artificially landscaped over 30 acres, adding orange and avocado trees, widened and surfaced trails, cleared hammock vegetation, and built four stone buildings, including a large garage. The crew also built a 10-acre fenced deer park so visitors could feed captive deer. The image below shows the deer park building with Phillips in the foreground. The 1933 structure still stands and is now the oldest surviving building within Everglades National Park. (Right, NPS; below, USNA.)

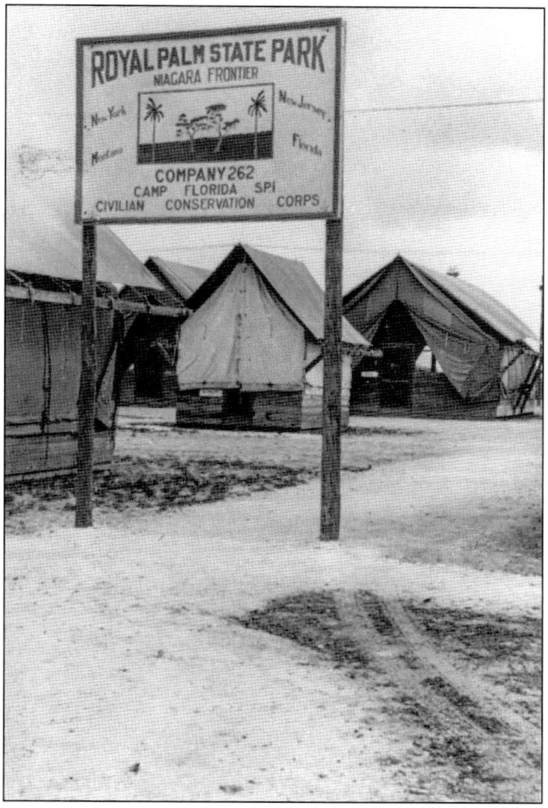

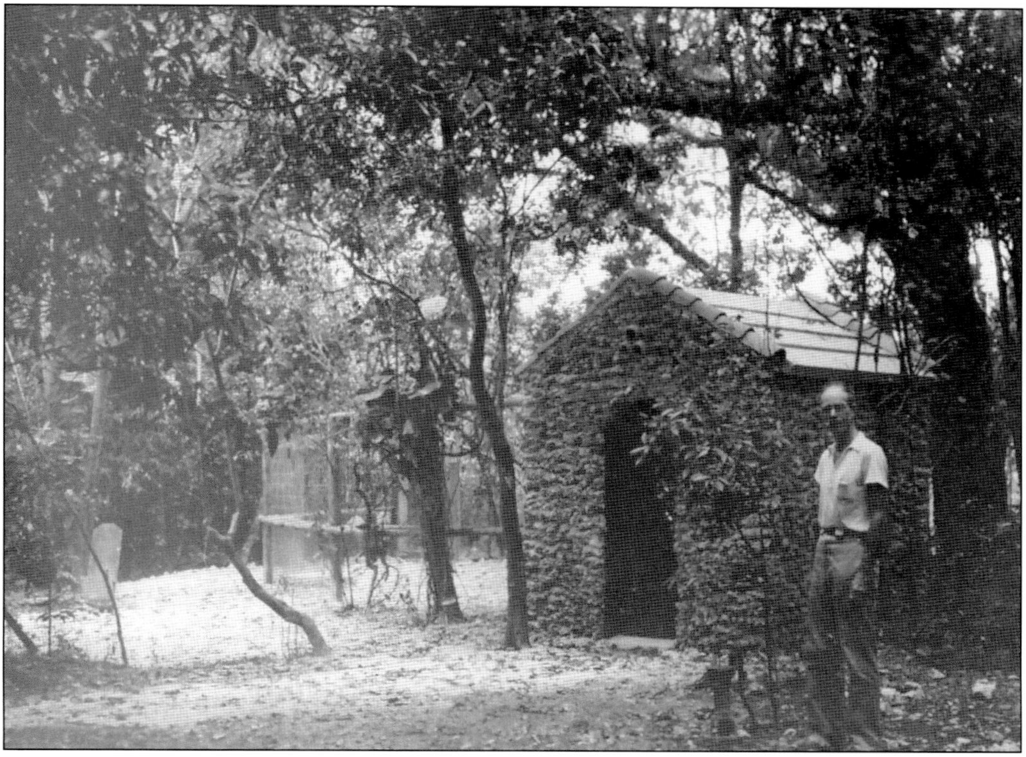

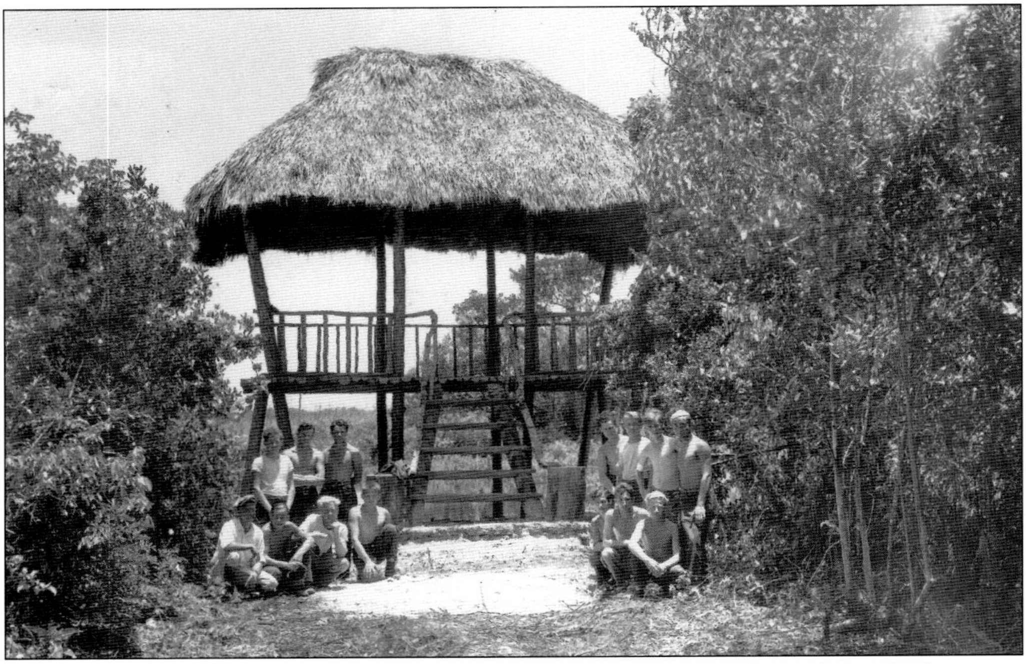

One of the Civilian Conservation Corps projects was to create an elevated thatched viewing platform from which visitors could see the Everglades of Taylor Slough. The image above shows the crew posing at the structure. Phillips also brought in heavy equipment (seen below). He blasted and dug out ponds, including a free-form lily pond, cementing the inside to keep the water from leaking out. Royal Palm State Park continued to attract carloads of visitors, and many more passed through the hammock on the way to Flamingo. In 1945, part of the hammock burned because drainage had robbed it of the age-old protection provided by a wet moat around the island. The Florida Federation of Women's Clubs managed Royal Palm State Park for 32 years, providing a historic waypoint toward creating a national park around it. (Both, UFMMJ.)

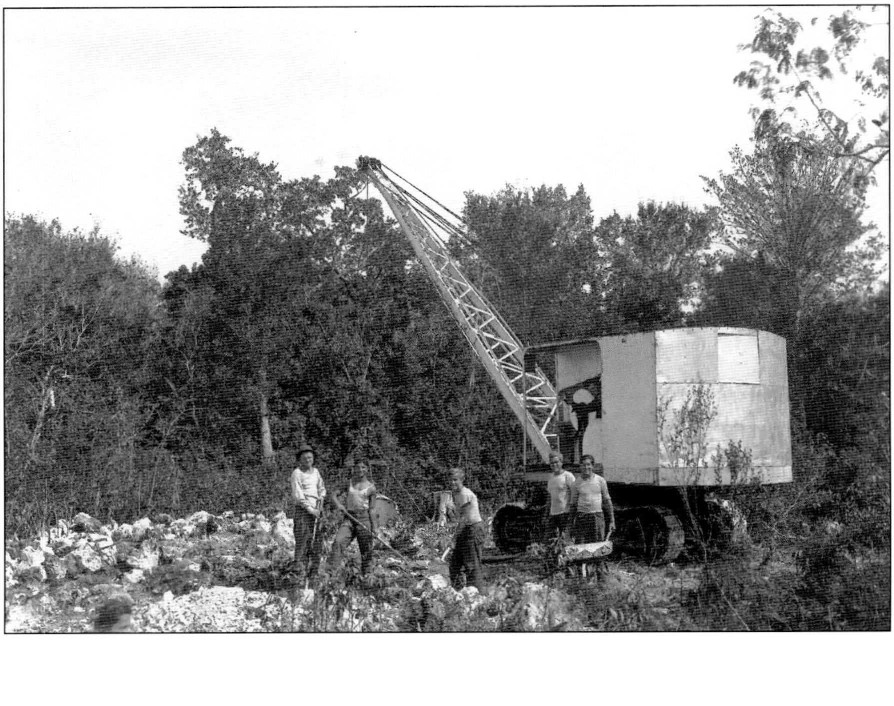

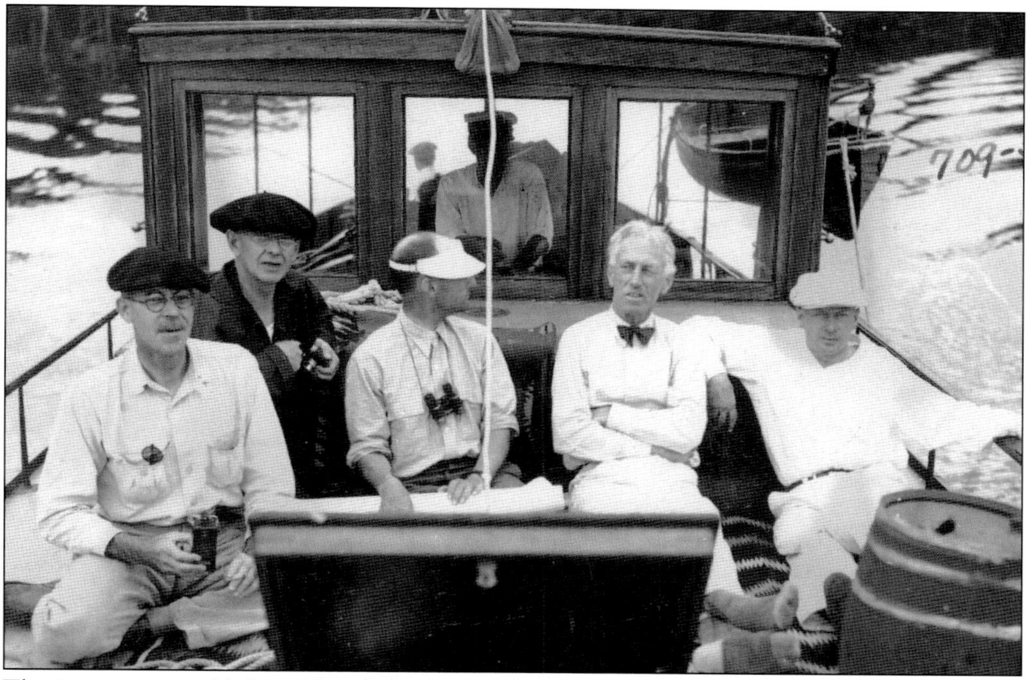

The journey to establishing Everglades National Park was long and difficult. Harold Bailey and the Florida Society of Natural History made a proposal as early as 1921, which inspired new member and new Coconut Grove resident Ernest F. Coe to found the Everglades Tropical Park Association in 1928. Coe spearheaded the effort relentlessly for years, leading many trips and tours to the Everglades. The image above shows Coe (with bowtie) leading one in 1929. In 1930, an official National Park Service tour by blimp (below) included such influential participants as T. Gilbert Pearson, president of the National Association of Audubon Societies; financier-naturalist J.B. Semple; Congresswoman Ruth Bryan Owen; Everglades Tropical Park Association president David Fairchild; National Park Service director Horace M. Albright; and American Museum of Natural History past director Herman Bumpus. (Both, HM.)

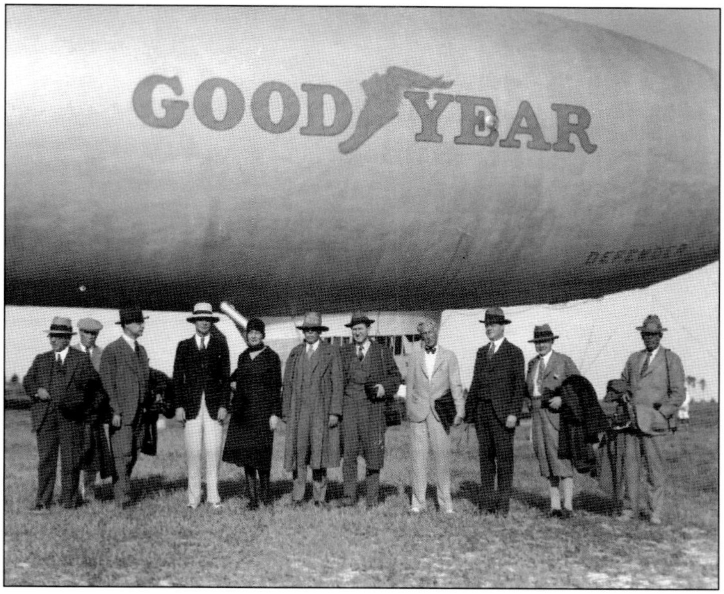

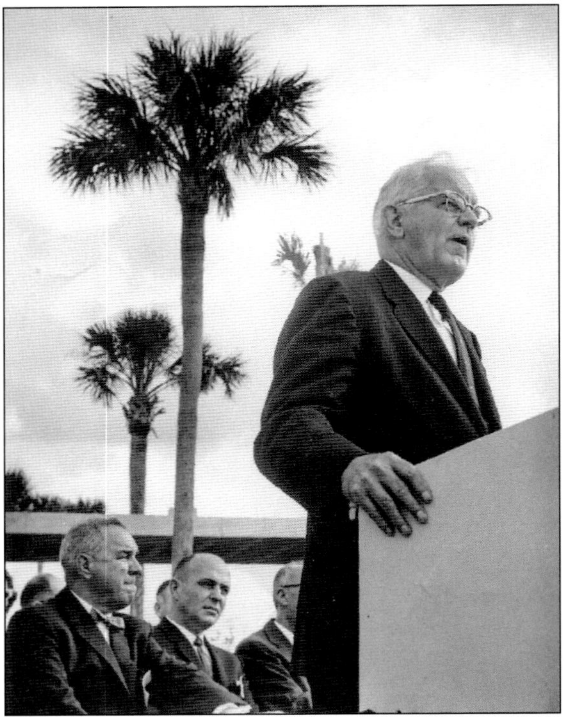

Among the prominent national park supporters were Sen. Spessard Holland and newspaper editor John Pennekamp. Holland led the federal campaign. Pennekamp, who had been asked by his publisher to secure state funding, impressed the legislative leadership in a poker game; they gave him the money. This later image shows Holland speaking at the 1961 dedication of the new main park visitor center. Pennekamp is seated behind him at left. (NPS.)

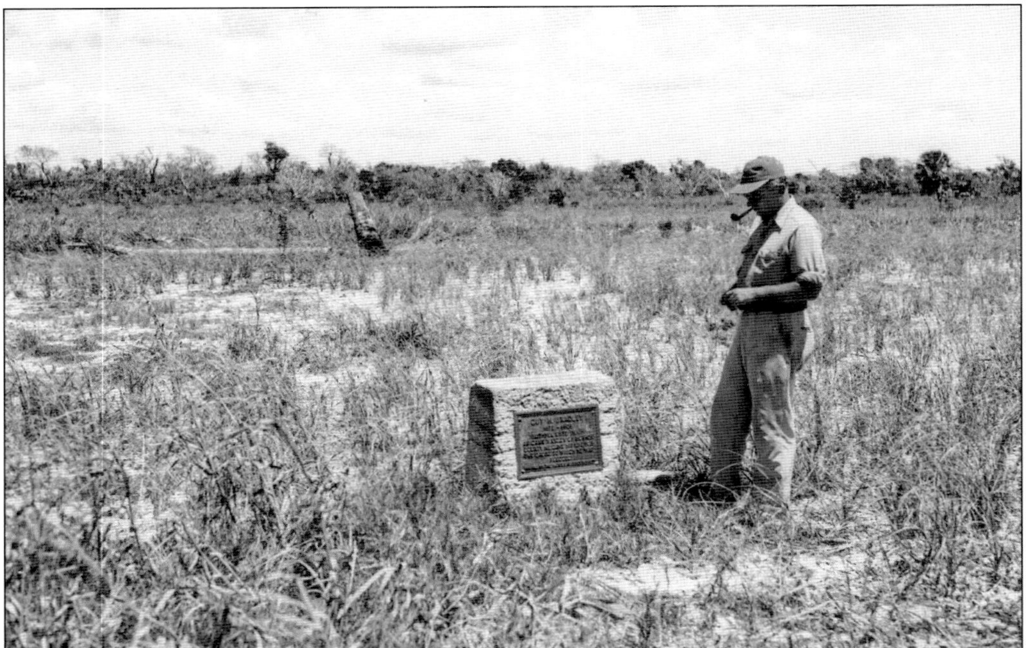

Crucial to defining what the park might be was a report by Daniel B. Beard, later the park's first superintendent. The park proposal was supported both by preservationists and those expecting a tourist attraction. Beard presciently cautioned about the "delicate task of adjusting human and wildlife use." This 1947 image shows Beard at the monument to Guy Bradley, whose death had brought conservation in the Everglades to national attention. (NPS.)

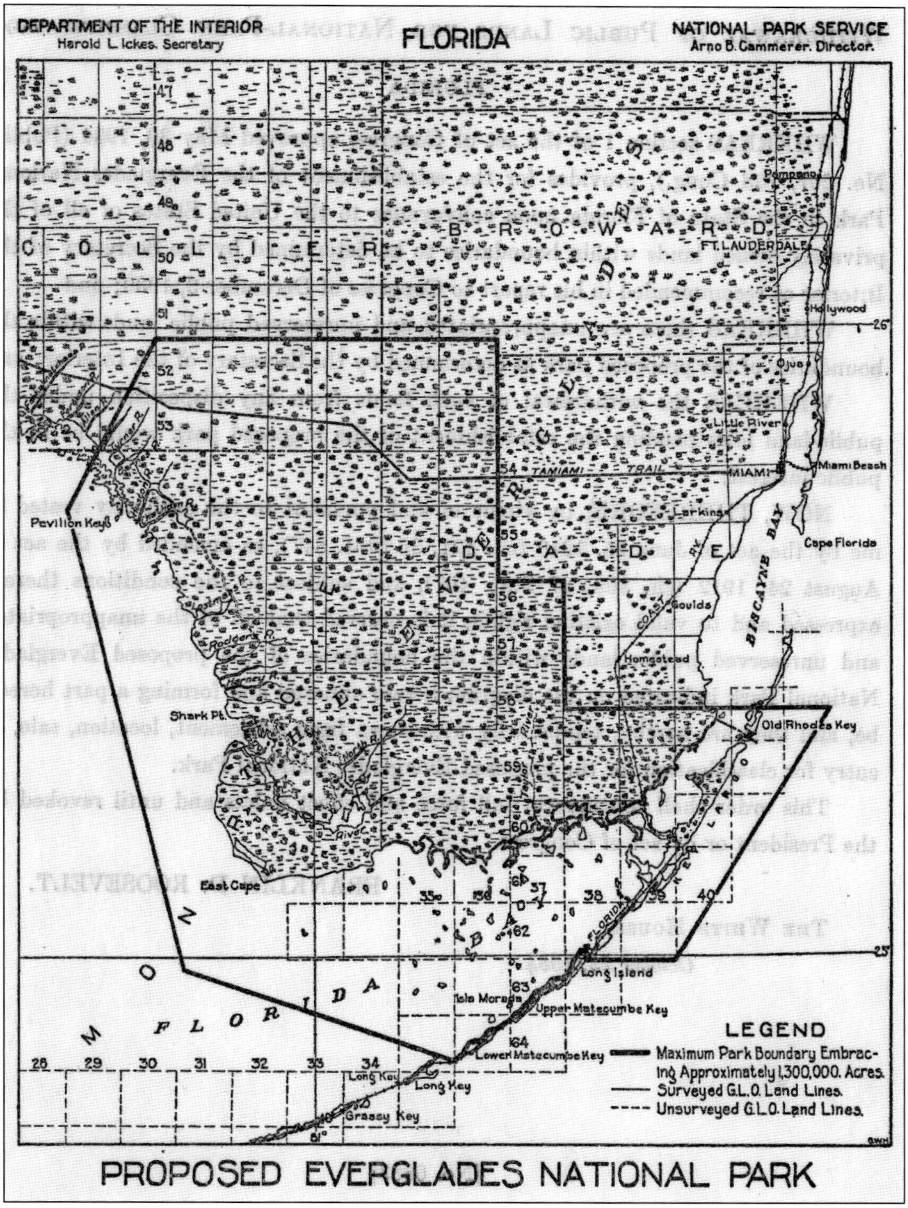

Daniel Beard's original biological reconnaissance suggested an expansive footprint for the park, one that revealed a brilliant understanding of the world-class diversity of South Florida's natural resources meriting protection. Ernest F. Coe vigorously supported such a boundary for the new park. It took in the core of the southern Everglades, southern Big Cypress Swamp, and the coastal mangrove forests. The proposed northern park boundary was north of Tamiami Trail to accommodate the important water flows from the northern Big Cypress Swamp. It extended through the Ten Thousand Islands, taking in all of the coastal keys and their bird rookeries south to Cape Sable. It included Florida Bay and its roosts and colonies of egrets, spoonbills, and great white herons and the coastal habitat of American crocodiles and West Indian manatees. Along the Florida Keys, the proposed boundary protected the outstanding West Indian tropical forests of northern Key Largo and the coral reef offshore. Inland, the boundary incorporated the headwaters of Taylor Slough and Royal Palm State Park. It was not to be. (SLAF.)

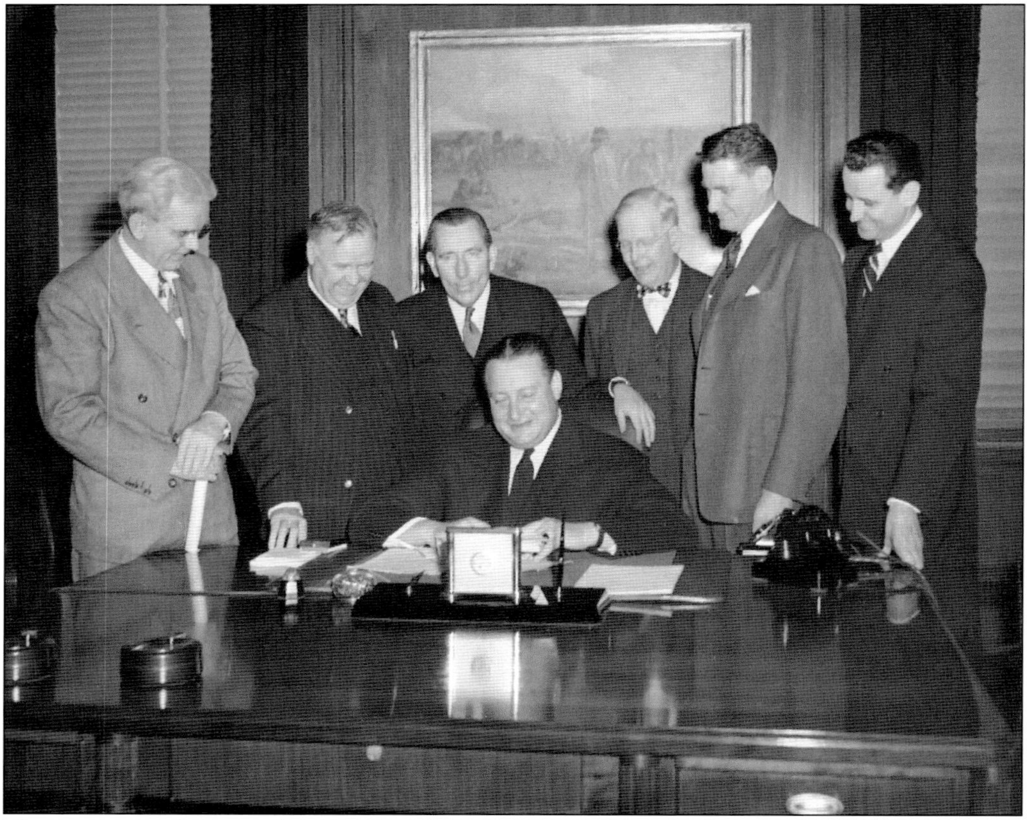

Thirteen years after its authorization, in June 1947, Secretary of the Interior Julius A. Krug (seated) filed an executive order creating Everglades National Park. In attendance were, standing from left to right, US senator Spessard L. Holland, unidentified aide, US senator Claude Pepper, US congressman Dwight Rogers, Florida governor Millard Caldwell, and US congressman George Smathers. A new national park had been born—a tropical, biological one. (SLAF.)

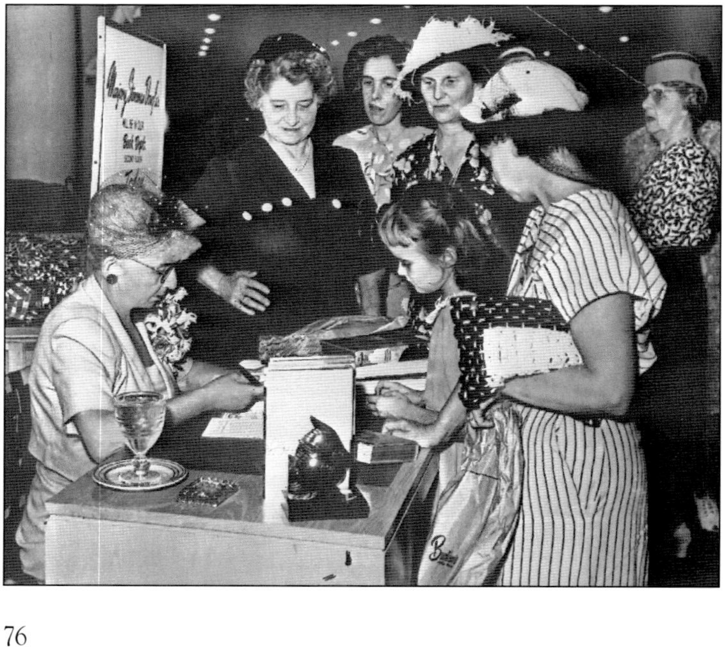

Also in 1947, the seminal Everglades book was published. Marjory Stoneman Douglas's *The River of Grass* was an instant hit as the first popular book on the history and nature of the Everglades. This image shows Douglas autographing her book in 1947 at Miami's historic Burdines department store. Decades later, she would re-engage with the Everglades as its fiercest defender and founder of the Friends of the Everglades. (SLAF.)

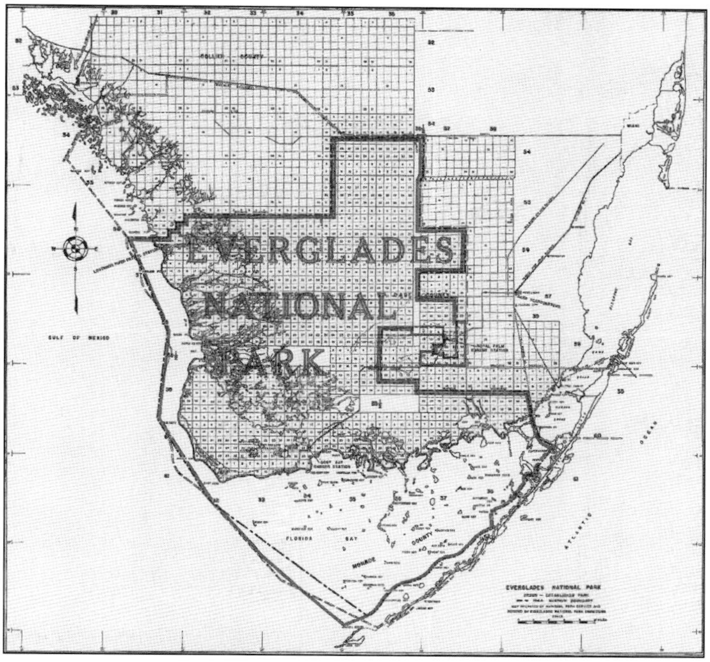

When finally settled upon in 1949, the park's first boundaries represented fiercely fought compromises. While incorporating western parts of the southern Everglades, Gulf Coast mangrove swamps, Cape Sable, and Florida Bay, it reduced the Coe proposals by zigzagging the border around any parcel thought to be of potential commercial value. The big gap in the middle of the park, coming to be called the "Hole-in-the-Donut," would prove especially problematic. (SLAF.)

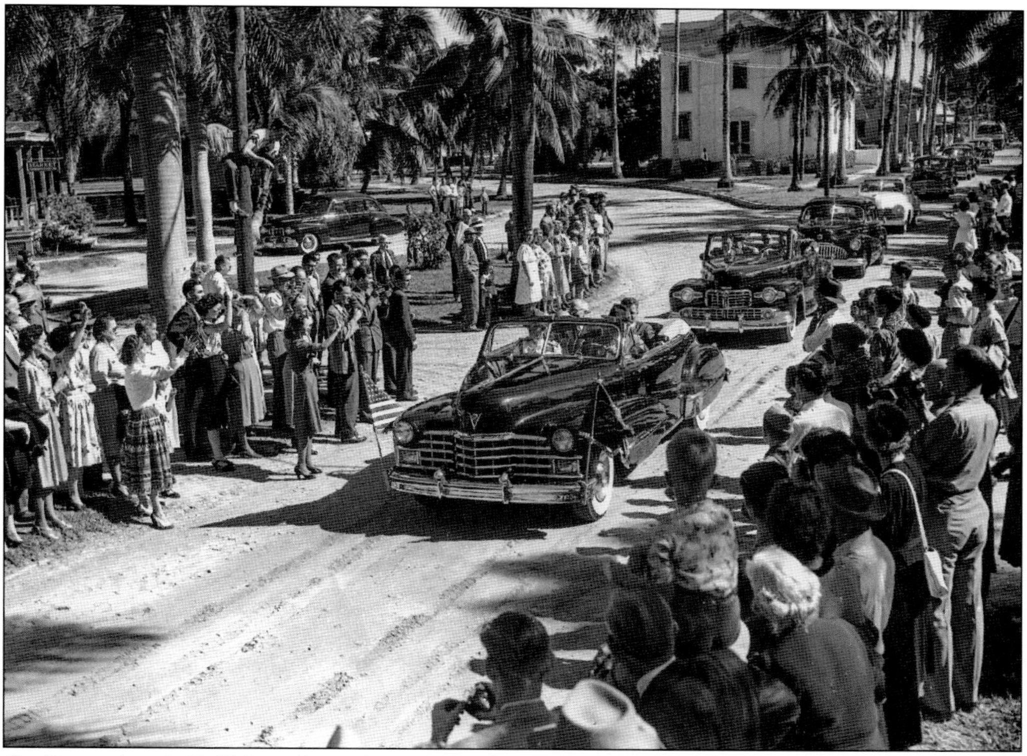

On December 6, 1947, President Truman, on the way to his winter vacation, stopped at the town of Everglades to dedicate Everglades National Park. The venue was chosen because it was named Everglades and Barron Collier had the money to sponsor the event. On arriving, the president headed to lunch at the Rod and Gun Club. The excitement throughout South Florida was as high as the expectation of economic benefits. (NPS.)

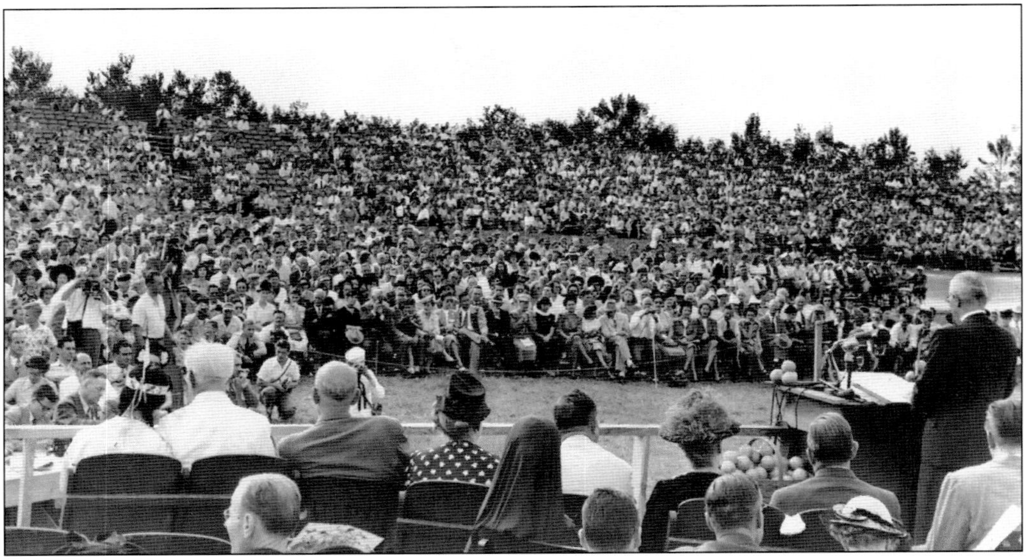

As seen here, the crowd was impressive. Over 4,000 people attended; bleachers were borrowed from Ringling Brothers Circus. John Pennekamp was master of ceremonies, Senator Holland spoke, and May Mann Jennings and Marjorie Stoneman Douglas were there. Ernest F. Coe attended only after much persuading, as he so objected to the boundary compromises. During the ceremonies, he was recognized for his fathering of the park; that recognition has grown with time. (NPS.)

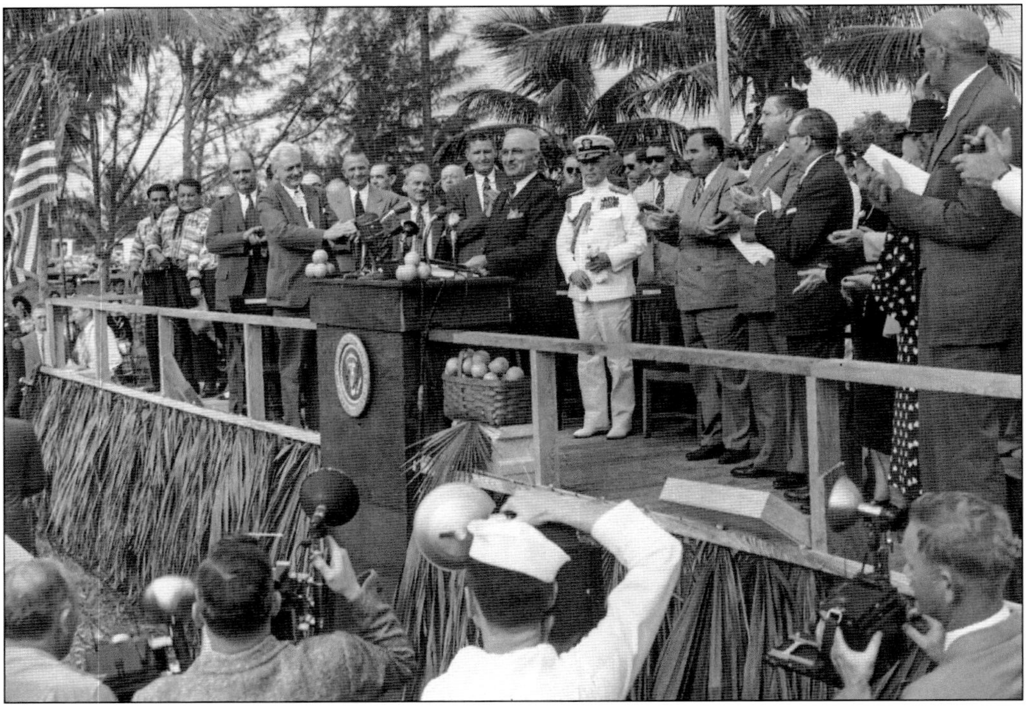

President Truman spoke about the park's essence: "Here are no lofty peaks seeking the sky, no mighty glaciers or rushing streams wearing away the uplifted land. Here is land, tranquil in its quiet beauty, serving not as a source of water but as the last receiver of it. To its natural abundance we owe the spectacular plant and animal life that distinguishes this place from all others in the country." (NPS.)

Five

THE EARLY PARK

There was much to be done to turn a watery landscape with a gerrymandered boundary into a national park serving multiple constituencies. There was no playbook for creating a biological park, nor for one adjacent to rampant urbanization. In 1945, the US Fish and Wildlife Service was given responsibility for the area as a national wildlife refuge. Oil rights issues had to be worked out. Commercial and sport hunting and random shooting needed to be curtailed. An immediate priority was protecting the bird colonies and roosts, until this time patrolled by private wardens and state game officers.

To become the economic engine many of its supporters expected, the park needed visitors; visitors needed roads, restrooms, interpretive trails, boardwalks, overlooks, parking lots, boat ramps, places to eat, picnic and camp sites, tours and programs, and gasoline. The park needed rangers and maintenance crews, some of whom were experienced South Floridians who knew the Everglades well.

Among the first complex tasks was to acquire and secure the land itself. Land in state ownership had to be transferred. State funds bought private properties. Over 200,000 acres had to be acquired from the Model Land Company. Smaller owners needed to be identified, and their parcels acquired. Occupied but untitled holdings and non-conforming structures needed to be dealt with. Even posting the park's boundaries was a significant task in the wet wilderness.

To sustain its environment, it needed to be better understood. One issue was the impact of commercial fishing, an activity not generally allowed in national parks. In South Florida, commercial and sport fishing were not always readily distinguishable. The roles of fire, hydrology, and water quality also needed to be better understood. The year the park was dedicated, 1947, was also when, after years of drought, South Florida flooded. The next year, Congress created the Central and Southern Florida Project for Flood Control and Other Purposes, which would end up controlling water coming to the park from the north. To provide better protection, the park's initial borders were expanded several times as opportunities arose.

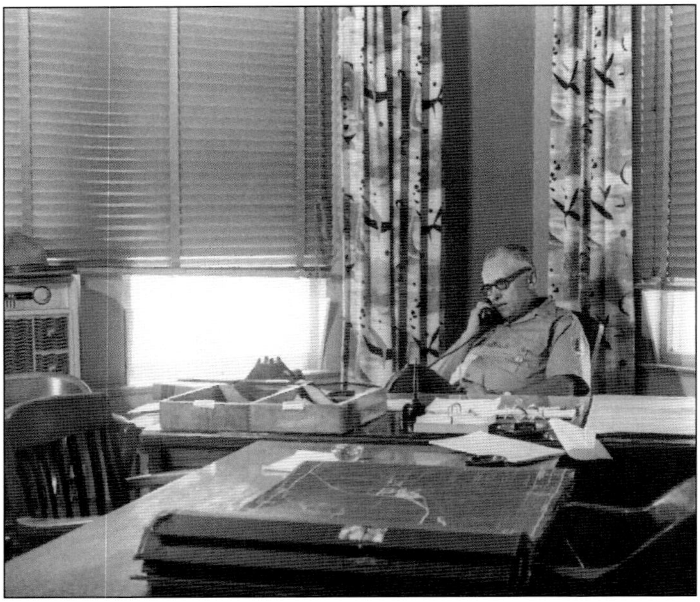

If Ernest Coe is the father of the park, Daniel B. Beard is its godfather. As an assistant wildlife technician in the Civilian Conservation Corps, he had recommended what the park should be and revealed the issues it would face. In 1945, Beard became manager of the Everglades National Wildlife Refuge and then the national park's first superintendent, a position he held for nearly a decade, from 1947 to 1956. (NPS.)

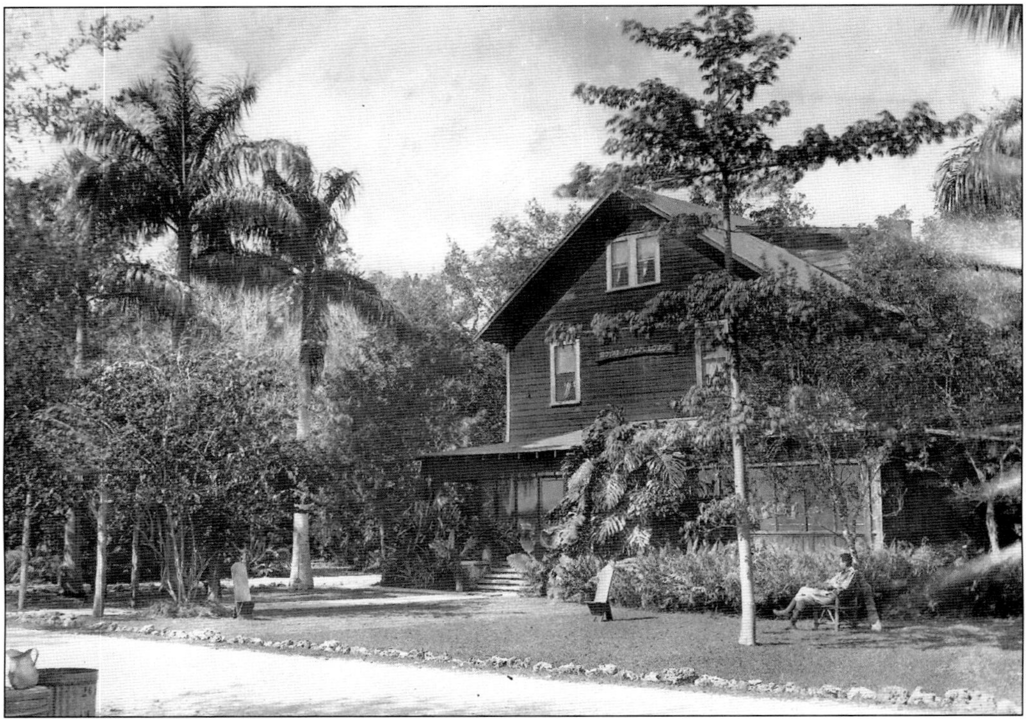

Royal Palm Lodge became the Royal Palm Ranger Station. This image shows how little it had changed over its decades of service. Not considered an appropriate facility for the future, in 1952 it was sold to Donald and Jeannette Sullivan, its last caretakers, who moved it to Homestead where it became Jack's Hotel and Motel until destroyed by hurricane Andrew in 1992, which also tore up Royal Palm Hammock itself. (UFMMJ.)

Park superintendent Beard started assembling his team, emphasizing local experience. Erwin Winte, Willard Dilley, and Barney Parker were the park's first rangers. Winte (shown in 1965) had been a state wildlife officer. Bringing law enforcement to a region that had hardly seen it before, and did not appreciate it, was a challenge. Hunters, fishermen, and poachers were not used to wildlife and trespass laws actually being enforced. (NPS.)

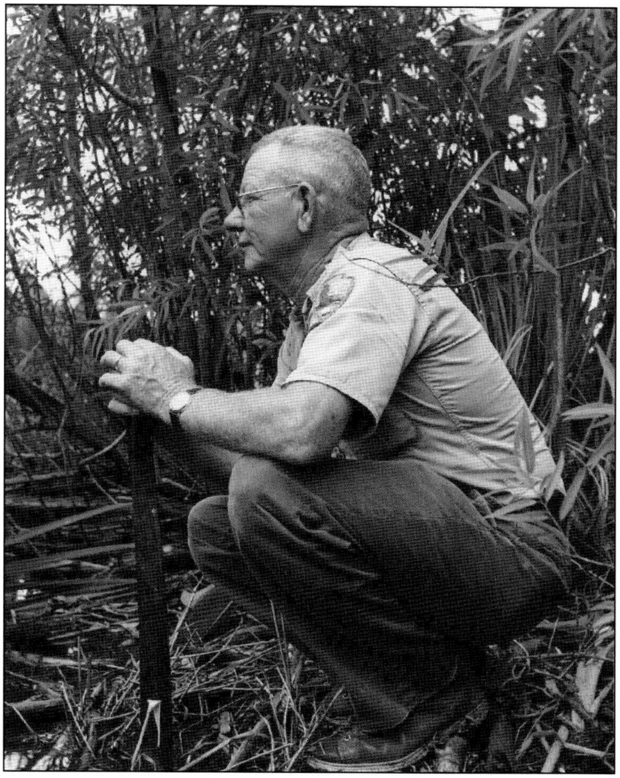

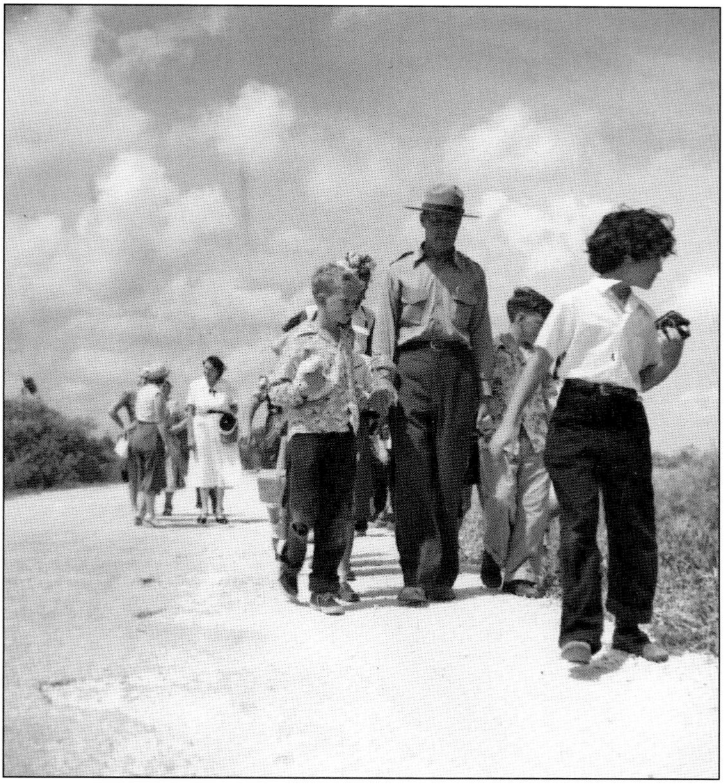

From the beginning, rangers performed many functions in addition to law enforcement, including resources management, visitor care, and interpretation. Early ranger Willard Dilley served as an interpretation ranger. This image shows him leading a group of schoolchildren from Miami Beach in 1952. Ranger-led walks and programs became a well-received part of the park experience. Providing such opportunities was an important aspect of planning for Everglades National Park's development. (UUL.)

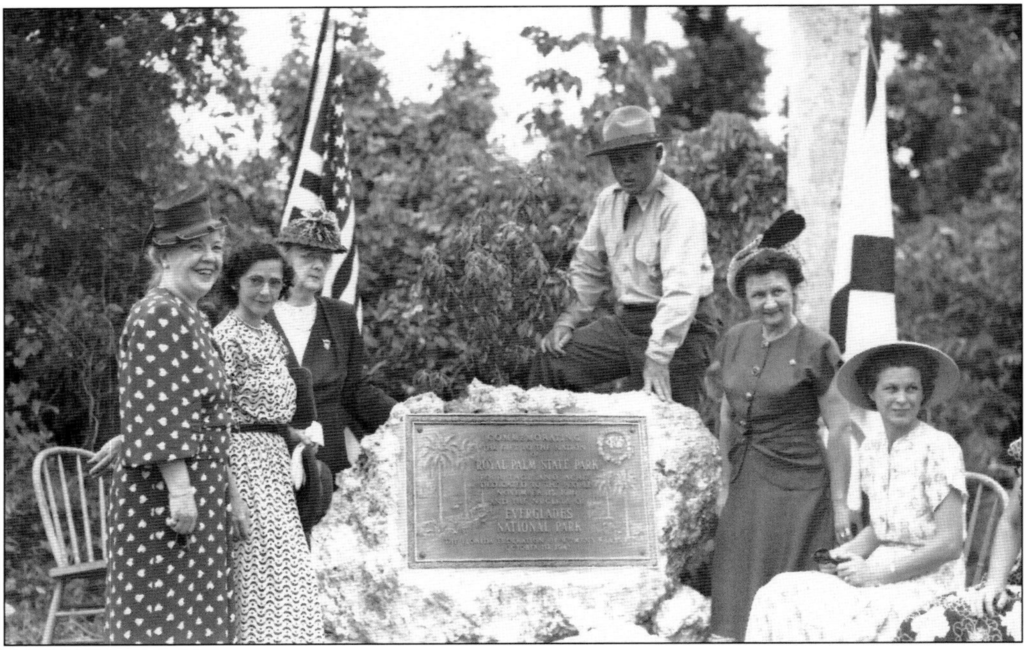

After three decades of stewardship, the Florida Federation of Women's Clubs turned Royal Palm State Park over to the National Park Service. The image above shows federation representatives unveiling a plaque commemorating the donation on October 10, 1947. Rangers took over interpreting the site for visitors, first from the Royal Palm Lodge and later from the Royal Palm Visitor Center. The 1957 image below shows ranger Clay Gifford talking to visitors on Royal Palm Hammock's Gumbo Limbo Trail, named after the popular peeling-bark tree. With the road passing through it, Royal Palm Hammock was a visitor's first stop in the park, often the only stop. The road through the hammock was abandoned when a spur was later built from the north. (Above, NPS; below, SLAF.)

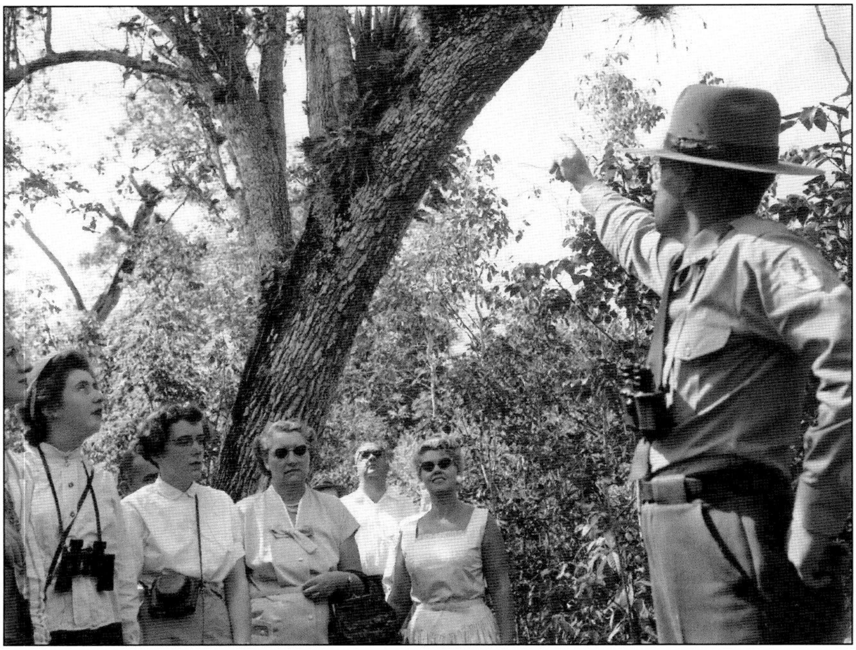

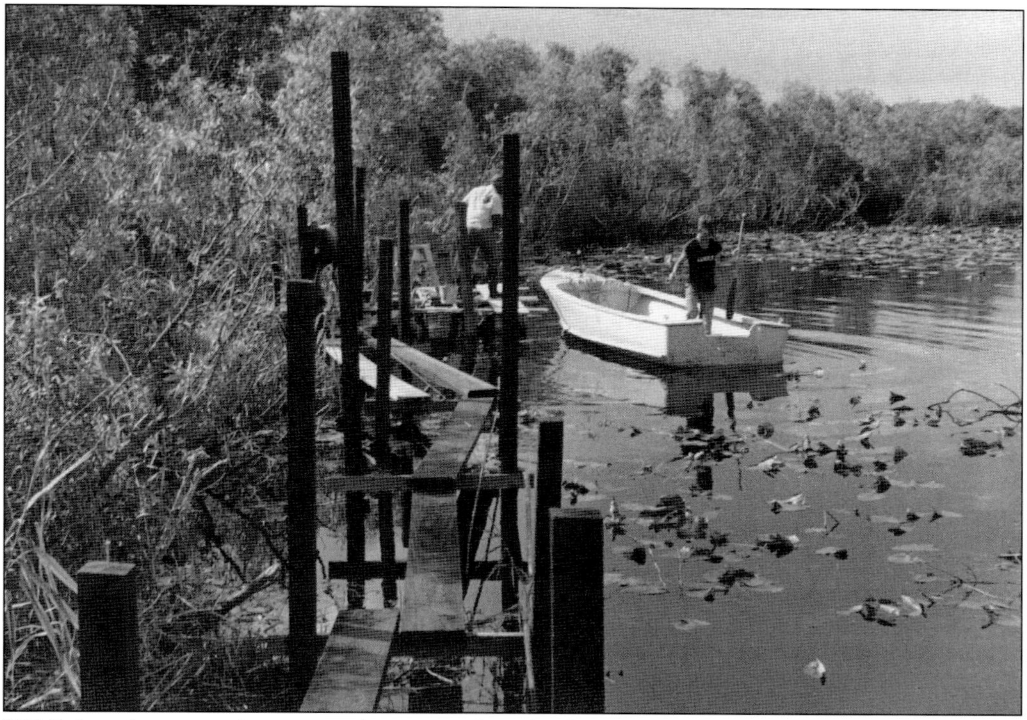

Wildlife gathering at the aquatic features at Royal Palm State Park had been keenly appreciated by decades of visitors, and the new national park chose to develop this site into its premier wildlife viewing location. The image above shows a rickety precursor to today's popular boardwalk. With safety improvements in place, Anhinga Trail became the gateway to the park, as the rather unrealistic image on the postcard below affirms. Seldom failing to provide wildlife views and opportunities for interpretation, the pond becomes especially active in the drying season when alligators accumulate by the dozens along with fish, turtles, and other wildlife, while water birds nest in the trees. This book's cover image shows visitors and a ranger with the trail's namesake, anhingas, nesting next to the boardwalk. (Above, NPS; below, KH.)

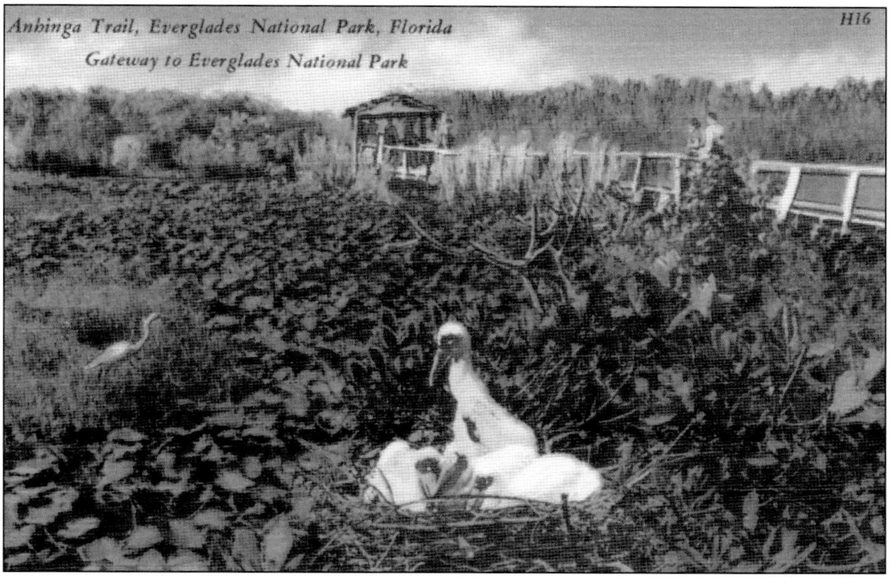

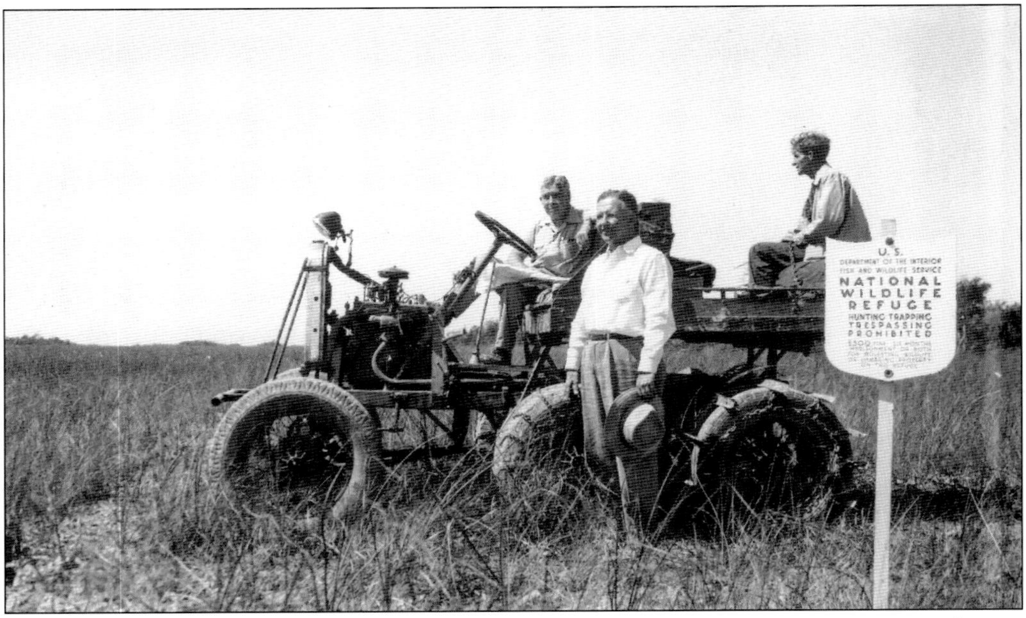

An early task to protect the park was marking its boundaries. It was not easy, requiring the use of a distinctly South Florida vehicle, the swamp buggy. Swamp or glades buggies were car frames, initially Model A Fords, fitted with airplane or tractor tires or tracks. Those with both were called half-tracks. This image shows a crew in a swamp buggy marking the Everglades National Wildlife Refuge boundary. (NPS.)

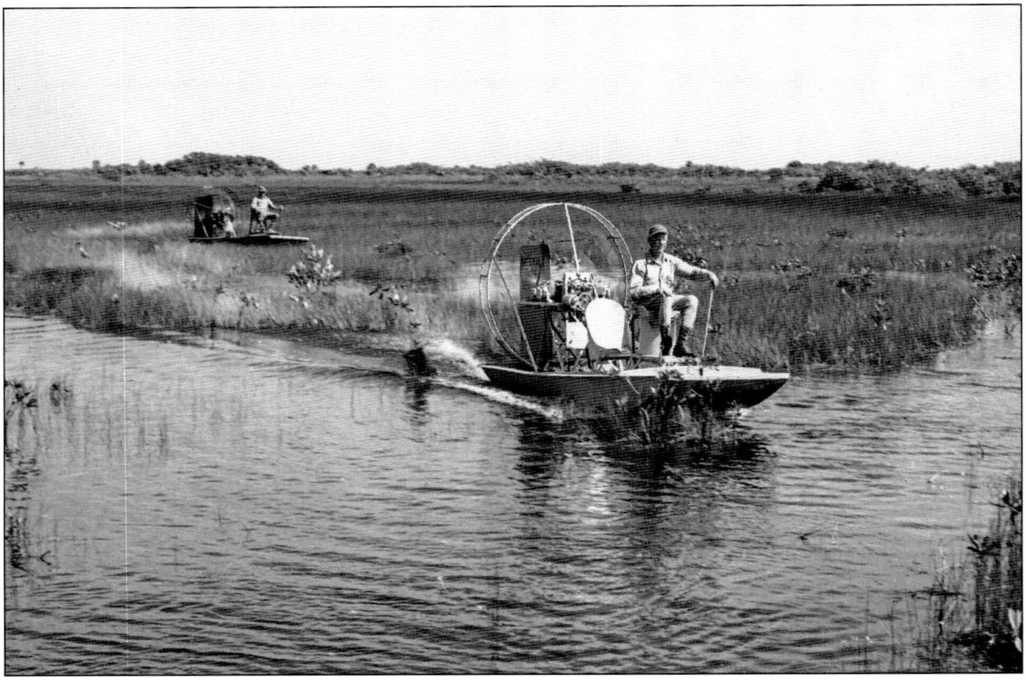

Rangers also needed to access the deeper marshes, and for this, they adopted another local transport method, the airboat. An airboat is a flat-bottomed skiff pushed by an airplane propeller powered by an airplane or car engine. Rangers patrolled by day and also by night, when much of the illegal hunting occurred. This image shows rangers on patrol in 1961. (NPS.)

Rangers also patrolled the front country, initially mostly dirt and gravel roads that could turn to mud in the wet season. Patrolling got easier as the roads were improved. This image shows a ranger and his car in 1958. The two-way radio enabled communication over the vast area of the park via repeater towers. Employees were given radio call identification numbers to use through dispatch. The superintendent's number was 001. (NPS.)

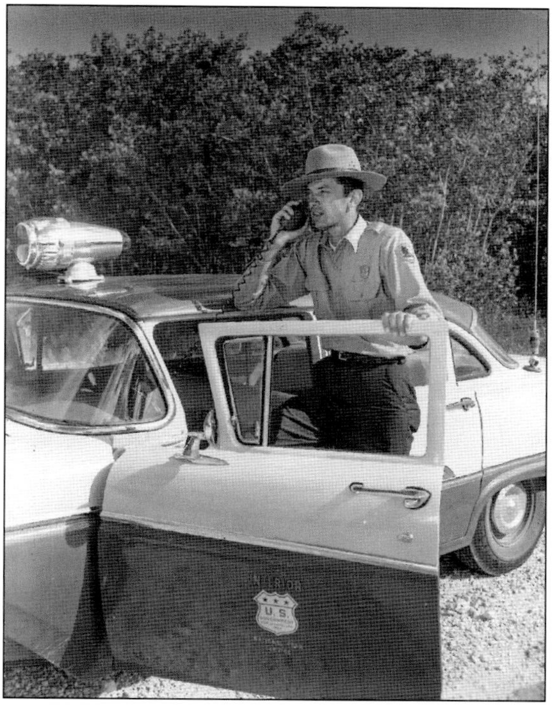

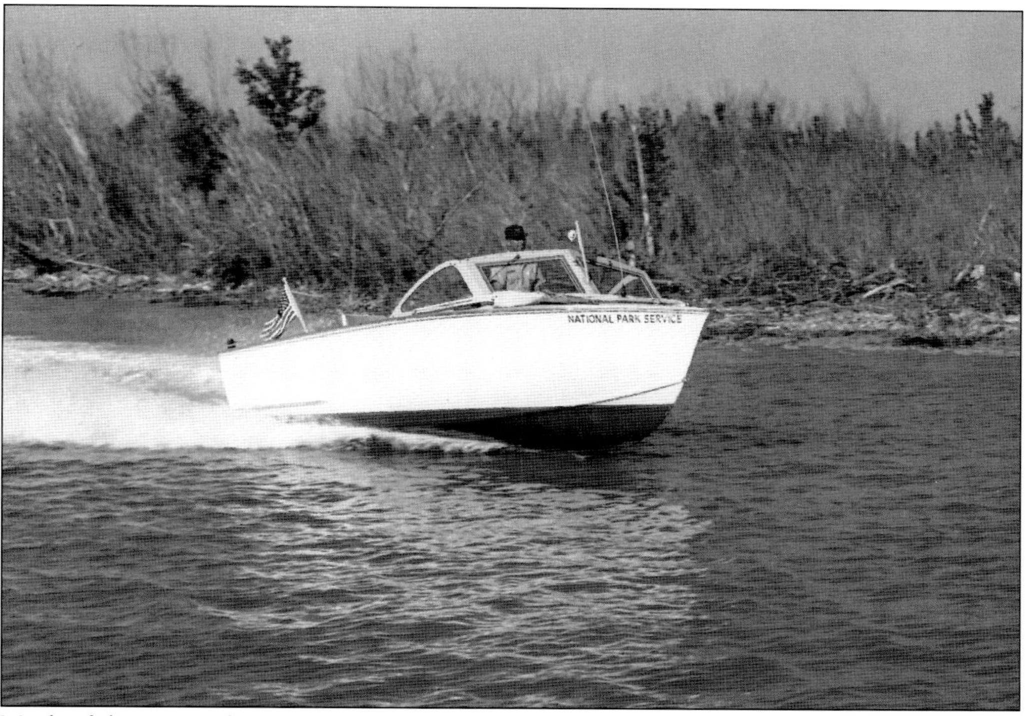

Much of the new park was water; the Florida Bay portion alone covered over 800 square miles. Patrolling required boats. Safety checks, breakdowns, fishing, poaching, and later smuggling and refugees were issues on the water. Barney Parker, previously a bird warden and state game officer, was the first ranger posted at Lostmans Ranger Station on the Gulf Coast. His first patrol skiff was named *Green Hornet.* (NPS.)

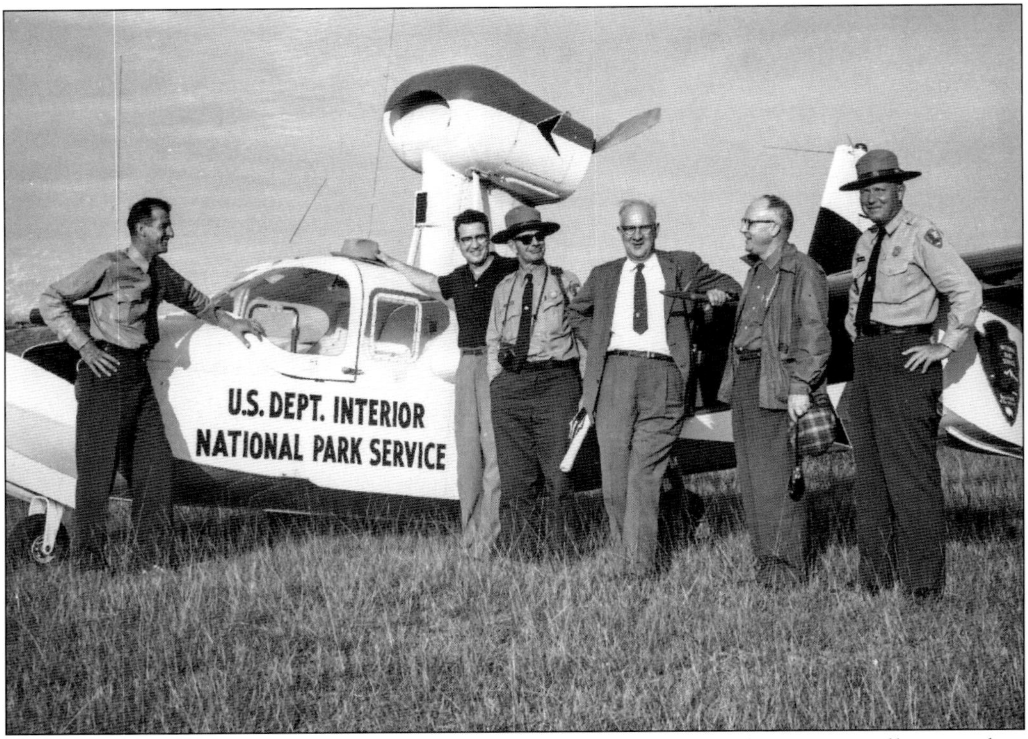

The best way to monitor the vast, mostly inaccessible park was from above, especially since deer poachers had airplanes too. The park's Lake Amphibian airplane with its aft-facing engine on its roof could land on water or land. Ralph Miele (far left), one of the park's first employees, became its chief pilot. Four people barely fit in the noisy cockpit. (NPS.)

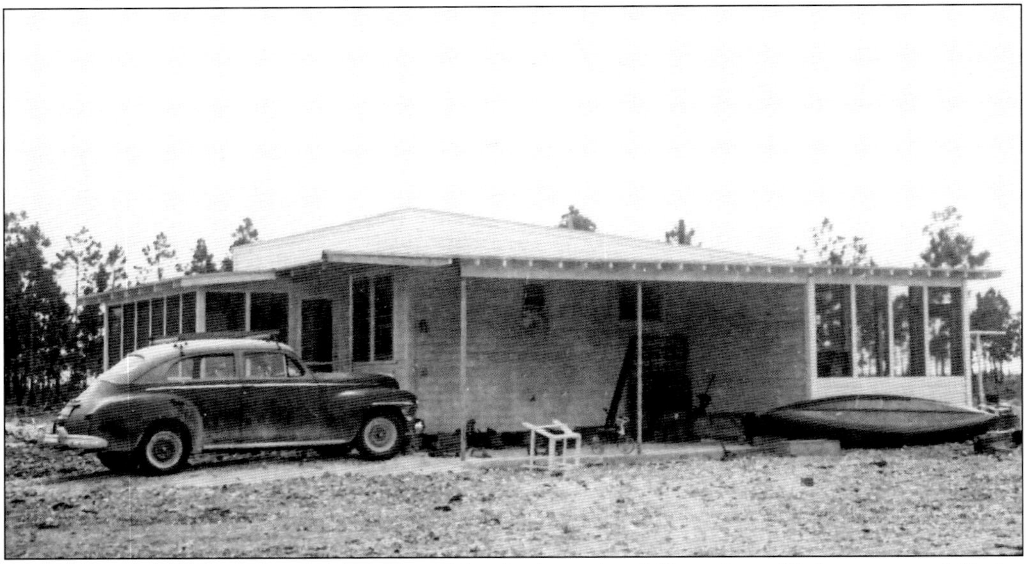

Park personnel needed places to live. Pine Island, where the old Ingraham Highway crossed Taylor Slough at its narrowest point, was chosen for staff housing and an airstrip and maintenance facility. Initial accommodations were simple but sturdy, as shown in this 1950 image. Rangers also lived at outlying district stations including Flamingo, Key Largo, Everglades City, and Tamiami Trail—first at Shark Valley and then at 40-mile Bend. (NPS.)

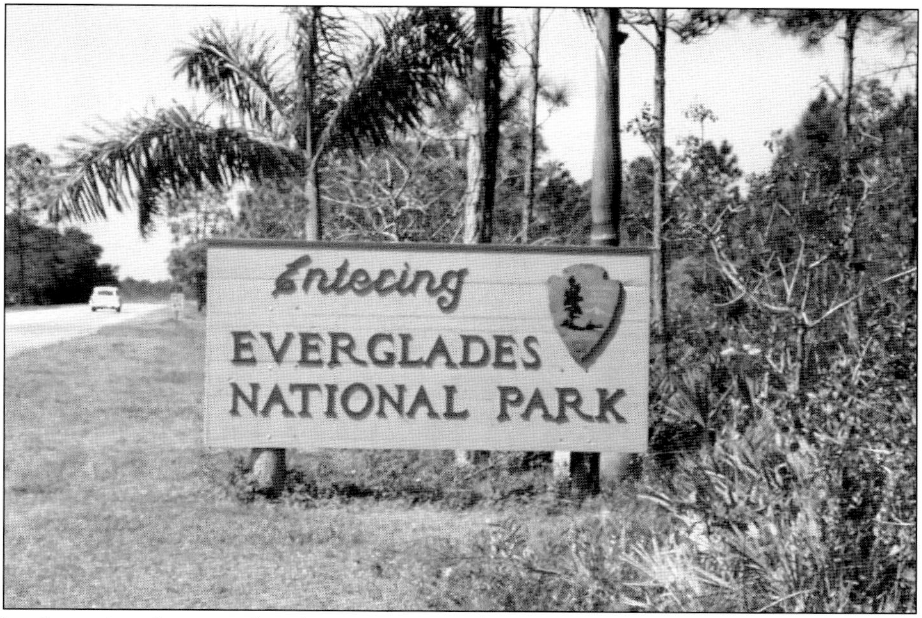

Unlike the railroad-oriented earliest western parks, by the time Everglades National Park was established, cars had taken control of park visitor transportation, so the park had to be made ready for them. Park headquarters initially was in Homestead. The main park entrance was approached from Homestead and Florida City following the Ingraham Highway. Crossing into the park, the entrance sign was always one of its most photographed installations, as visitors stopped to have their commemorative pictures taken. The image above shows the 1960 version. The main park entrance station was situated just beyond. The image below shows the chickee-themed entrance booth in 1953. Rangers stationed there greeted visitors by the carload, offering information on the park, a tradition that continues today. (Above, SLAF; below, NPS.)

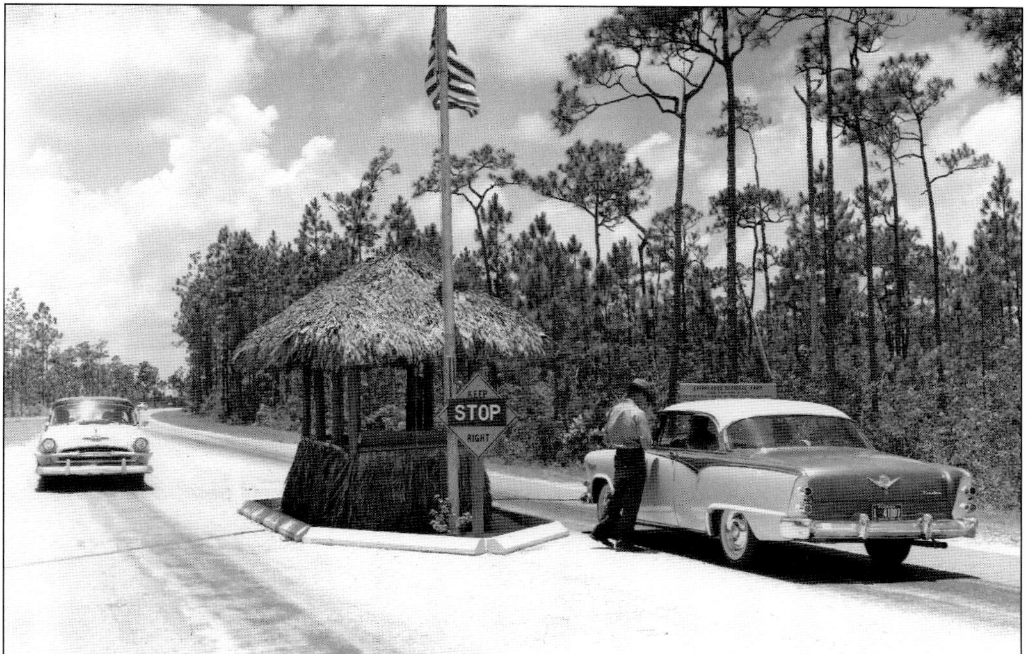

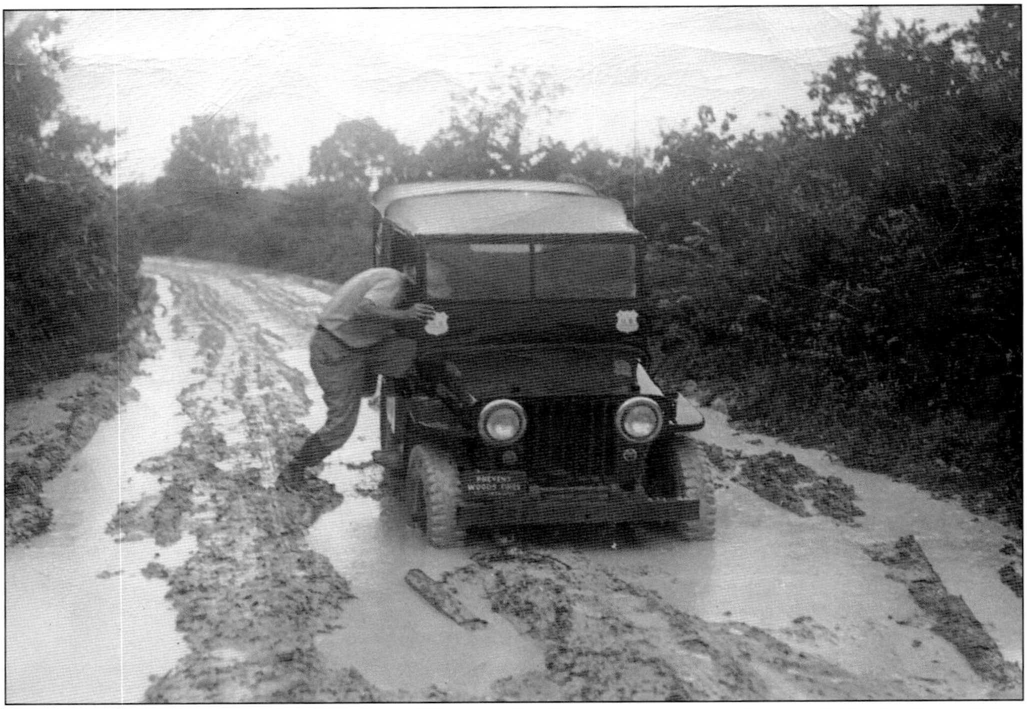

Ingraham Highway posed difficulties. The roadbed was narrow, weak, canal-flanked, straight, badly surfaced, poorly culverted, passed through privately-farmed land, and was out of sight of the actual Everglades. Parts flooded in the wet season. Among the decisions facing the new park was whether to improve the old road or build a new one. Deliberation was prolonged. The compromise was that the road started on the Ingraham route, then looped scenically north of Long Pine Key before turning south, picking up the Ingraham track again. This route avoided the farmed lands and provided access to new observation points. Built in sections from 1955 to 1963, it used fill from scattered borrow pits rather than the locally customary roadside canal. The aerial view below shows a borrow pit, Pine Glades Lake, and its access road. Culverts maintained water passage. (Both, NPS.)

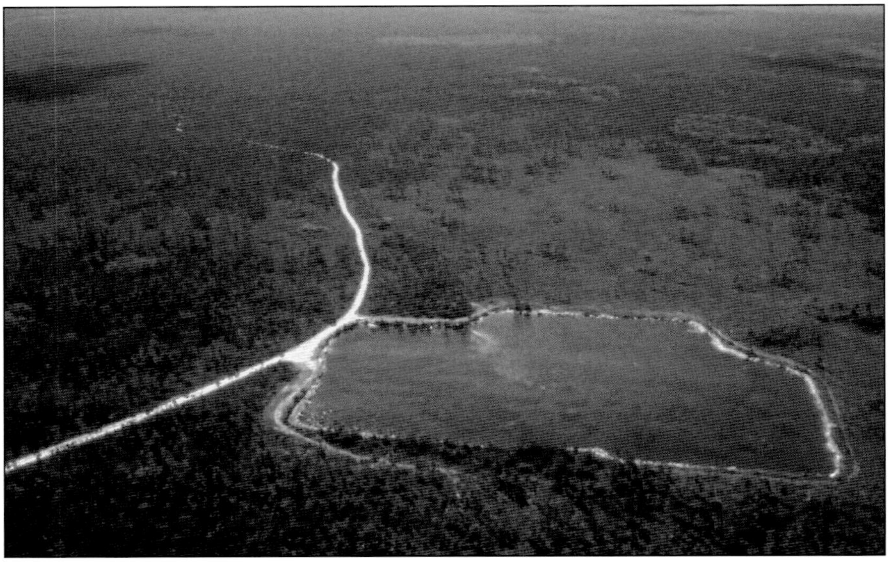

The new park road's placement created opportunities for interpretive stops. One of the more distinctive was Mahogany Hammock, an example of the near-coast palm-ringed tree islands that supported mahogany (or madeira) trees, shown here in 1960. Harvest of South Florida's mahogany trees had started centuries before but somehow missed this hammock where visitors were able to view the national-champion mahogany tree along the trail. (SLAF.)

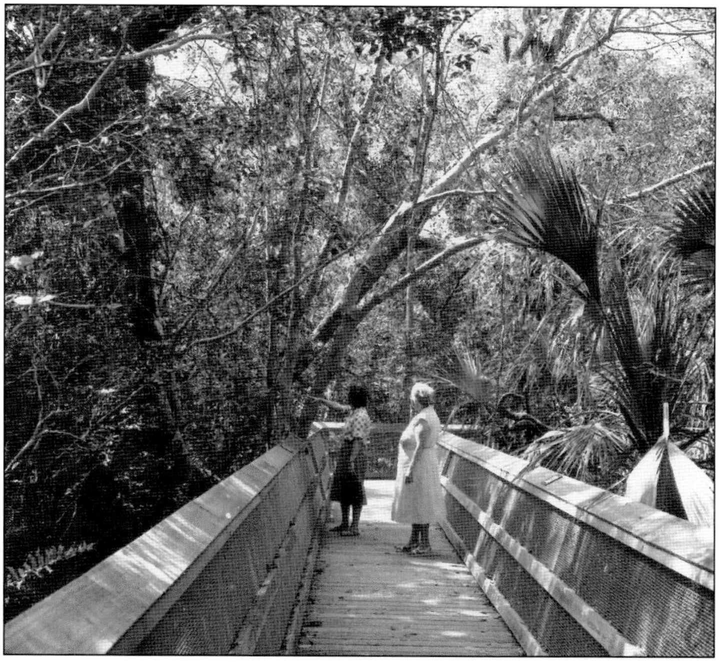

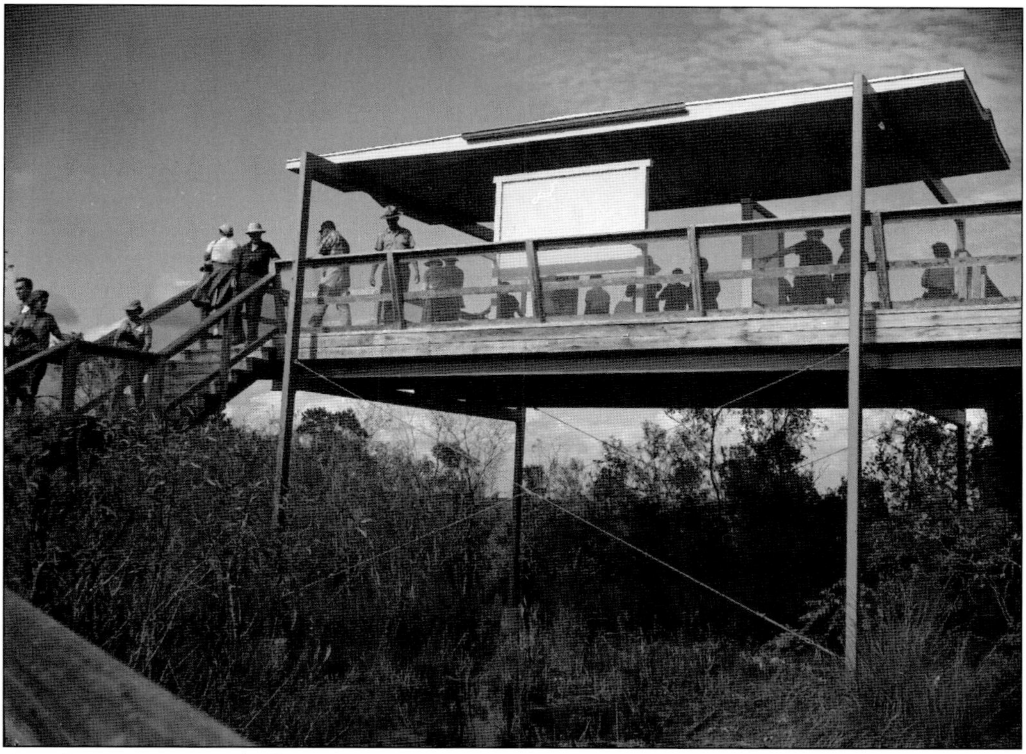

A perhaps surprising challenge was finding ways for visitors to actually see the Everglades marsh itself. As ground-level viewing lacked the perspective needed to appreciate the marsh, a spur off the main park road accessed an overlook called Pa-Hay-Okee, a name borrowed from a Mikasuki concept of a grassy place. The raised observation platform shown here provided an elevated view of the grassy plain of the Everglades extending to the horizon. (NPS.)

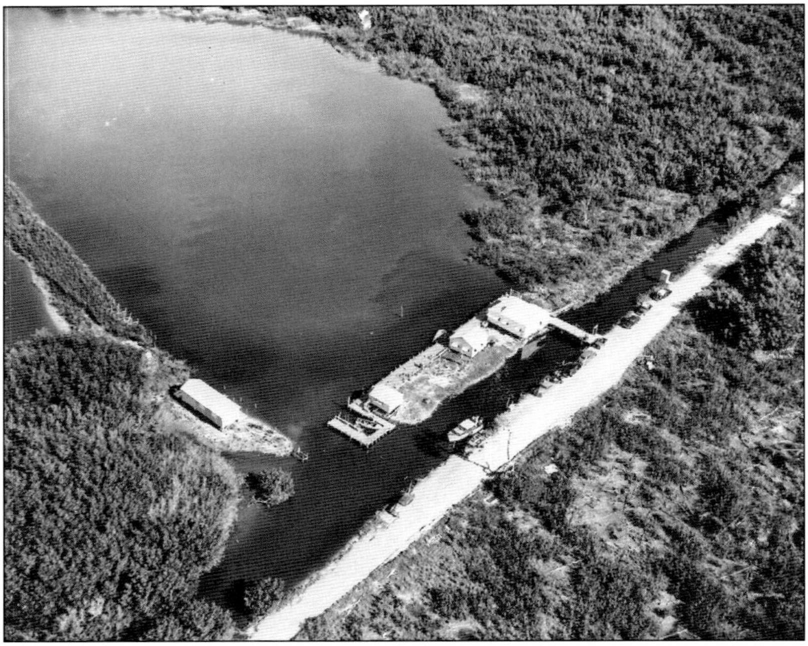

Shark River Fishing Company's fishing camp on Coot Bay was chosen as the park's southern mainland ranger station and visitor contact area. It was on Ingraham Highway, accessed by a fill drive across the Homestead Canal (above). Visitors and journalists encouraged more visitor-oriented facilities, and by 1950, the marina had gained a snack bar and gas station and had replaced its by-then infamous outhouse, which had been publicized in an article critical of the pace of the park's development. The marina serviced park and private boats (below), which could head to Whitewater Bay and Shark River via Bear Lake or to Florida Bay via the Flamingo spur of the Homestead Canal. Getting there by car via the Ingraham Highway continued to prove challenging when it rained. (Above, NPS; below, HM.)

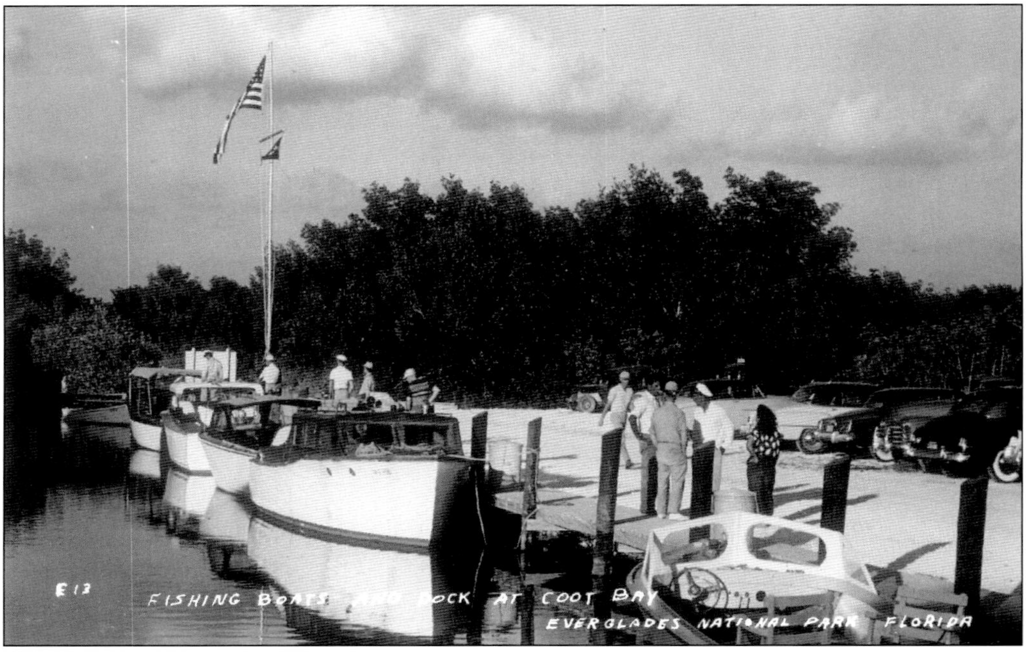

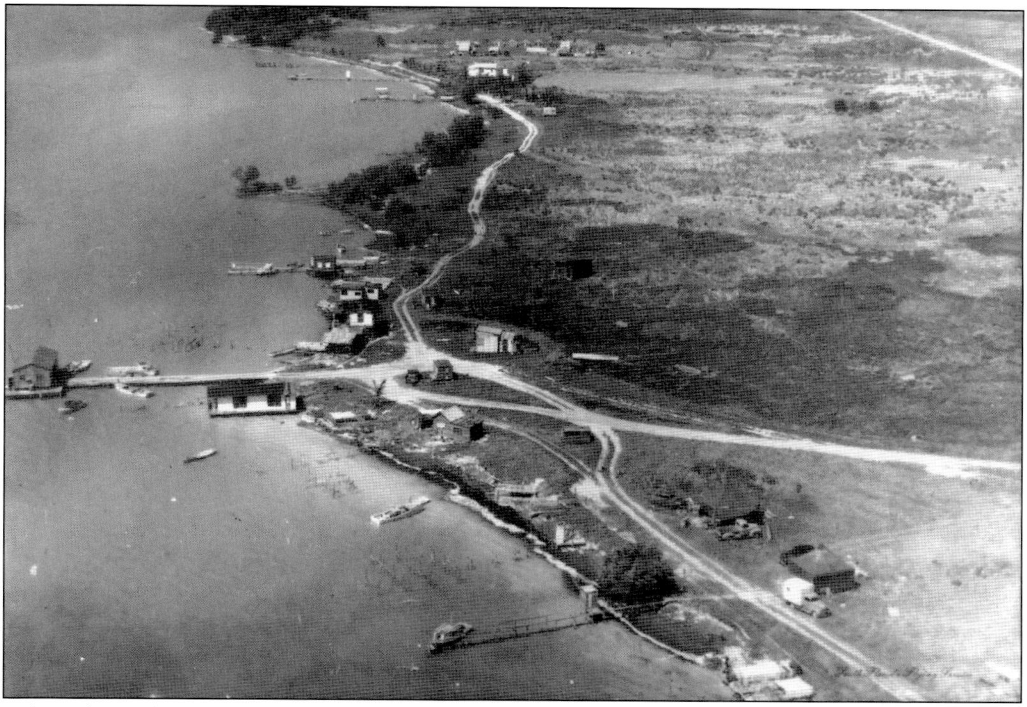

When the park was established, Flamingo consisted of 34 major structures as well as docks and minor buildings used by residents and related businesses dispersed along the bayshore (above) and the Flamingo Canal (below). Early park planning expected the community to remain, but this would have conflicted with the legislated purpose of the park and pose significant challenges to resource protection. Lloyd House, Coleman Irwin, and Loren Roberts, who ran fish houses, were bona fide property owners; other residents were not and legally became squatters on government-owned land. When compensated, the Flamingo fish houses moved their businesses elsewhere. The nearby E.C. Knight fish house on Snake Bight moved to Tavernier in 1950. Coleman Irwin's sturdy house became a ranger outpost. Many residents were quite uninterested in leaving, showing their feelings by tearing down the park's gate and sign. (Both, HM.)

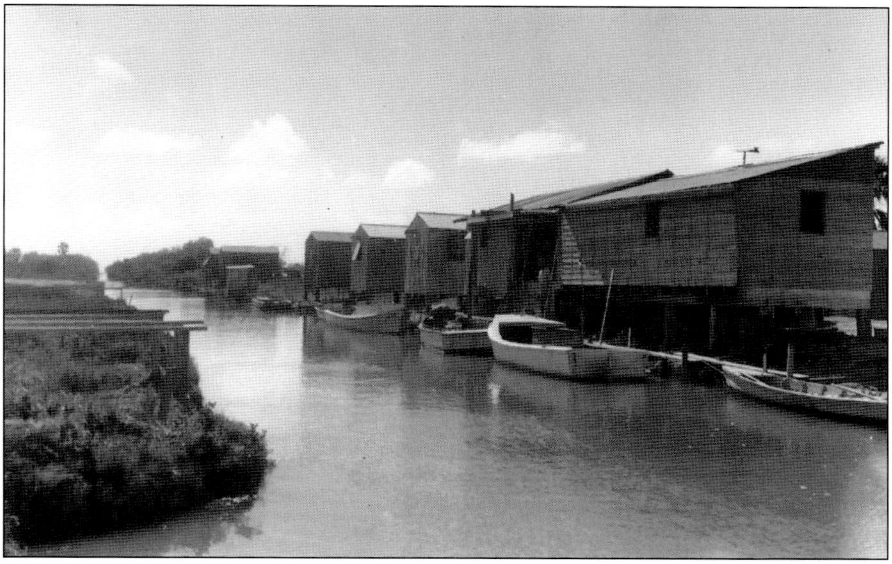

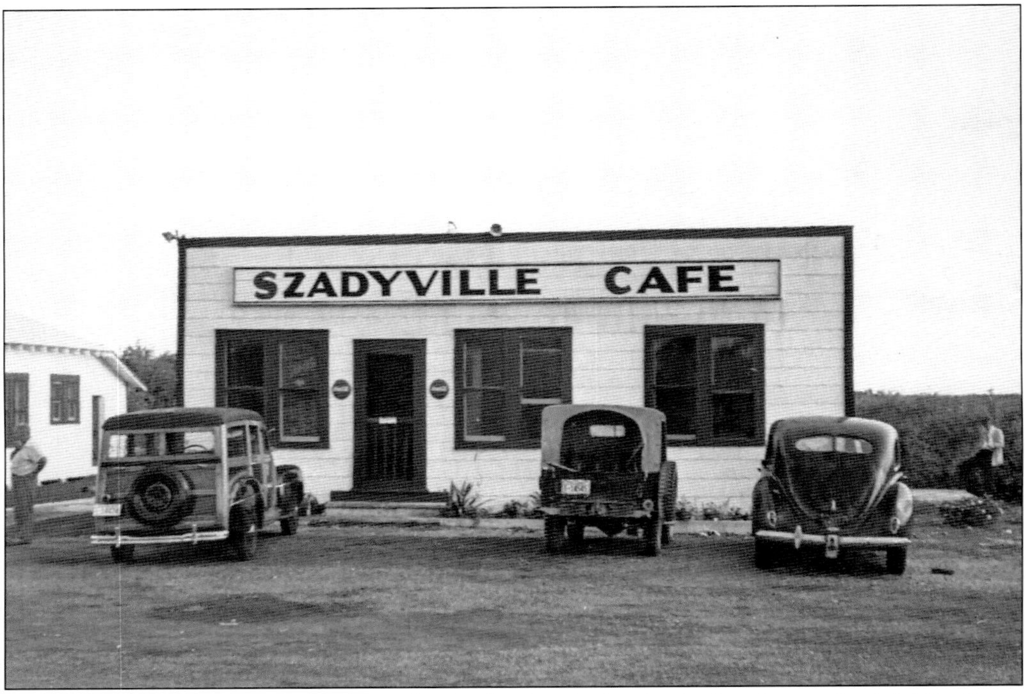

Other Flamingo businesses, such as the Szadyville Cafe, also had to leave. On Middle Cape, Edwin Lunsford had built a cabin and airstrip for a luxury resort. He bought more property, even after being appointed to the Everglades National Park Commission. Despite being an insider, his plan never happened. Following a court order, non–property owners had departed the Flamingo area by end of June 1951, and most structures were eliminated. (NPS.)

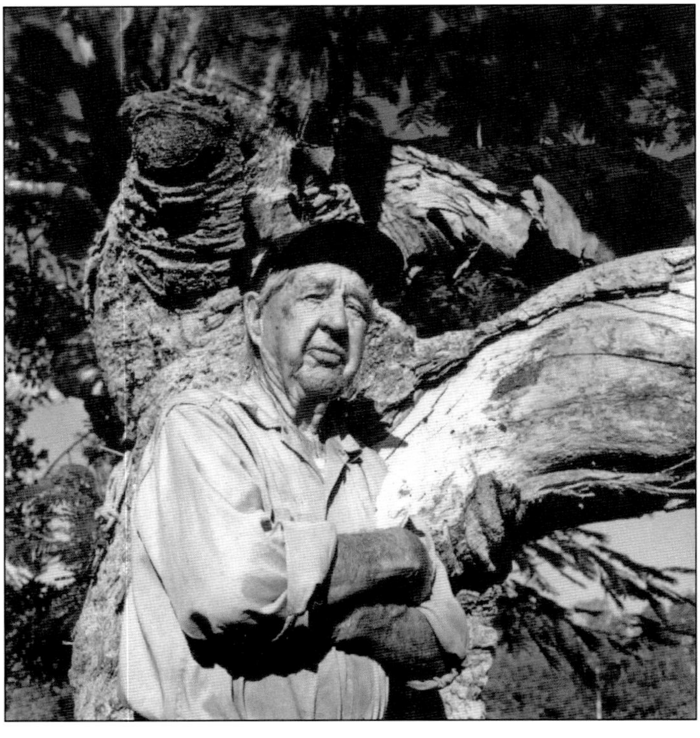

Settlers remaining along the Gulf Coast also did not own their cabin sites and moved on. The Ten Thousand Islands above Lostmans River, added to the park in 1954, also hosted a few isolated residents. Arthur Darwin on Possum Key (shown here), Ed Braddock at the Watson Place, and Roy Ozmer on Pelican Key were allowed to stay until hurricanes or age encouraged them to move on. (SLAF.)

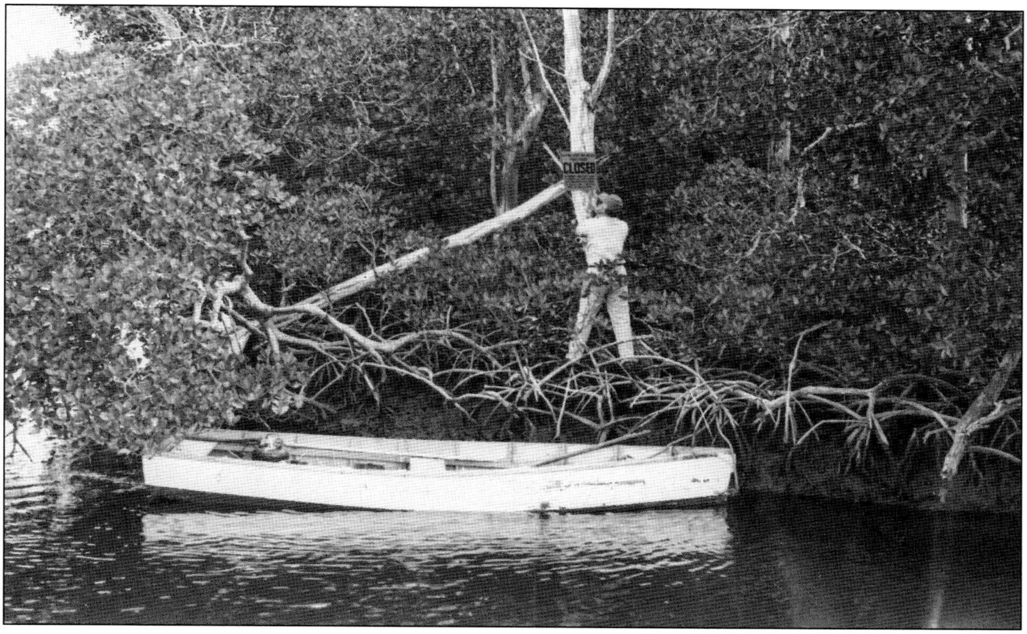

Protecting waterbird colonies and roosts was a high priority for the new park. The park's initial boundaries encompassed the famous bird colony at Rookery Branch of the Shark River. Federal protection began prior to the park itself with the establishment of Everglades National Wildlife Refuge. This 1947 image shows Daniel B. Beard, then refuge manager, posting a no-entry sign at the access creek to the colony. (NPS.)

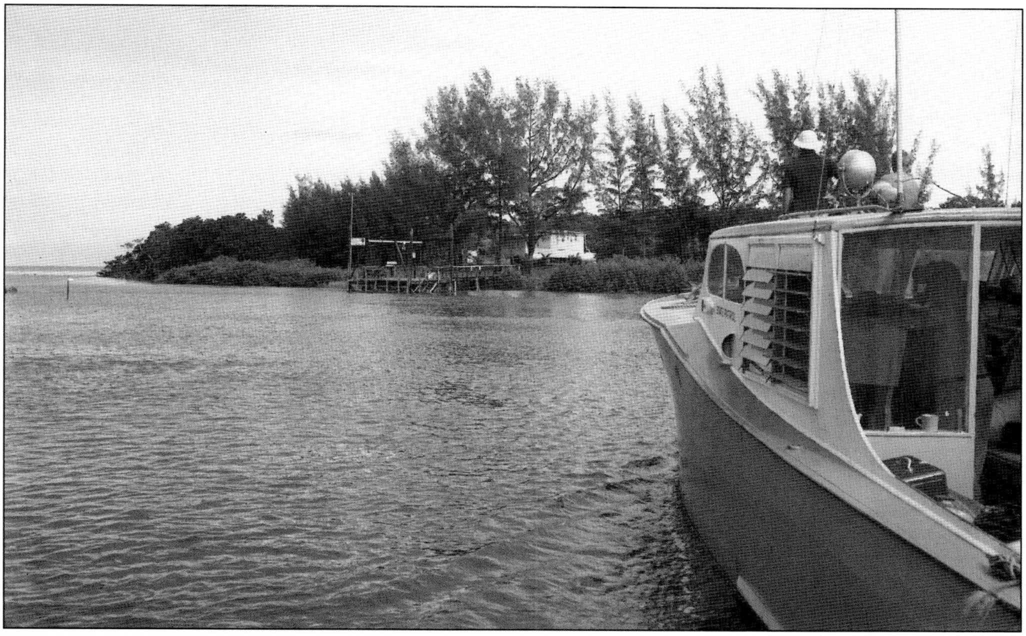

After the park's establishment, the Gulf Coast bird rookeries were patrolled from the ranger station at the mouth of Lostmans River. Ranger Barney Parker lived on a houseboat until a structure was built. This 1957 image shows a boat approaching the station. Settlers and generations of Indigenous people had long occupied this well-situated high ground. Hurricane Isbell destroyed the station in 1964. (SLAF.)

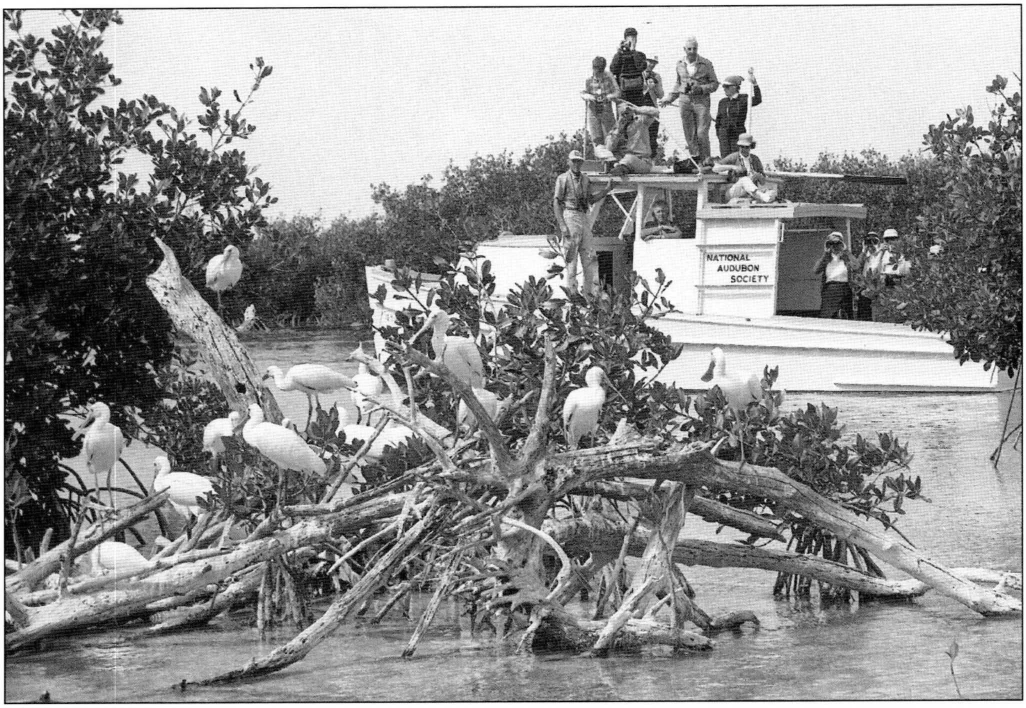

Cuthbert Rookery was the most famous of the waterbird colonies needing protection within the new park. The colony was located on small mangrove-covered islands within Cuthbert Lake, which connected via Long Lake to West Lake. This made the colony accessible by boat from the Ingraham Highway. The narrow channels were kept open by periodically trimming ever-encroaching mangrove branches. The Audubon Society ran monthly tours to the colony before and after the park's establishment. These 1950s images show the tour boat with nesting birds in the foreground above, followed by a participant lunch on the West Lake shore below. Visitors to Cuthbert Rookery could learn much about the park's history—the massacre of egrets during the plume trade, the death of Guy Bradley, the founding of Audubon societies, and the movement to create a park. (Above, DPL; below, NPS.)

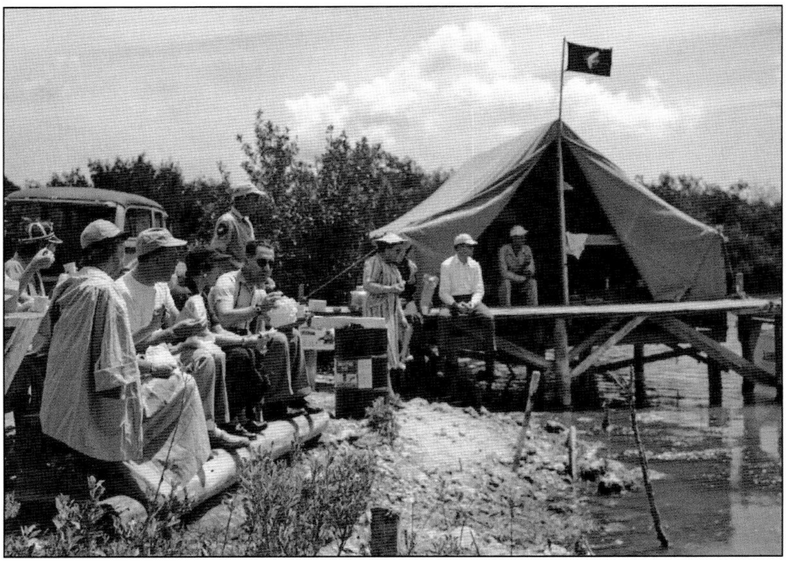

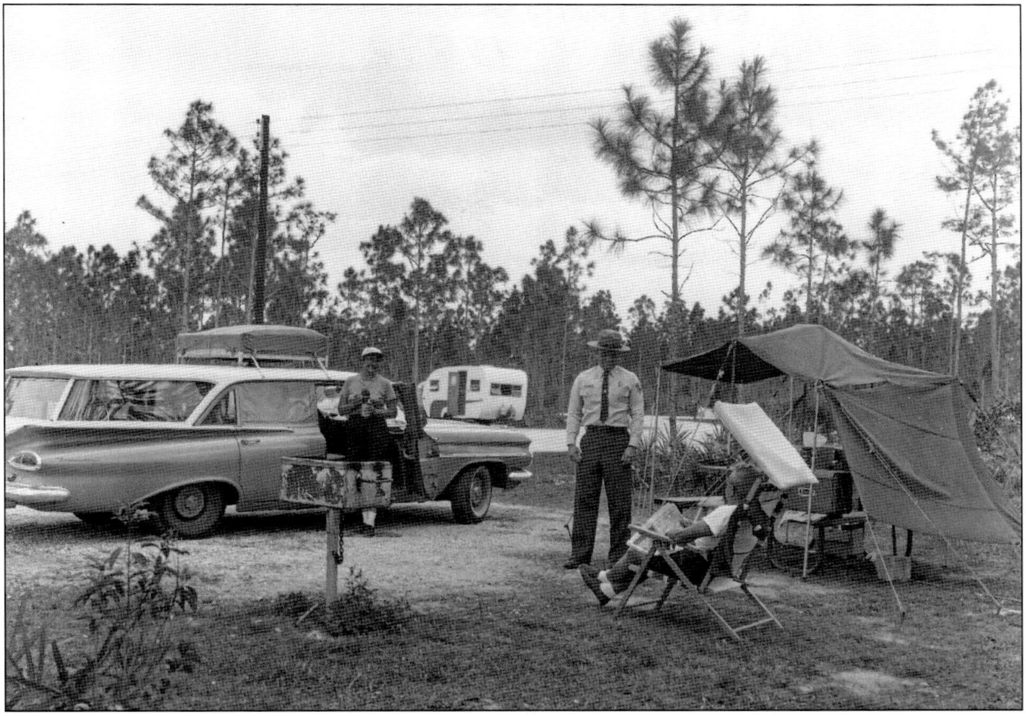

Initially, it was assumed that park visitors would mostly take day trips, but demand for camping soon developed. Early on, some camping was allowed at Royal Palm, but an extensive car-friendly campground was developed farther west on Long Pine Key. The campground, shown here, included a shallow artificial lake, an outdoor auditorium, and nature and hiking trails among fire roads in the pine rocklands and through adjacent wet prairies. (NPS.)

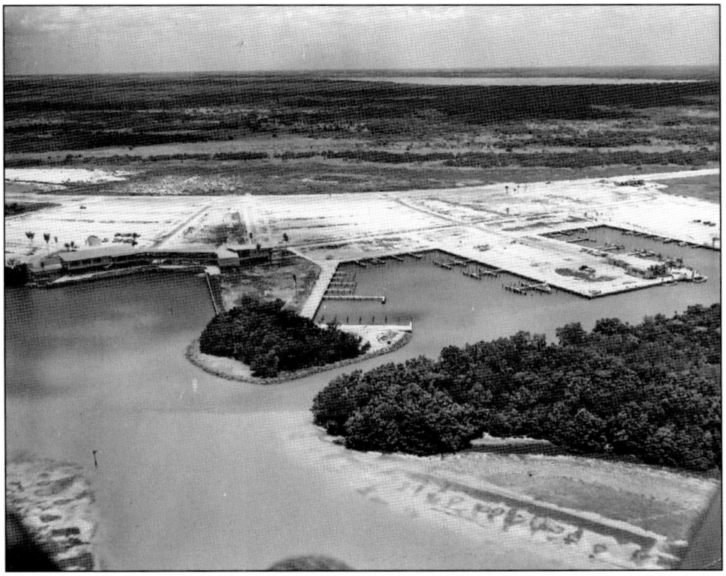

It was decided to concentrate southern park operations at a new Flamingo developed area, including those from the Coot Bay Ranger Station and visitor facilities that had been planned for Cape Sable where the Ingraham Highway ended. Dredging for the development began in 1955. In 1957, park operations moved to the new Flamingo, shown here. The Coot Bay station was disassembled, and the site was fully restored. (NPS.)

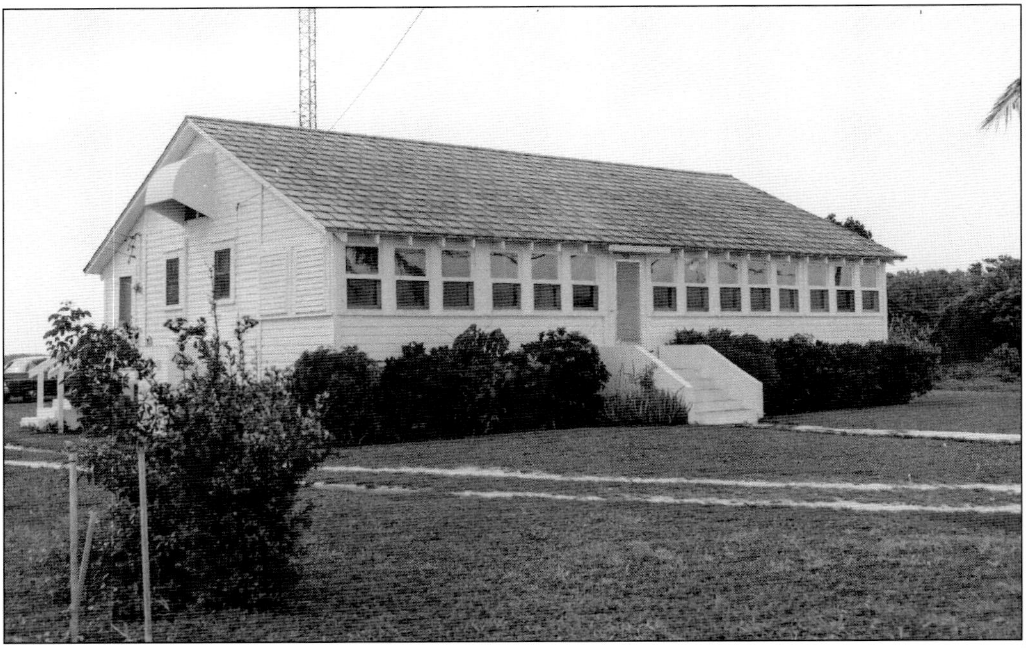

Flamingo provided rangers ready access to Florida Bay, but the bay's size and extensive network of boat-blocking shallow banks inhibited patrolling all of it from there. In 1954, a site was purchased for a ranger station on Key Largo, shown here in 1960. From there, rangers could better keep an eye on disturbances to nearby bird nesting islands and monitor sport and commercial fishing activities. (NPS.)

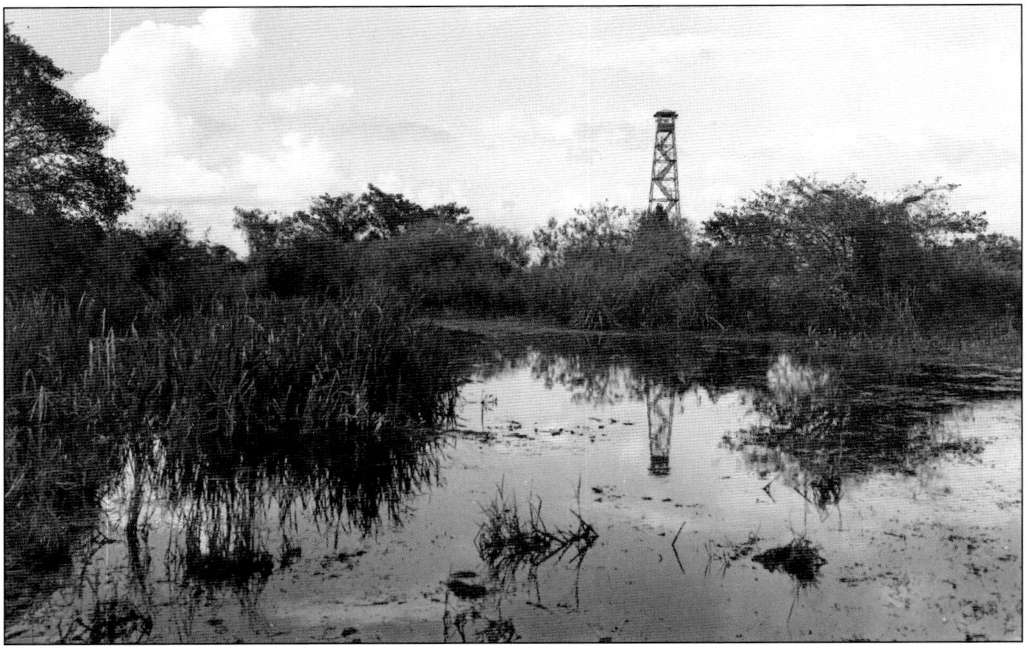

At the park's northern boundary, a visitor experience opportunity was presented by a seven-mile road built in 1946 to access two unsuccessful oil well sites. In 1952, a fire tower was built on the pad at the end of the road. Ranger Erwin Winte was the district's first ranger. In 1952, a ranger station was established at the 40-mile Bend site of the Zady Tamiami Trail wayside station. (NPS.)

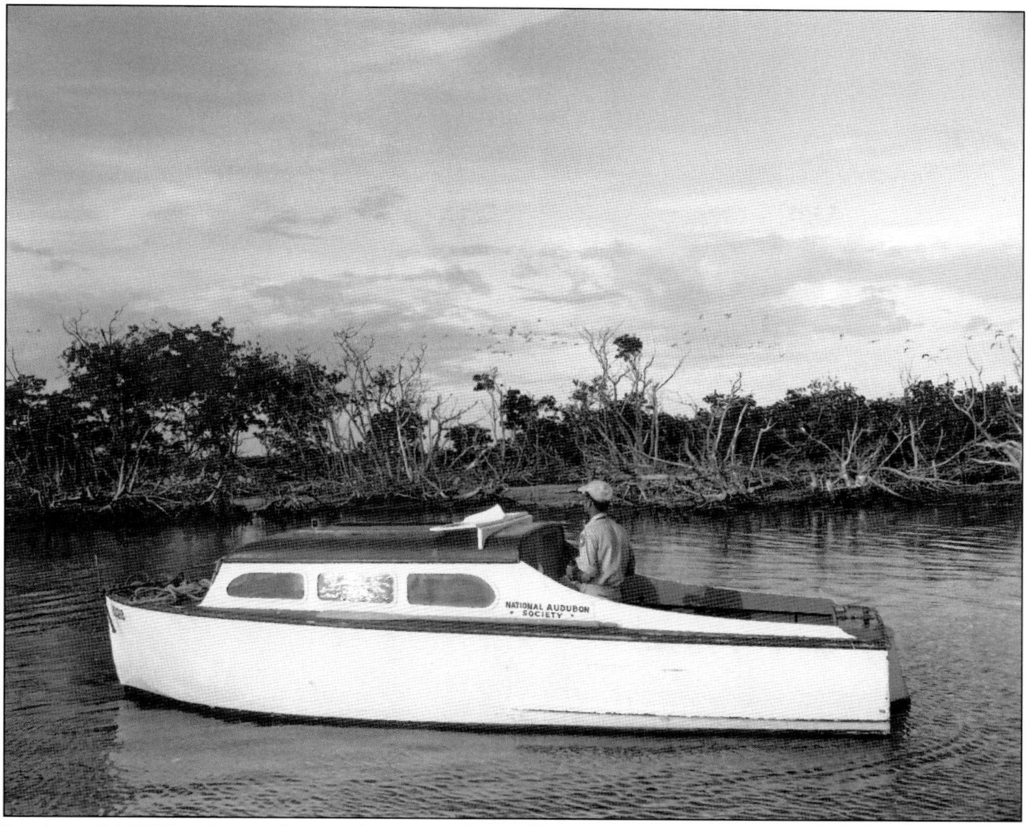

In the mid-1950s, the park's northwestern boundary was extended north, incorporating parts of the Ten Thousand Islands. The extension's jagged interior boundary became known as the "Stairsteps." The extension incorporated the famous Duck Rock where tens of thousands of waterbirds roosted during their non-nesting season. This 1952 image shows an Audubon Society warden patrol before the park's extension. (SLAF.)

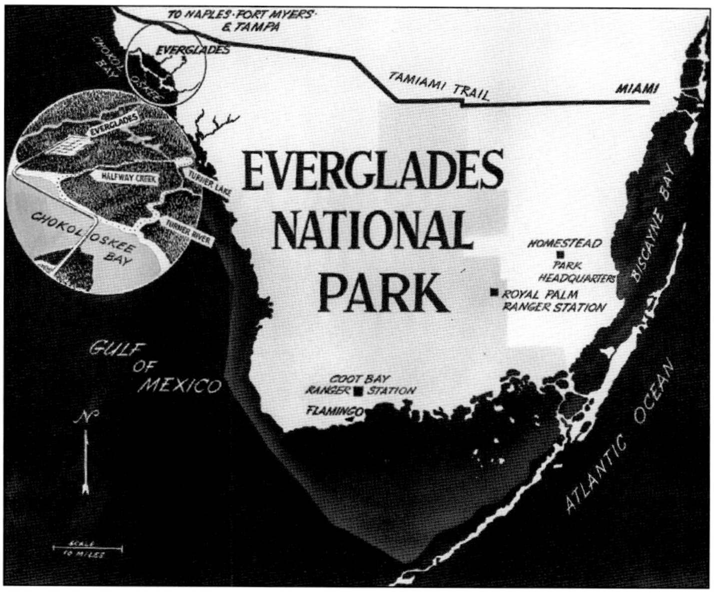

The town of Everglades was chosen as the park's western gateway. The 1950s park expansion authorized purchasing land for an in-town ranger station. Collier interests donated additional land as an incentive for tourism. This advertisement shows a western waterway boat tour of the national park. The 1961 television program *The Everglades* was about a ranger patrolling out of an Everglades City sort of community. (NPS.)

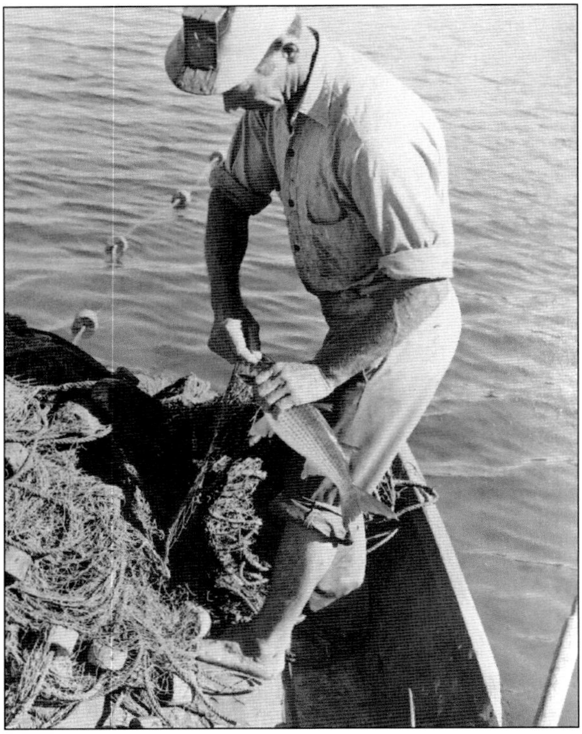

With extractive uses of resources being incompatible with a national park, the management of fisheries was problematic from the start. When the park was established, in addition to sport fishing, commercial fisheries operated out of Flamingo, Chokoloskee, Everglades, and the Florida Keys. Commercial operations, mostly using nets, were allowed to continue while the park service studied and deliberated the issues. This image is from the Ten Thousand Islands. (SLAF.)

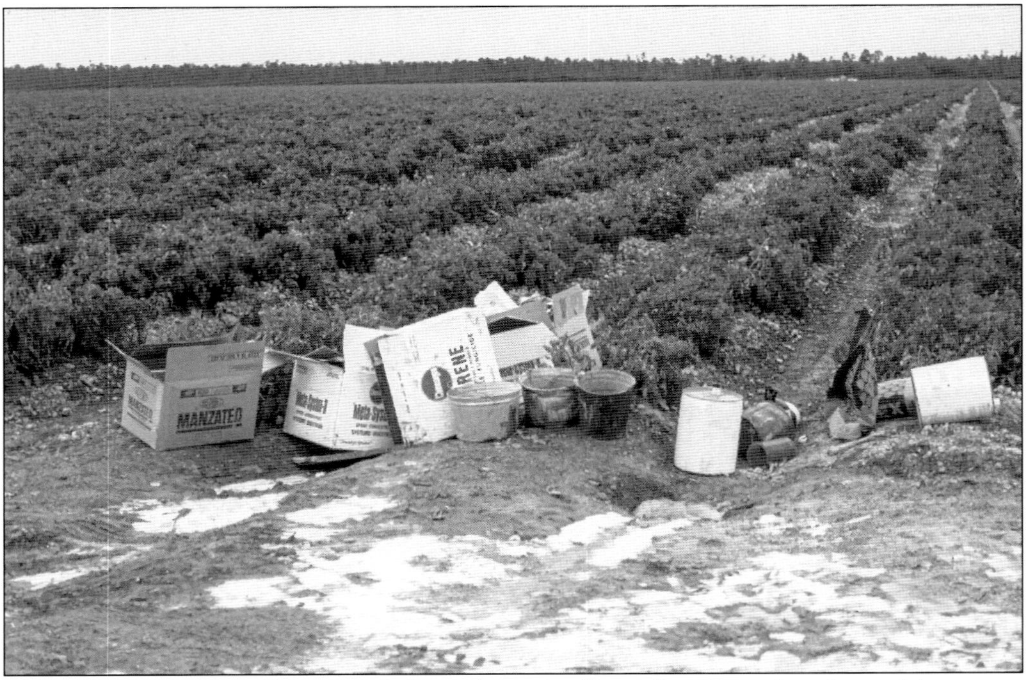

The park's original boundary excluded parcels south of Long Pine Key, where limited dry-season farming had occurred. Soon after the park's establishment, the limestone was pulverized into soil, enabling extensive winter farming. Called the Hole-in-the-Donut, this inholding used pesticides and fertilizers and allowed unregulated access, including by hunters. The 1950s park expansion authorized the area's inclusion in the park, though farming continued into the 1970s. (NPS.)

Six

A Park for Birds and for People

From the mid-1950s to the mid-1960s, plans for the basic design of the park were in place, its worldwide fame was well secured, and its infrastructure was being constructed. Research was producing a new understanding of the park's ecology, the effects of extractive activities like commercial fishing were becoming documented, the potential consequences of upstream water management were being noted, and the impacts of hurricanes were becoming clearer.

Starting in the mid-1950s, timed to the bureau's 50th anniversary, the National Park Service undertook a 10-year program called Mission 66 to expand visitor services, a program championed by long-serving National Park Service director and landscape architect Conrad Wirth. Departing from national park tradition, Wirth advocated modernist structures of concrete and glass. There was to be ample accommodation for visitors' cars. The program was timely for the then underdeveloped Everglades National Park.

In 1960, Hurricane Donna roared through the park causing extensive structural damage and killing 50–70 percent of the park's western mangrove forest. Recovery of both the natural and built environment was slow. Similarly damaging, the water management systems north of the park came into full operation in the early 1960s. The resulting manipulation of surface water flows into the park caused unnatural drying out during dry years and flooding during wet years. As the importance of water quality and natural seasonal water flows became better understood and litigated, programs emerged to modify the existing water management system delivering water to the park. In 2000, Everglades restoration was born.

Everglades restoration aimed in large part to restore pollution-free water to the park in the quantities, distribution, and timing its environment requires. Progress was made as historic flow ways were recreated and bridges replaced levees. Florida panthers and American crocodiles expanded their ranges. In some years egrets, storks, and ibises nested in numbers reminiscent of the past. Visitors found new and diverse ways to see more of the park off its main road. As the idea of the Everglades continued to capture imaginations around the world, the famous Everglades National Park provided real-life in-person opportunities to experience, understand, and appreciate America's Everglades.

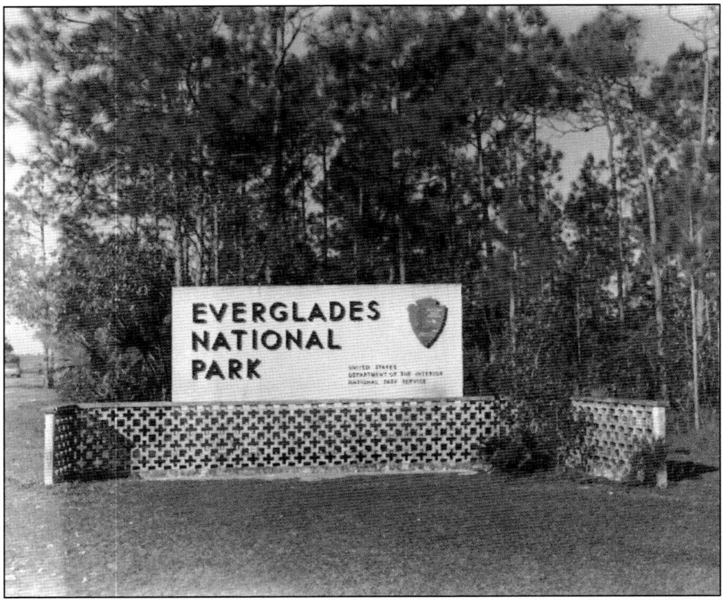

The 1960s evolution of the park infrastructure may be illustrated by the second-generation entrance sign along the main park road, shown in 1970. Its concrete latticework matched the new visitor center nearby. In each of its iterations, the entrance sign on the main park road greeted visitors as the developed and agricultural lands instantly gave way to natural pine forest when they crossed the park's boundary. (NPS.)

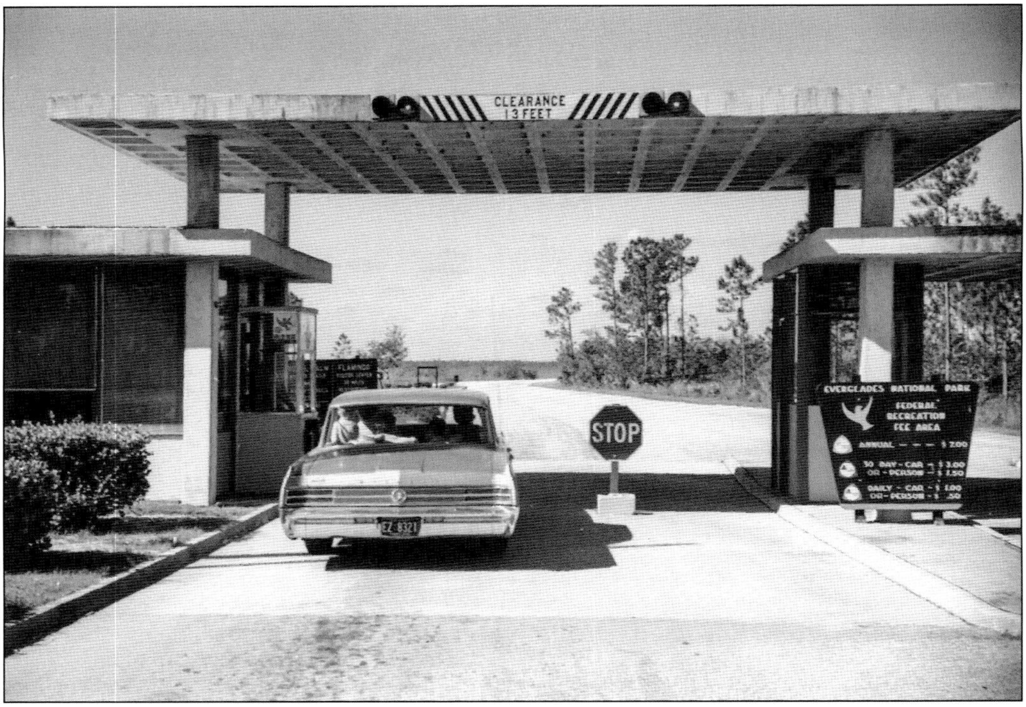

Mission 66 brought a new entrance station to the park, replacing the simple hut of the early days. This image from 1966 shows the heavy-duty concrete replacement, this time providing a bit of shade. Park personnel and volunteers continued to greet visitors as they drove through on their way to Anhinga Trail and, perhaps, Flamingo. It was replaced by the current, more soaring structure after Hurricane Andrew. (NPS.)

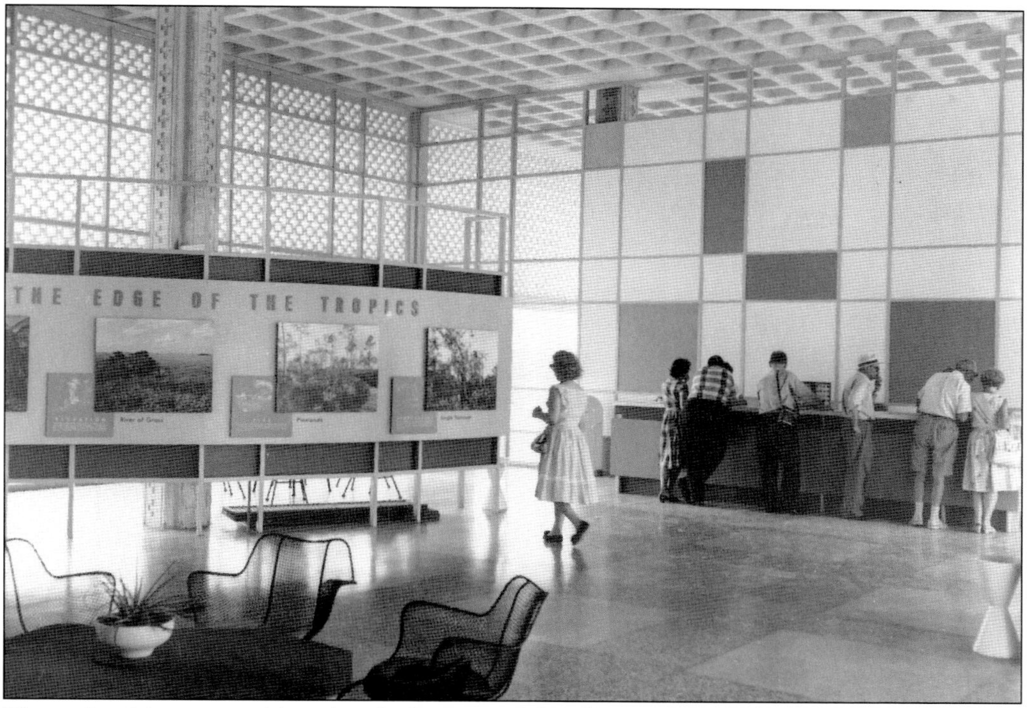

The main visitor center (above) and adjacent park headquarters opened in 1961. Superintendent Beard had advocated continuing the park's welcome center in Homestead, but the center was placed on Parachute Key, which Beard had named in case his proposal was not adopted and the visitor center could then "parachute" into the park. The main visitor center was damaged in 1965 by Hurricane Betsy and again in 1992 by Hurricane Andrew, requiring repairs to the headquarters and complete replacement of the visitor center building. The new visitor center (below), dedicated in 1995, was named to honor the father of the park, Ernest F. Coe. The multi-purpose building was designed with a contact station, bookstore, exhibit space, and theater with an observation pavilion and a boardwalk nearby. (Above, NPS; below, RWB.)

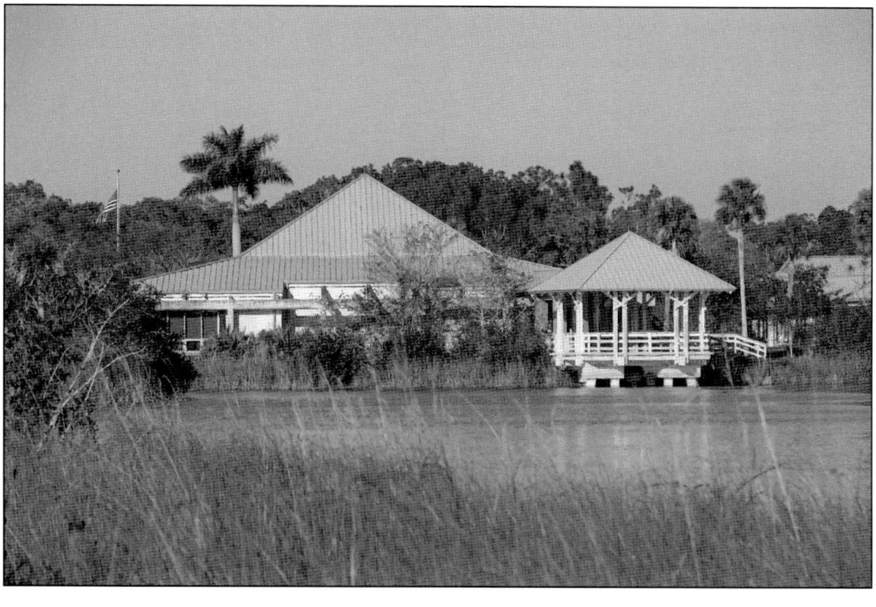

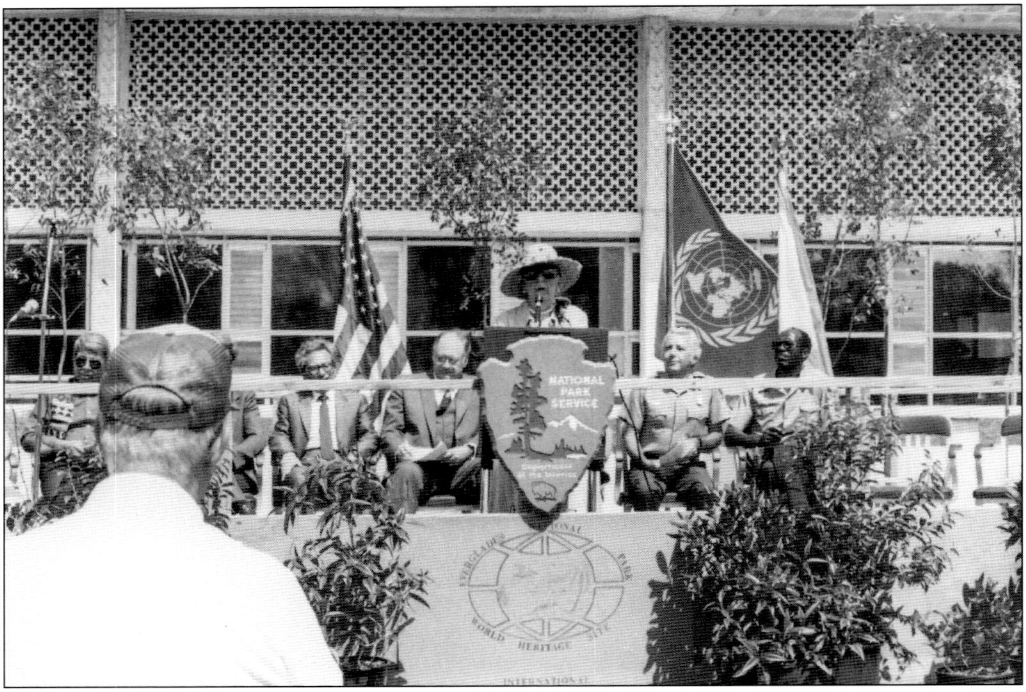

In 1982, the original main visitor center was the site of Everglades National Park's dedication as an international biosphere reserve, acknowledging its achievements in melding biodiversity conservation with sustainable use. This image shows Marjorie Stoneman Douglas speaking at the ceremony. The park was recognized in 1979 as a world heritage site by UNESCO, and in 1987 as a wetland of international importance by the Ramsar Convention on Wetlands. (NPS.)

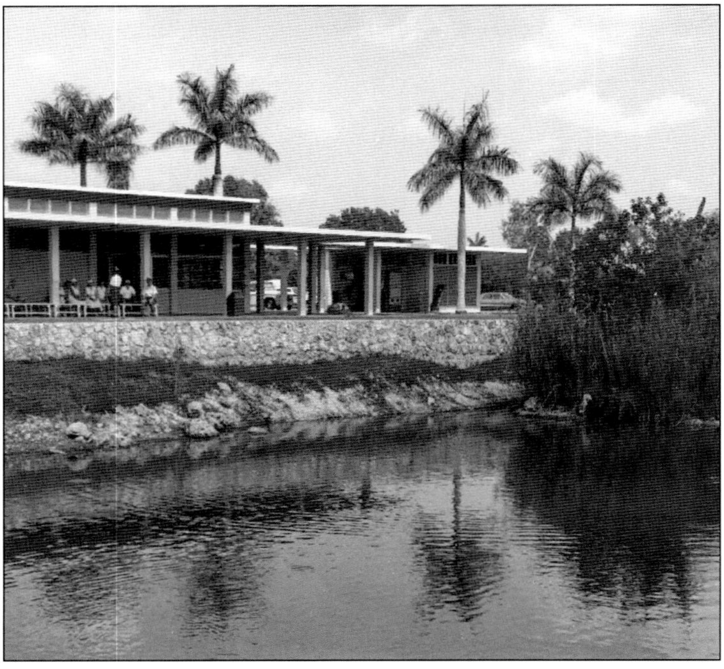

At Paradise Key, a new Royal Palm Visitor Center was built in 1951. The stark concrete structure, shown in 1965, was one of the early examples of modernist park architecture. It provided meeting space, a ranger office, comfort station, and exhibit space with interpretive panels inspired by the work of modernist artist Charley Harper, known for his stylized wildlife images. The exhibit space was replaced by a shop in 2006. (NPS.)

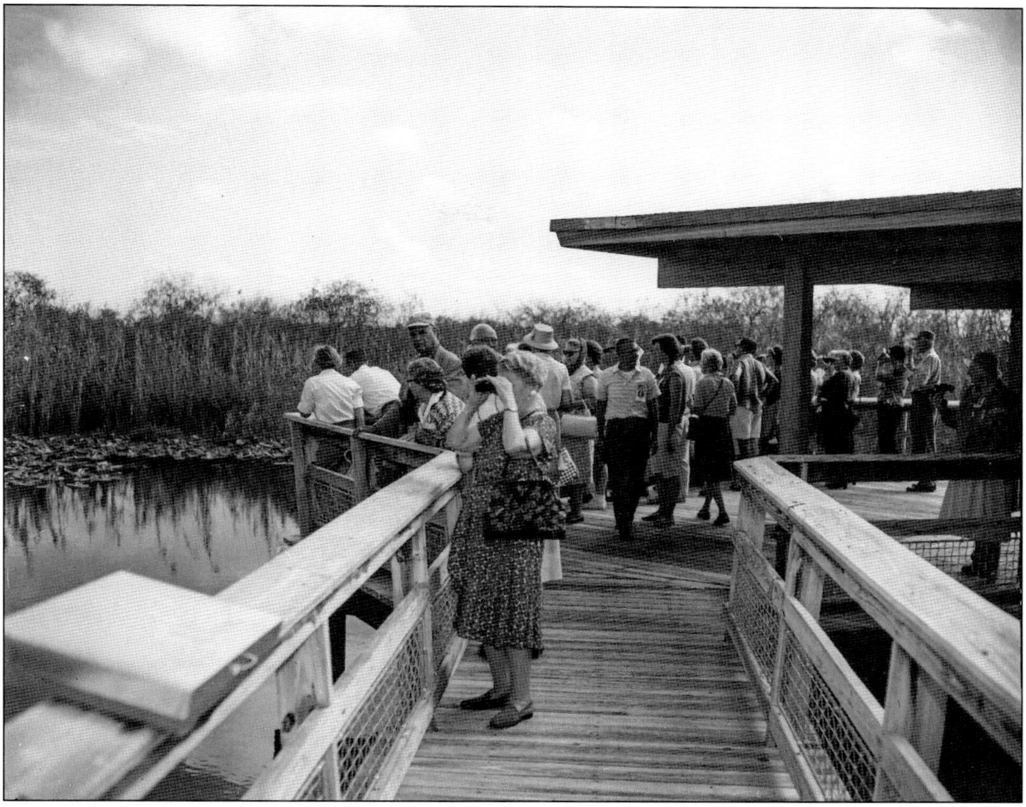

Anhinga Trail was substantially improved in 1961. It incorporated parts of the old Ingraham Highway and a boardwalk loop. Visitors would crowd the boardwalk in the winter tourist season, as shown in this 1965 image, to see anhingas and alligators, especially as water levels dropped in the drying season and the old borrow pit became essentially a huge alligator hole. (NPS.)

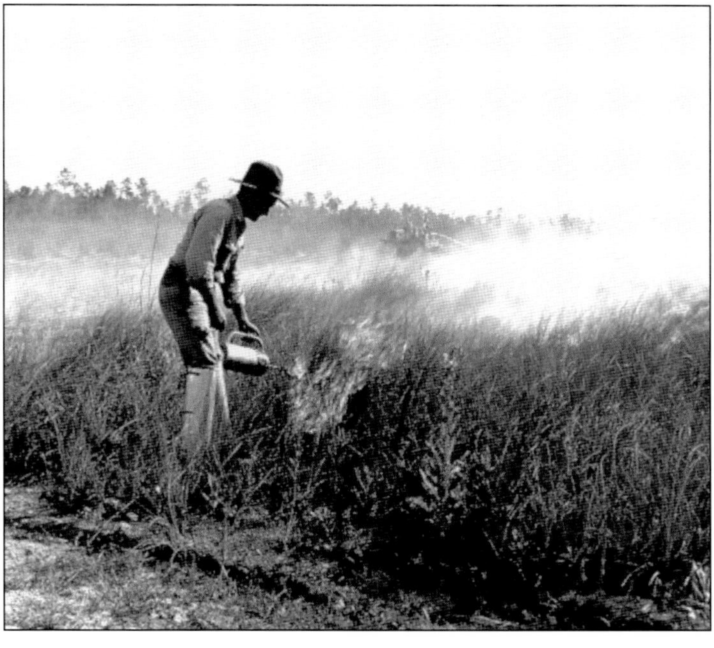

Paradise Key's neighbor Long Pine Key is covered by some of the last remaining stands of South Florida's pinelands, called pine rockland; only two percent of the original pineland is left, mostly in the park. Research at the park in the early 1950s found that the pinelands required periodic burning to persist. This image shows the first prescribed fire being purposely set to imitate the natural burning cycle. (NPS.)

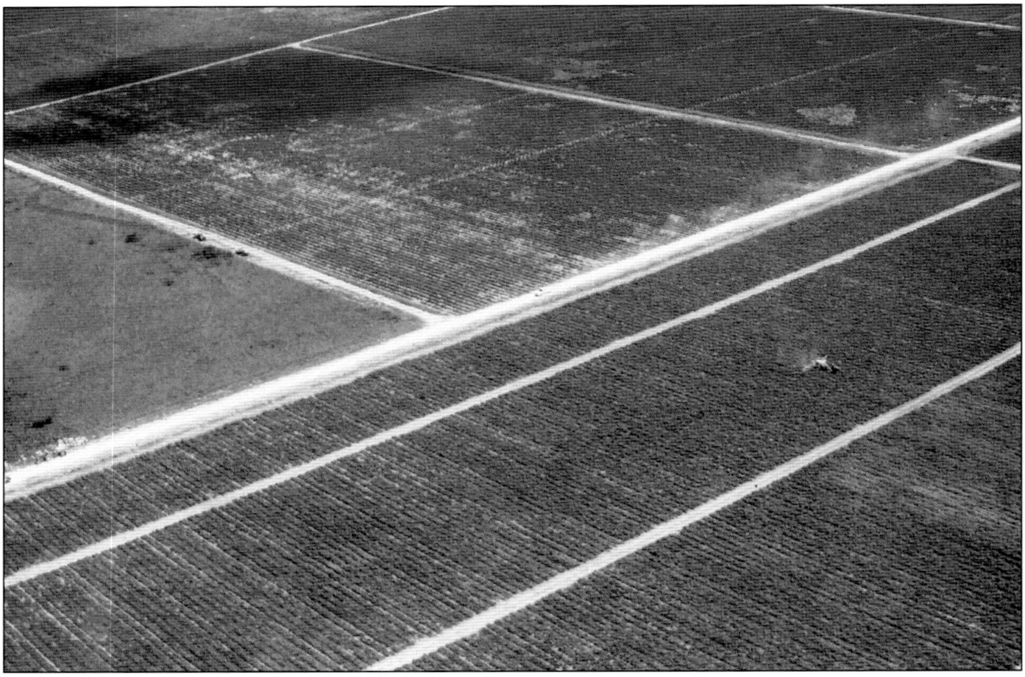

The large-scale farming begun in the mid-1950s in the Hole-in-the-Donut (above) continued after Congress authorized the addition of the land to the park. In 1961, an opportunity became available when one of the earliest and largest operators, Iori Farms, defaulted on a government loan. By 1975, all the farmed lands and other holdings in the area had been procured by the government, and farming ended. However, the much-altered soil encouraged non-native plants, notably Brazilian pepper. Starting in the mid-1990s, the area's 6,300 acres became the site of an extensive restoration effort (below). The woody vegetation was mechanically cleared, and the artificially pulverized topsoil scraped away down to limestone to restore conditions suitable for native wetland vegetation to colonize. The massive project was a huge success in restoring the environment to favor native plants. (Both, NPS.)

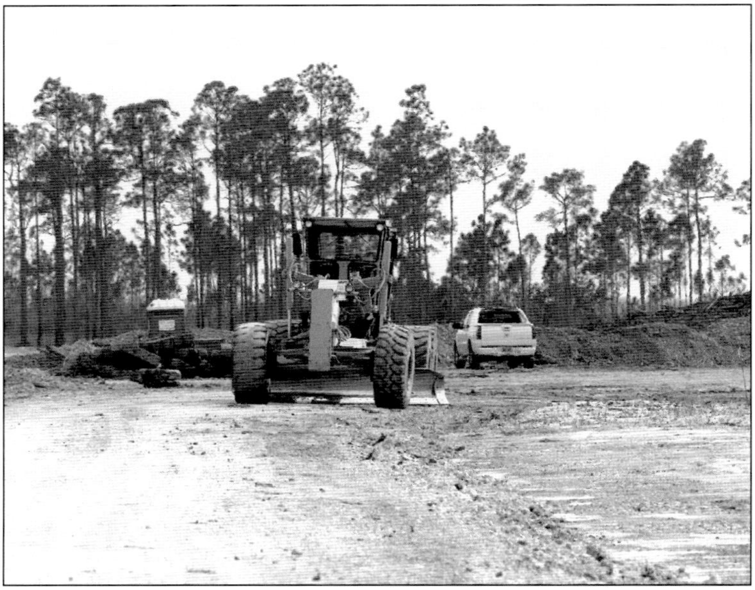

Iori Farms' buildings were repurposed. This 1969 image shows the senior author's Jeep outside the Iori bunkhouse, which was then being used by the University of Miami as a research lab. In 1975, when the author was a park wildlife biologist, the building was renovated to become the new South Florida Research Center, the establishment of which accelerated research in the park. The Farm Road became known as Research Road. (KH.)

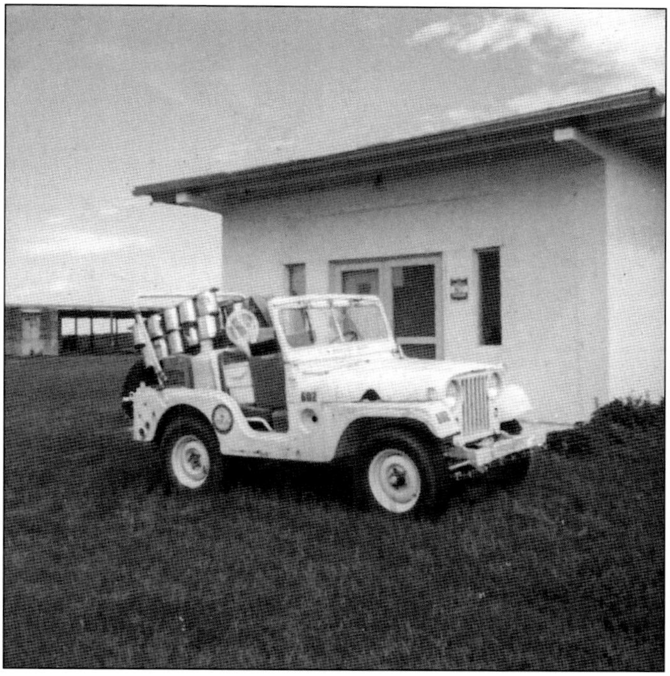

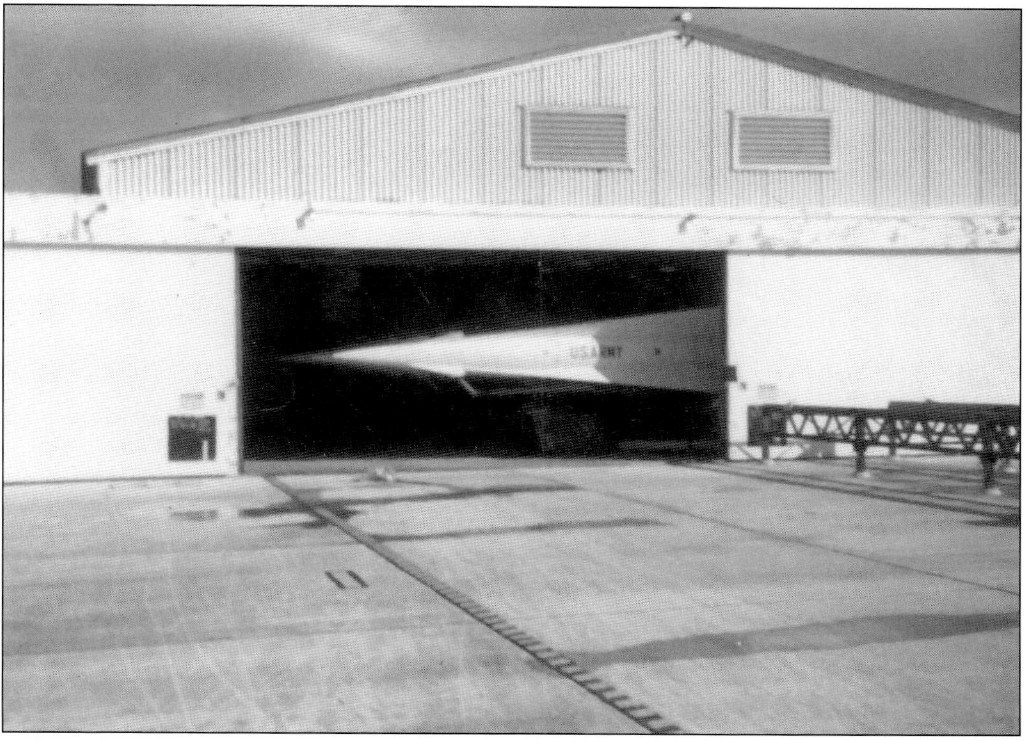

Hole-in-the-Donut also housed a missile base. Moved onto former Iori Farms land in 1965, Base HM-69 housed nuclear-loaded Nike Hercules missiles to provide surface-to-air defense for the Miami-Homestead area. Deactivated in 1979, it was listed in the National Register of Historic Places in 2004. The administrative and barracks building in the battery control and administration site was repurposed as the Daniel Beard Research Center. (NPSWRE.)

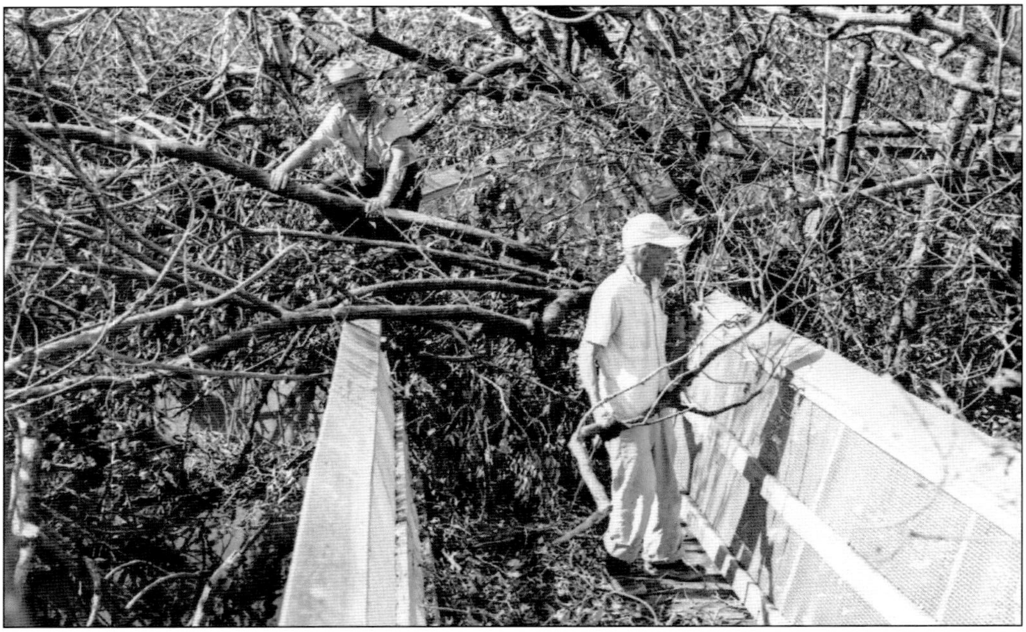

Nature was not kind to the park's vegetation. Hurricanes, such as those in 1960, 1965, 1992, and 2005, caused impressive changes. The image above shows Frank Craighead Sr. examining downed branches on the Mahogany Hammock boardwalk following Hurricane Donna; ranger Ernst Christensen is climbing in the foliage. Dr. Craighead studied the recovery of vegetation from the storm. Many of the park's ancient mahogany trees, some eighty feet tall and four feet in trunk diameter, were toppled in the storm. Hurricane Donna also devastated mangrove forests along the Gulf Coast. The image below shows mangroves killed by Hurricane Betsy in 1965. Hurricanes are a natural phenomenon, but recovery may take decades or centuries. Or a hurricane might change the vegetation altogether. In South Florida, the environment is always changing due to the forces of nature. (Both, NPS.)

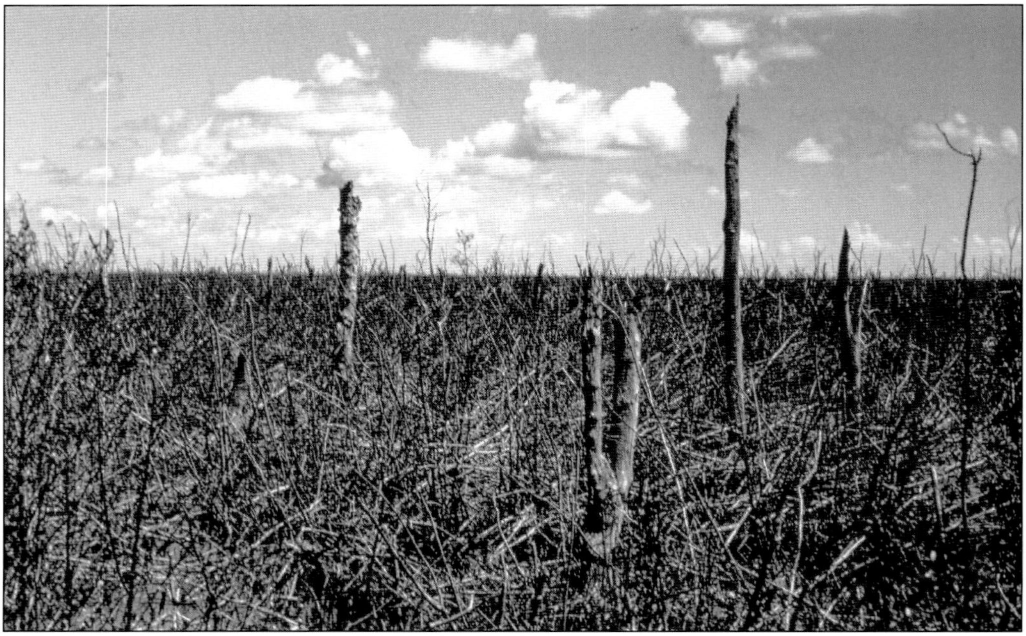

Since the days of the Ingraham Highway, West Lake has provided access to the park's shallow mangrove-lined lakes and coastal bays. This 1963 image shows visitors soon after permanent facilities were built. West Lake is the beginning of an eight-mile canoe trail connecting to Garfield Bight in Florida Bay through lakes and mangrove-arched creeks. Crocodiles nest along the lake's shore, and rafts of waterfowl converge there in winter. (NPS.)

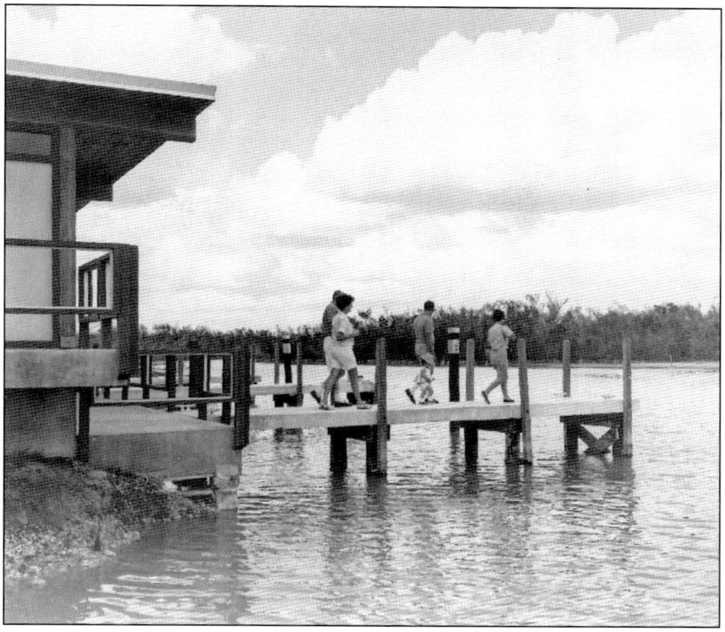

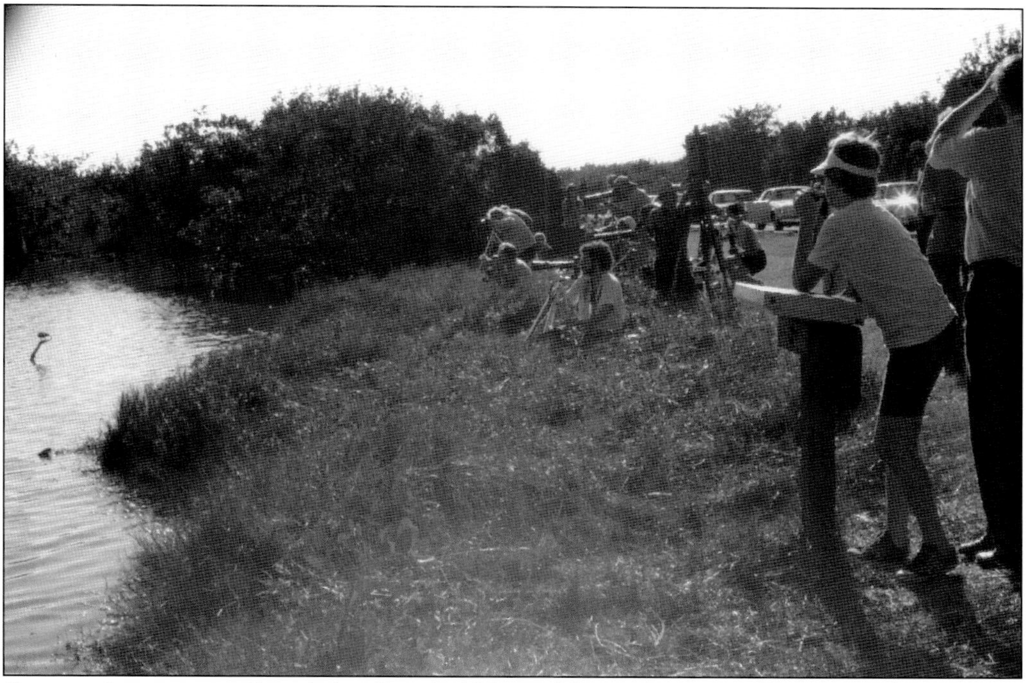

Canoes also put in at Everglades City Gulf Coast Visitor Center, Hell's Bay Trail, Bear Lake Trail, Flamingo, Nine Mile Pond, and Coot Bay Pond, which is attached to Coot Bay by a canal dug by Lewis Watson in 1945. A roadside pond, Mrazek Pond (shown), became world famous for birders and photographers when water levels drop in the late winter, concentrating fish and attracting birds. (SLAF.)

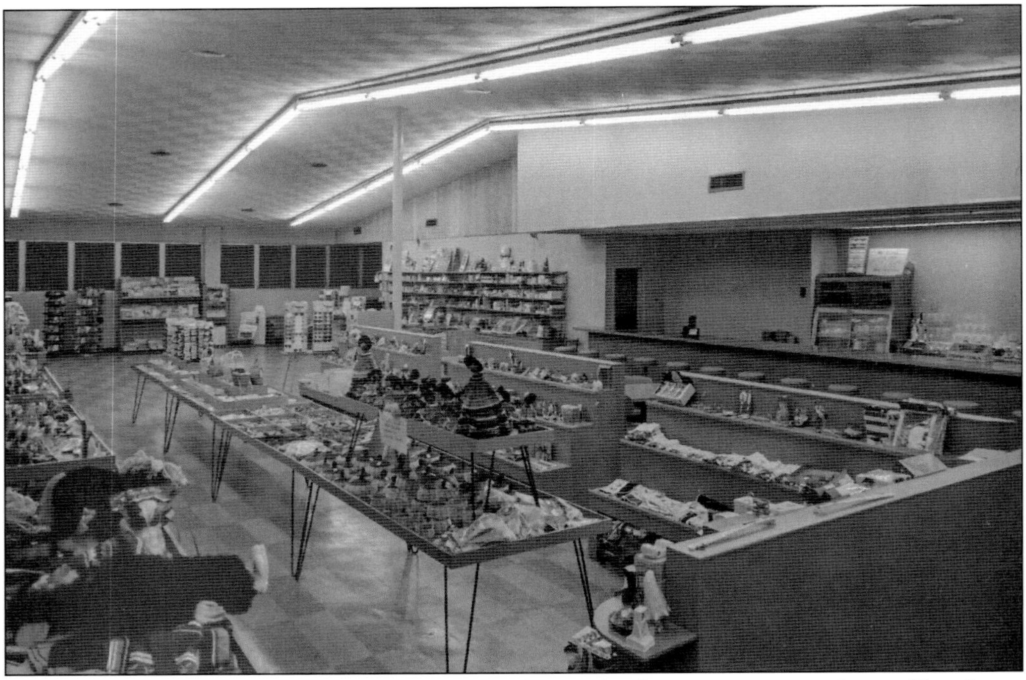

The developed area at Flamingo was extensive. Given the distance to town, almost 50 miles, it was designed to provide a full range of visitor and park management facilities. It included the ranger station, a marina with launch ramps, boat rentals, tours, a restaurant, a store and gift shop (above), comfort stations, and a gas station. Flamingo needed to provide housing for both visitors and park and concessionaire personnel. The development included an extensive campground for tents and campers and the Flamingo Lodge, a five-building, 60–guest room motel that opened in 1957 (below). Building a full-scale lodge was controversial, but included in the plan when Florida governor LeRoy Collins made it an implicit understanding when agreeing to transfer state lands for the 1950s park expansion. (Both, NPS.)

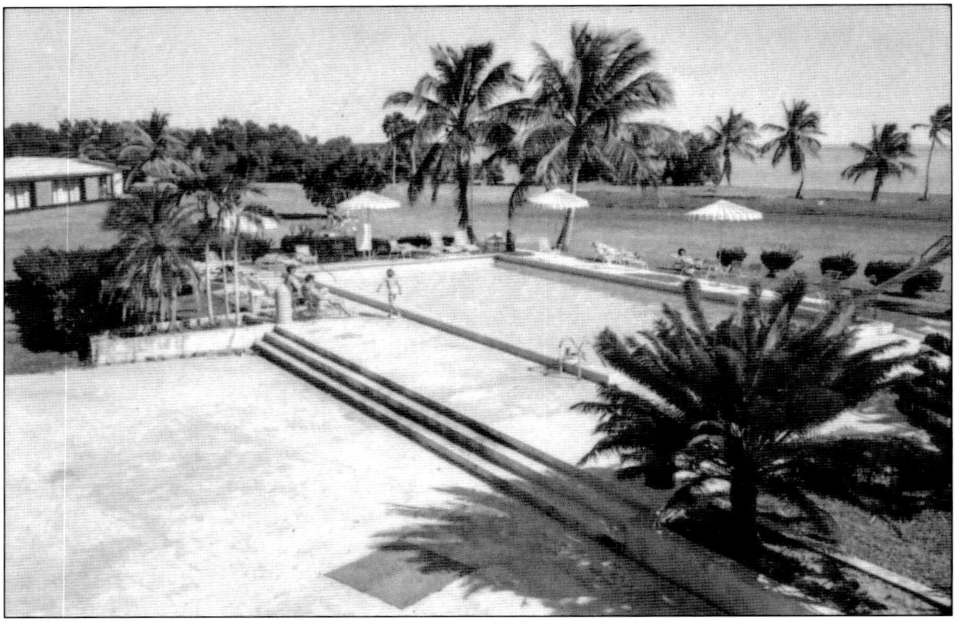

Flamingo's principal multipurpose structure was built perched high on piles. One building was the Flamingo Visitor Center; the other was the concessionaire's restaurant and gift shop. The connecting walkway offered a second-floor view of the entrance to the Buttonwood Canal and Florida Bay. Opening in 1957, the drastically horizontal and flamingo-pink building actually fit in rather nicely, echoing the storm surge–accommodating stilt houses that were its historical precedents. (NPS.)

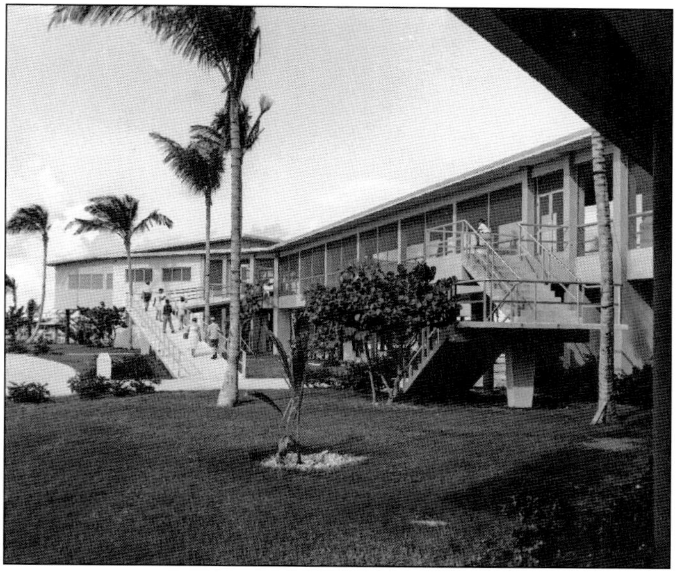

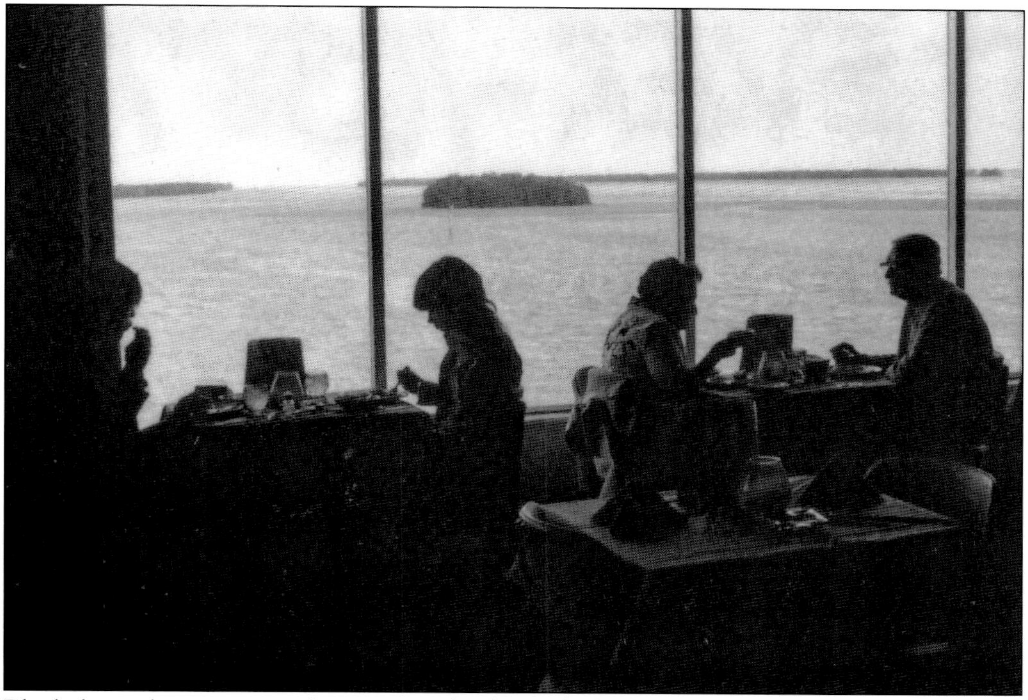

The lodge and restaurant evoke memories for those who had the opportunity to experience them. After the long drive through the park, finding screened-off accommodations and food with an elevated view of Florida Bay was a treat. Views from indoors also were a treat because Flamingo's wet-season mosquitoes, no-see-ums, and deer flies were world-famous. This 1970 image shows the diners' view of Florida Bay out the restaurant windows. (NPS.)

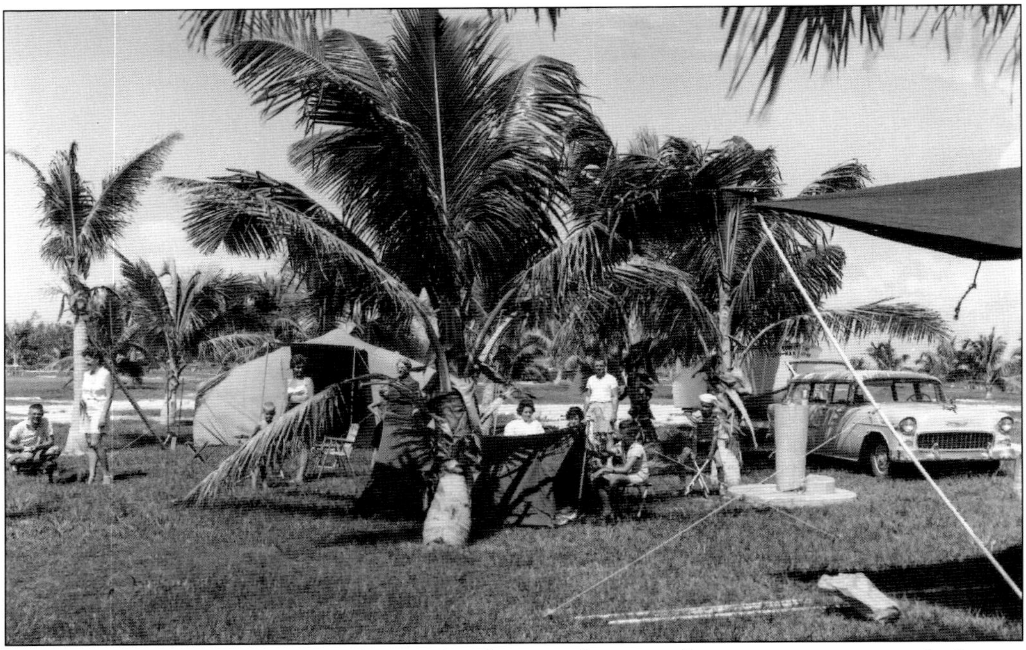

The Flamingo Campground was designed with spaces for car and tent camping, an amphitheater for ranger-led programs, and hiking trails along the Florida Bay shore following old roadbeds. The campground opened for the 1958–1959 winter season with 54 camping and 60 picnic sites, as well as the all-important comfort stations. The Flamingo Campground, overlooking Florida Bay, is shown in 1961. (NPS.)

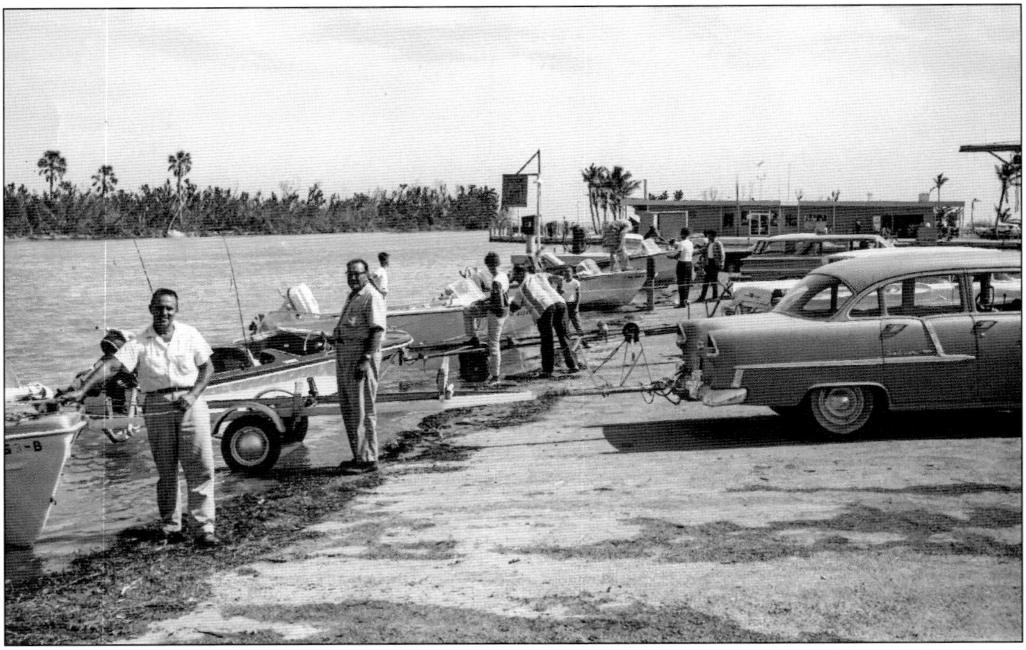

Flamingo became a boater's gateway, as suggested in this 1960 image. Boaters launched into the Buttonwood Canal, from which they could head to Coot Bay or Florida Bay. However, the canal also allowed saltwater intrusion into the interior of Coot Bay, so a dam was added in 1982. After that, boaters picked which side to launch on. (NPS.)

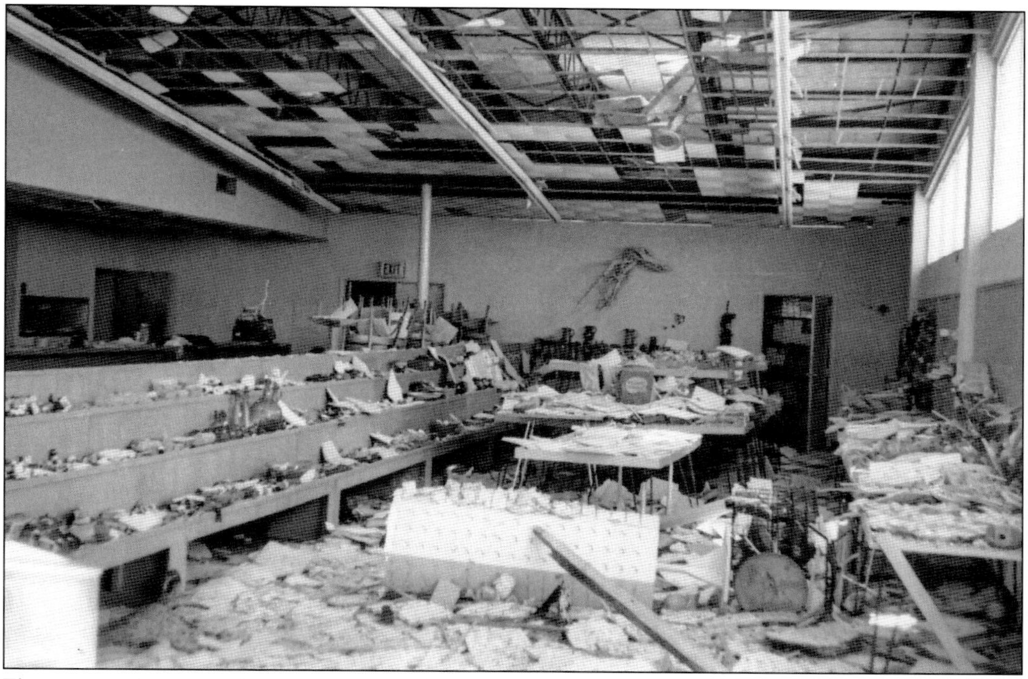

Flamingo is low and Florida Bay is shallow, so during hurricanes, Florida Bay ends up on top of Flamingo. Hurricanes were first recorded as devastating structures in Flamingo in 1909 and 1910 as its settlement was getting underway. Storm surge from the 1926 and 1935 hurricanes eliminated farming on the prairies. The 1948 hurricane destroyed frame houses, many of which were rebuilt from the debris. In 1960, Hurricane Donna mowed down Flamingo. Shown are the gift shop (above, compare to page 108) and a comfort station (below) post-hurricane. It also washed out Guy Bradley's monument. Hurricane Andrew caused $40 million in damages in 1992. The 2005 hurricanes, Katrina and Wilma, blasted Flamingo's infrastructure with 10-foot waves against the then 58-year-old Flamingo Lodge and its cabins, which had to be closed. The buildings were removed in 2009. (Both, NPS.)

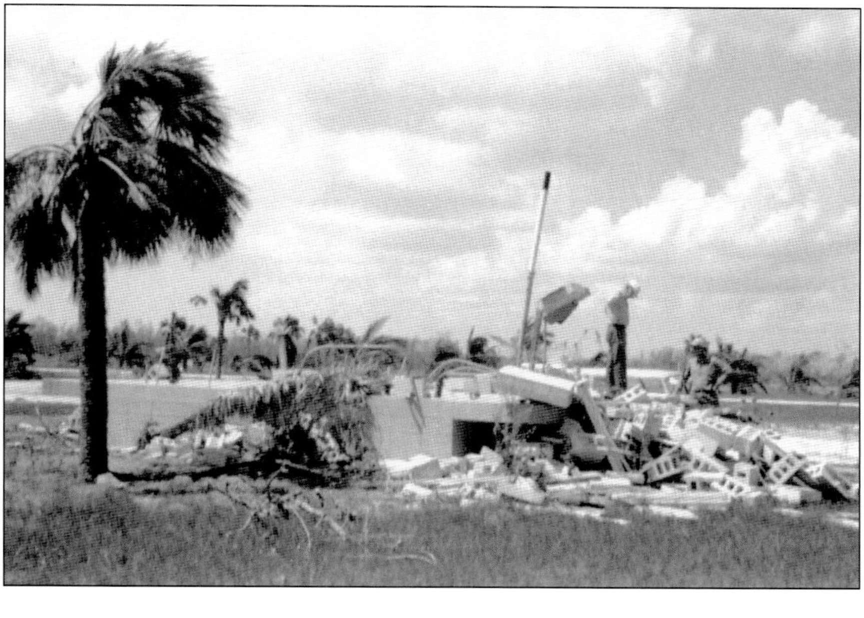

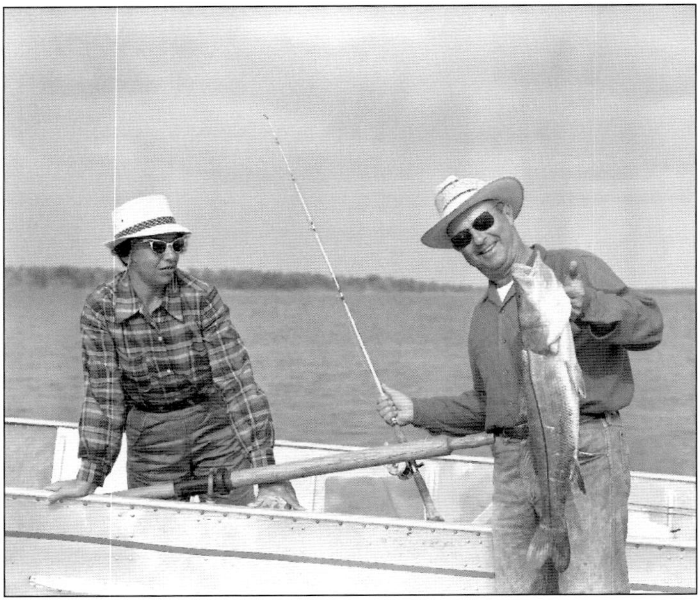

The Flamingo fishing community was reborn as a headquarters for sport fishing on western Florida Bay and the interior mangroves. This 1963 image shows outdoors writer Charles Waterman displaying his snook. Following decades of deliberation, consultation, and research, in 1986, commercial fishing was prohibited in the park, and bag limits were placed on sport fishing. Snook is one of the species that faced population declines and now is strictly regulated. (SLAF.)

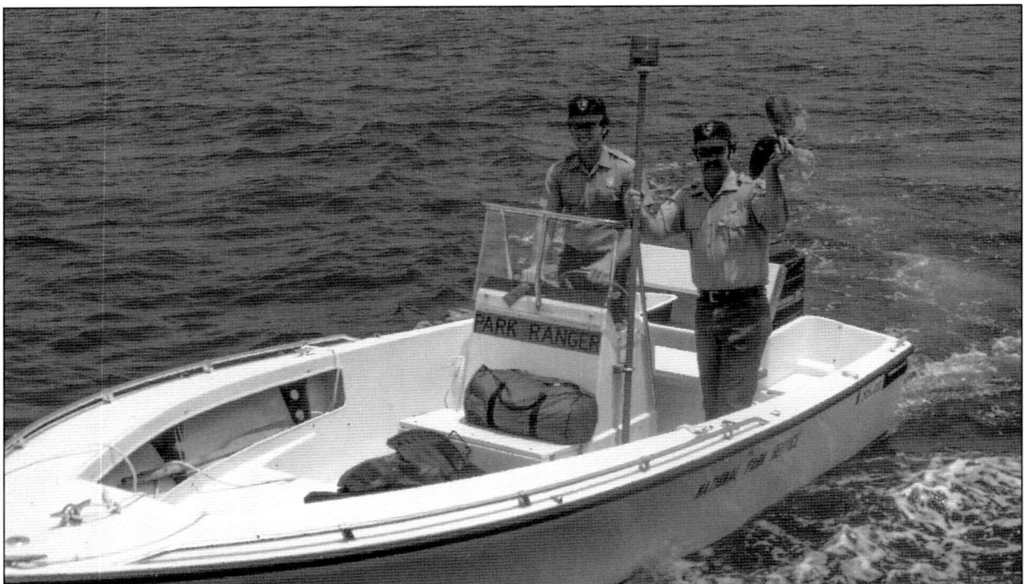

Heavy visitor boating activity in shallow water required extensive ranger patrolling. This ranger is displaying a common experience, a dinged propeller. Along the Gulf Coast, propellers may encounter sand, rock, or oyster reefs. In the shallows of Florida Bay, propellers can scar seagrass beds. To protect the bay bottom, in 1978, over a half-million acres of the park's submerged marine bottoms were officially declared to be wilderness. (NPS.)

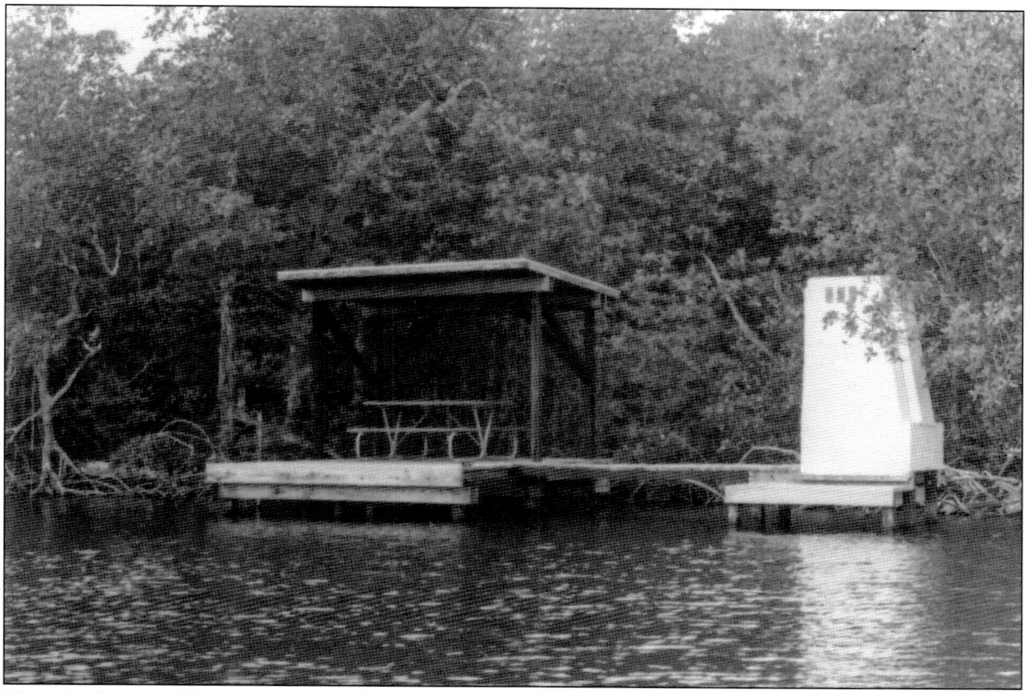

The Wilderness Waterway is an inland route covering 99 miles between Flamingo and Everglades City. Ranger Dick Stokes created it in the mid-1960s by clearing a connection between the Broad River and the Harney and the Shark Rivers. Now called "the Nightmare," powerboats go around the narrow, intricate passage. Ranger William G. Truesdell wrote the first guidebook. It is a 7-to-10-day paddling trip with en route campsites, such as this elevated platform shown in 1973. (NPS.)

The Wilderness Waterway is an example of Everglades National Park being paddling territory, especially in relatively bugless winters. For millennia in the Everglades, canoes were the means of transportation for Indigenous people, Seminole War troops, and pioneer settlers. Coconut Grove's Kirk Munroe was a leader in recreational canoeing in the early 1900s. This image is of a family paddling in the mangroves in 1969. (SLAF.)

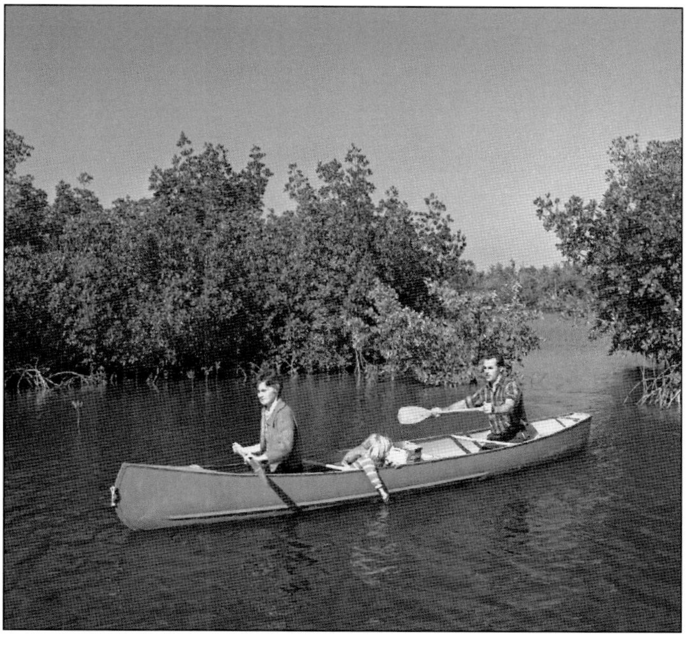

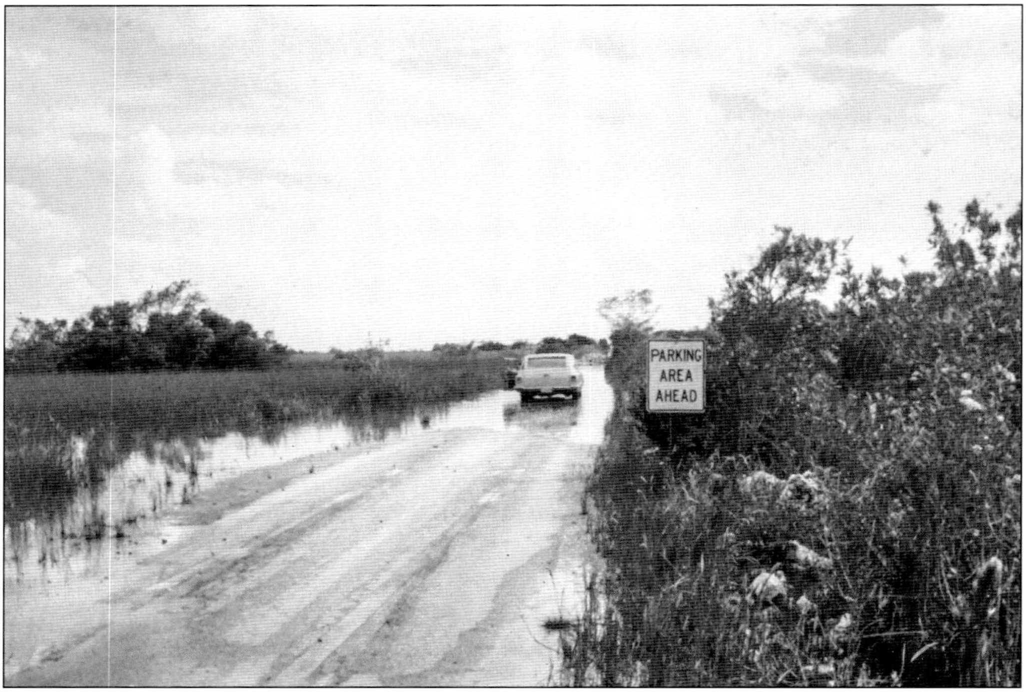

Along Tamiami Trail, the park converted the abandoned oil well road into a prime wildlife viewing opportunity called Shark Valley—the valley part being a bit ironic in such a flat landscape. A curvy eastern leg was added, creating a 15-mile loop. Initially, visitors could drive their cars (shown in 1966) one way, passing 17 roadside exhibits. Flooding in the mid-to-late 1960s closed the road to private cars. (NPS.)

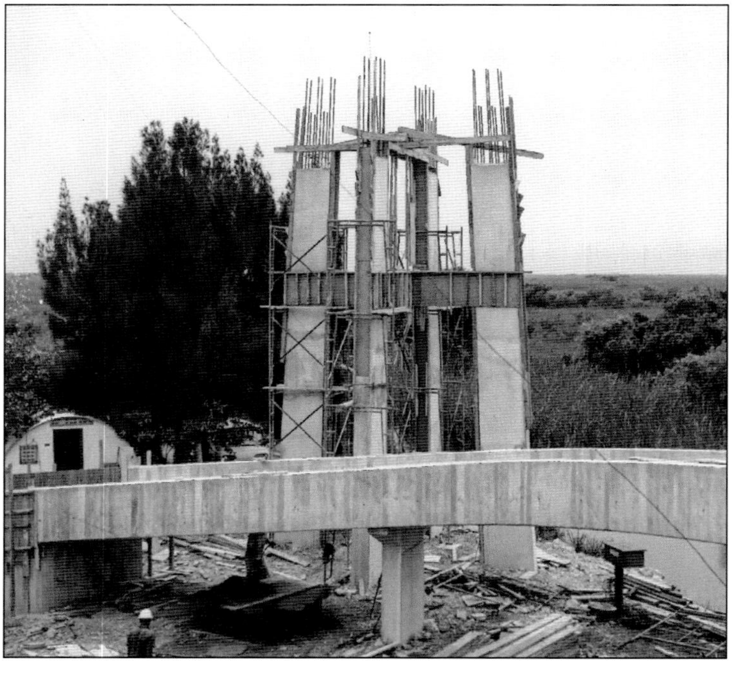

Viewing opportunities for visitors were much enhanced in 1965 when the fire tower at the end of Shark Valley Road was replaced by a modernist concrete observation tower. The image shows the tower under construction. It reached 65 feet, with a 360-degree observation platform topped by a fire lookout cab. The tower's bird's-eye view of the Everglades from the observation platform is shown in this book's introductory image. (NPS.)

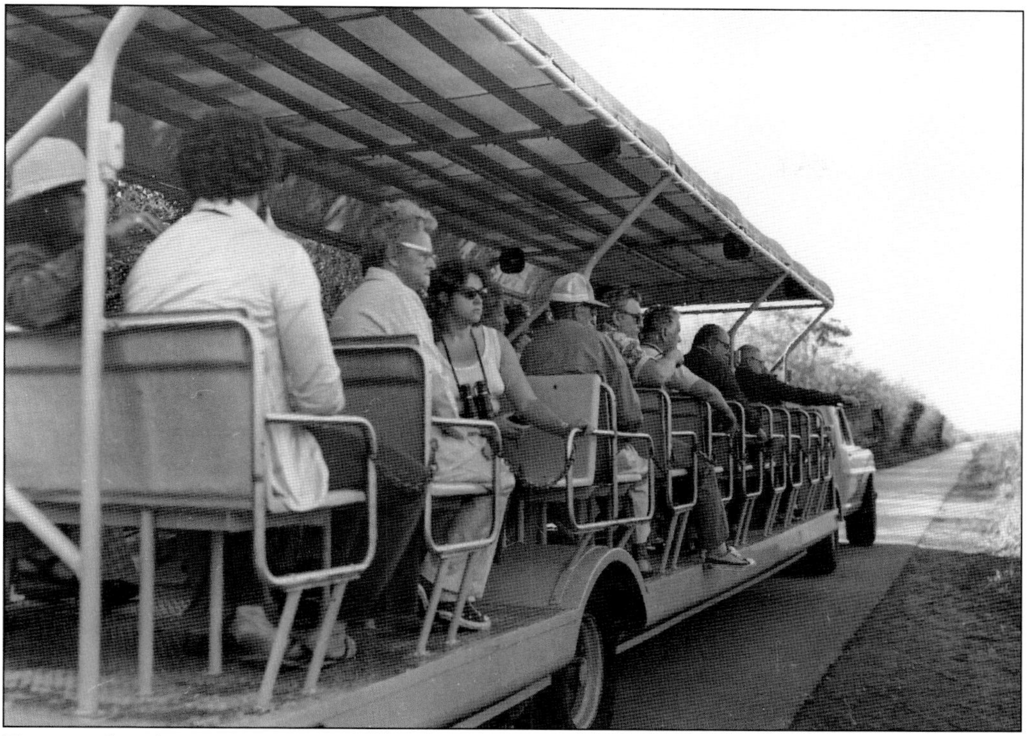

Trams replaced private cars in 1972, and, two years later, bike tours started, both still popular ways to see the wildlife sights at Shark Valley. Early tram drivers included local Miccosukee dressed in their traditional patchwork shirts. The commentary on the trams was initially taped and timed. Rangers tended to school groups, including taking them fishing. This image shows tourists on a tram tour in 1977. (NPS.)

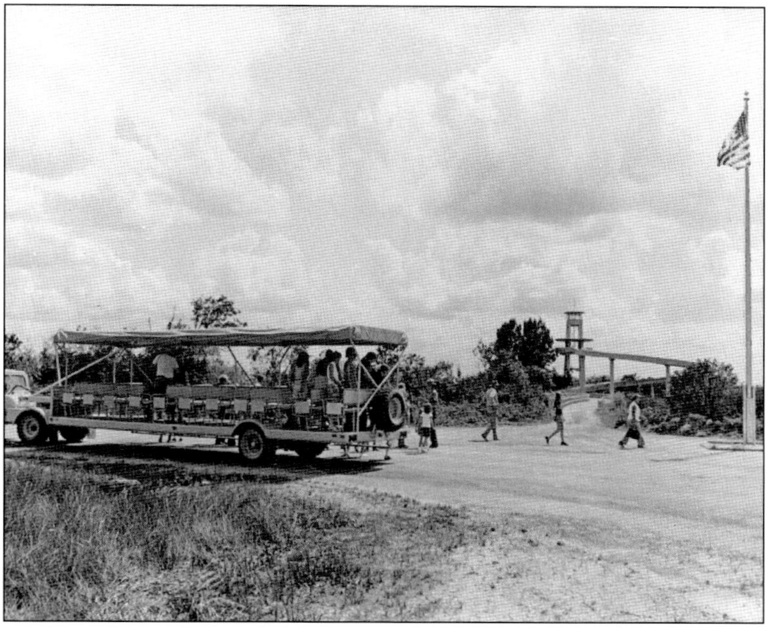

In this early 1970s photograph, visitors walk from the tram to the tower, ascending via a long, curving ramp seen in the distance. The view from the overlook is of the Everglades to the east and southeast and the Big Cypress Swamp to the west. In the borrow pit dug for the old oil well, alligators, fish, and large soft-shell turtles gather in the annual spring drying season. (NPS.)

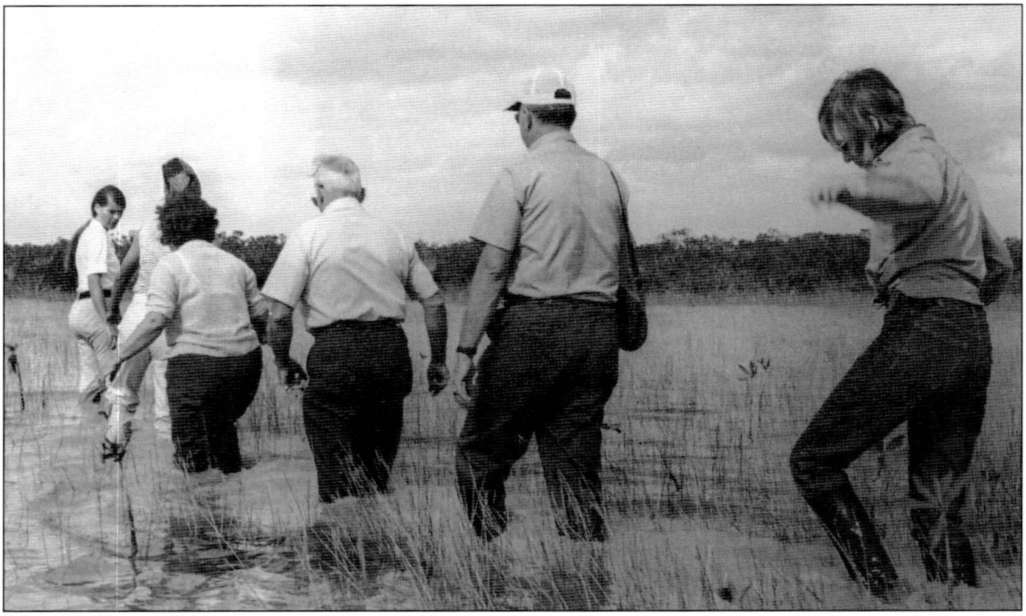

Although many park experiences were designed to accommodate visitors in cars or trams, there was no better way to experience the glades than by wading through it. This image from 1973 shows a ranger-led hike into the marsh. Coming to be called slough slogs, hikes were wet, muddy, and inevitably memorable. (NPS.)

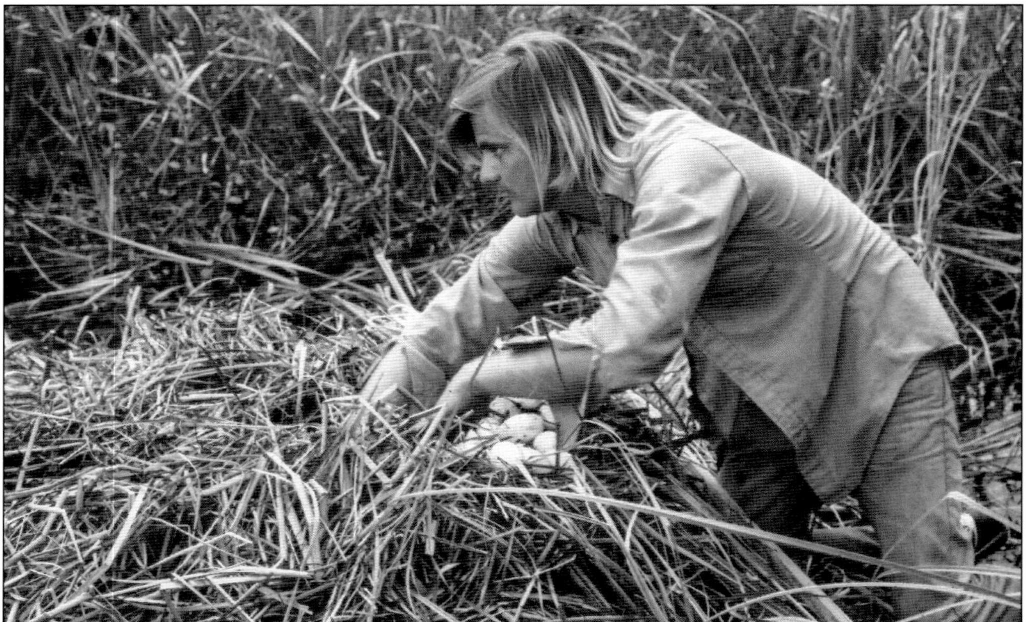

Everglades means alligators. Alligators were always a matter of management concern, first from poaching, then from artificially-enhanced dryness, and then from too-high water levels during nesting season. Alligator nests could flood if water discharges into the park became too high after alligators laid their eggs. This image shows the senior author examining an alligator nest and eggs in 1977, seemingly a bit concerned about the nest-guarding momma gator nearby. (KH.)

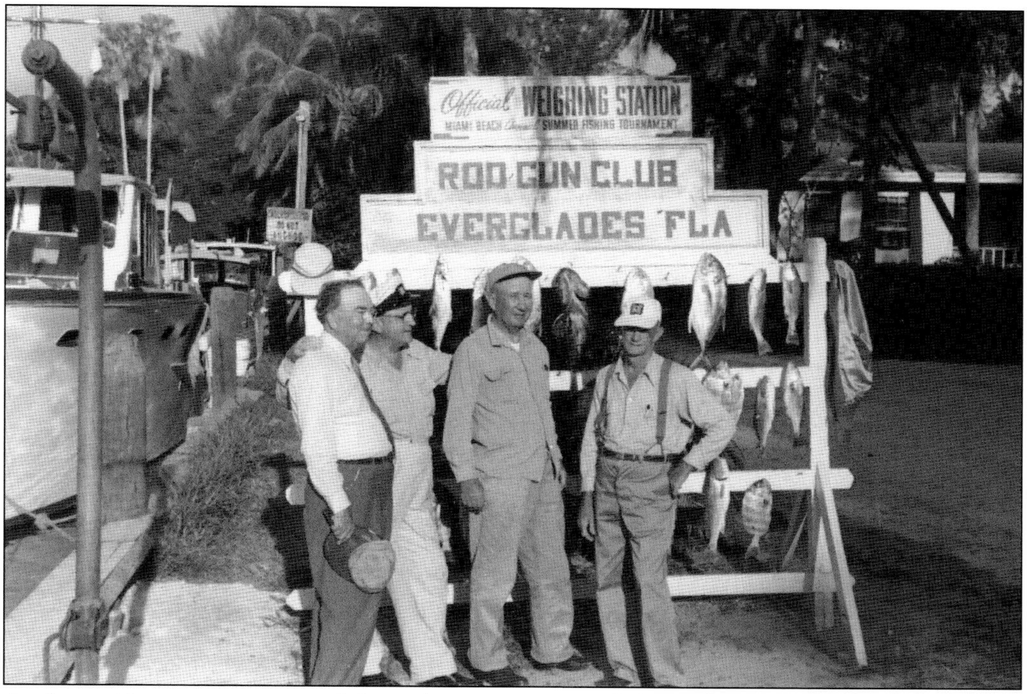

At the park's western gateway, fishing the mangroves and channels was a main attractor to the park, as this 1961 image at the Rod and Gun Club attests. Local fishing charters were developed to put visitors on tarpon, pompano, snook, snapper, or largemouth bass in fresher water. For private boats, better charts over time and GPS helped to navigate narrow passes, shallows, and oyster bars. (SLAF.)

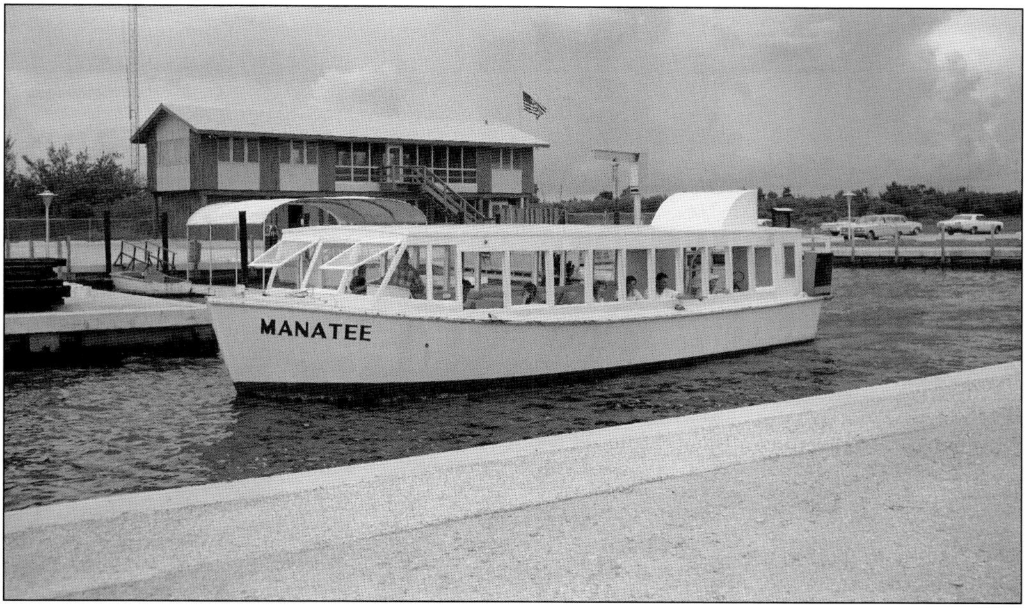

Non-fishing alternatives for western Everglades National Park visitors were tour boats. Tours took visitors around Chokoloskee Bay and through Indian Key Pass. This 1967 image is of the *Manatee*, one of a succession of concession-operated tour boats that took visitors on narrated tours from Everglades City into the Ten Thousand Islands. (SLAF.)

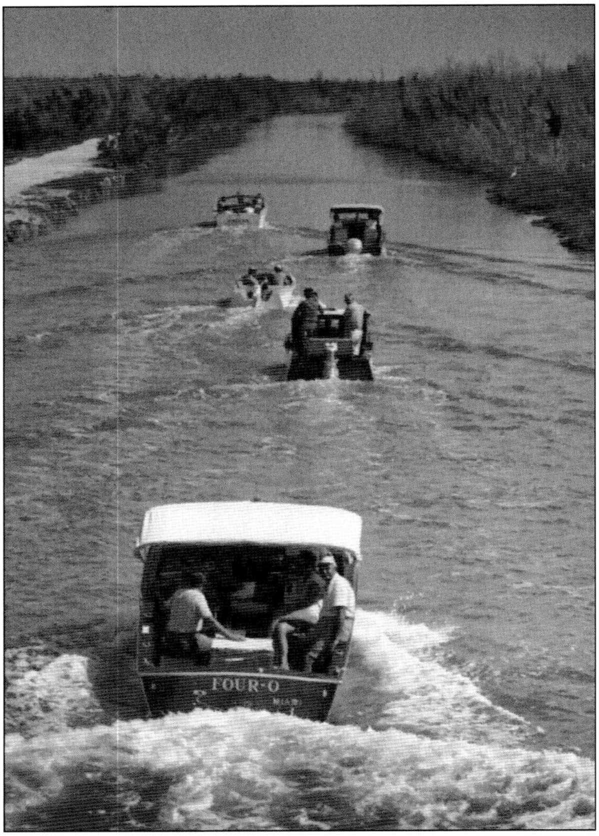

An early approach to allow visitors access to the tricky waters of the Gulf Coast was an organized flotilla called a boat-a-cade. Rangers led a string of private boats from Everglades to the Lostmans River Ranger Station or inland into the rivers and back. Overnighting on their boats introduced guests to a wilderness experience, and its mosquitoes, an experience the senior author had in the late 1950s. (NPS.)

Along the Gulf Coast, evening flights of waterbirds at Duck Rock and other roost sites became an attraction for visitors. The Audubon Society operated the tours. In this aerial view of Duck Rock, each white spot is a roosting bird, which could number in the tens of thousands. Most of the birds were white ibis. Duck Rock's vegetation and soil were swept away by Hurricane Donna in 1960. (NPS.)

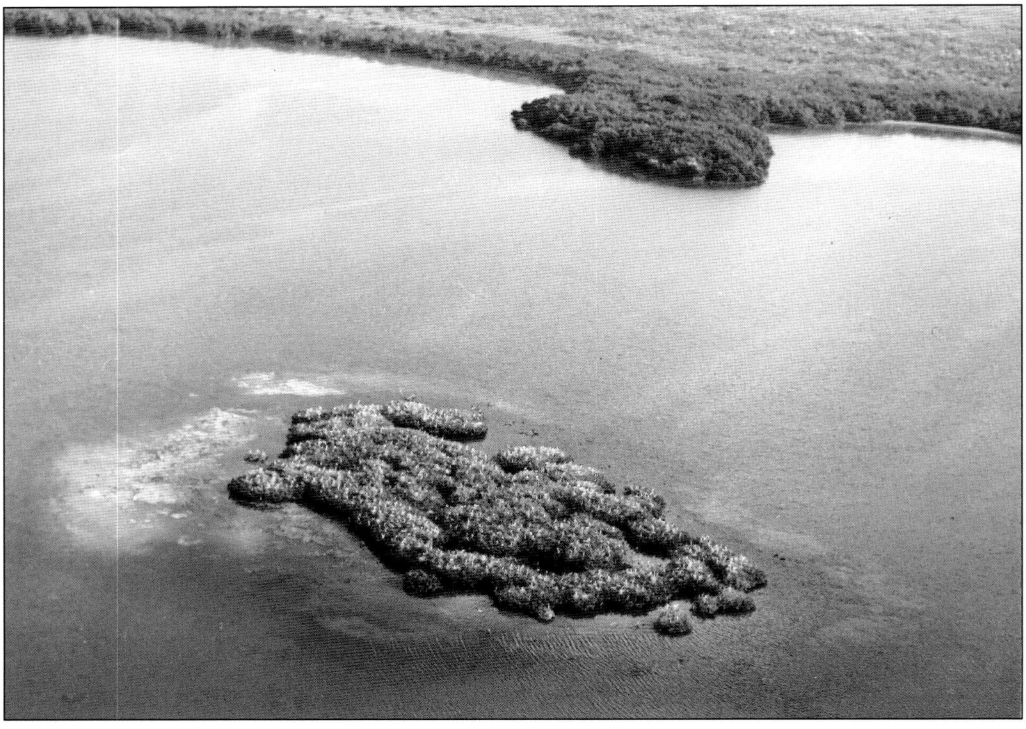

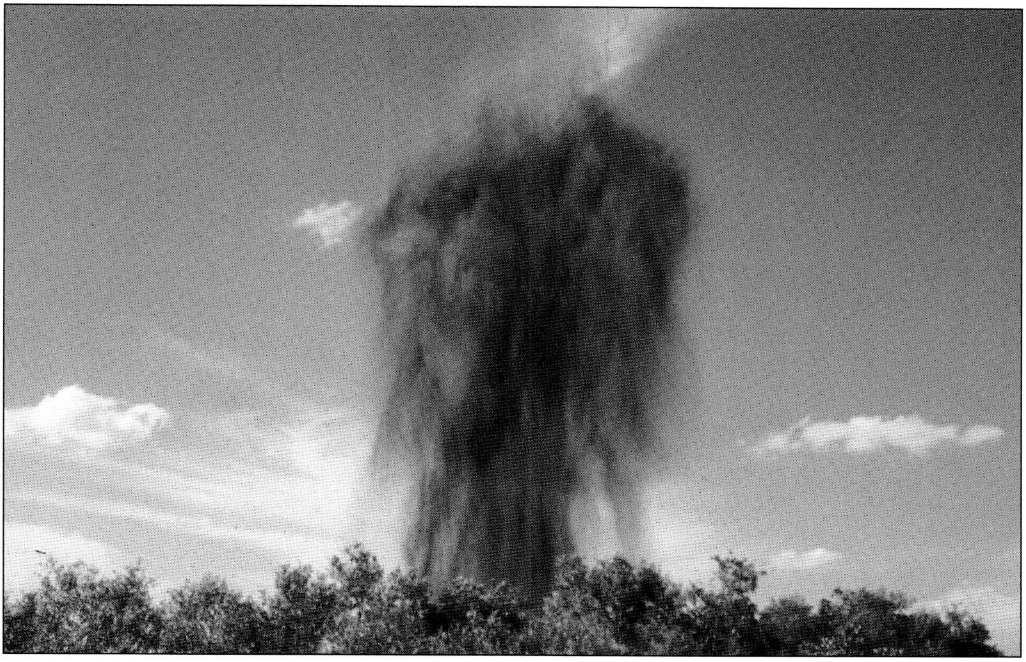

Protecting the ecology of a national park at the end of its drainage basin was not easy. Starting in 1949, the US Army Corps of Engineers and the State of Florida began constructing levees and canals to tame the Everglades' natural seasonal and episodic water level fluctuations. By 1962, Lake Okeechobee had become a leveed reservoir with outflows by canals directly to the Atlantic and Gulf of Mexico rather than south into the Everglades. The remaining Everglades north of the park were leveed off into water conservation areas. In the dry year of 1962 when the system was completed, surface water flow into the park was cut off. The park dried, animals died, and fires burned. Artificial gator holes were blasted to provide water for wildlife (above) and water was pumped into the Anhinga Trail pond (below). (Above, KH; below, NPS.)

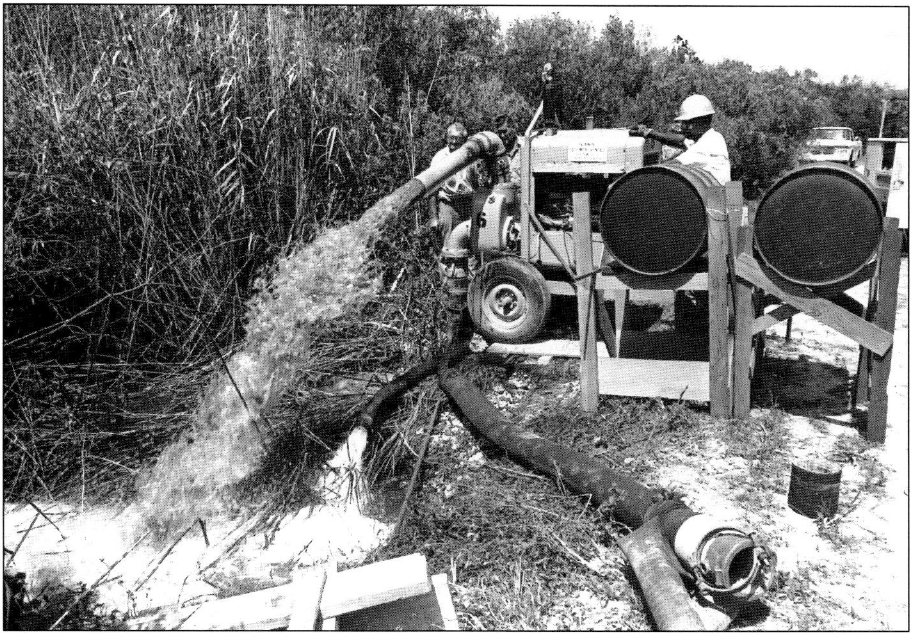

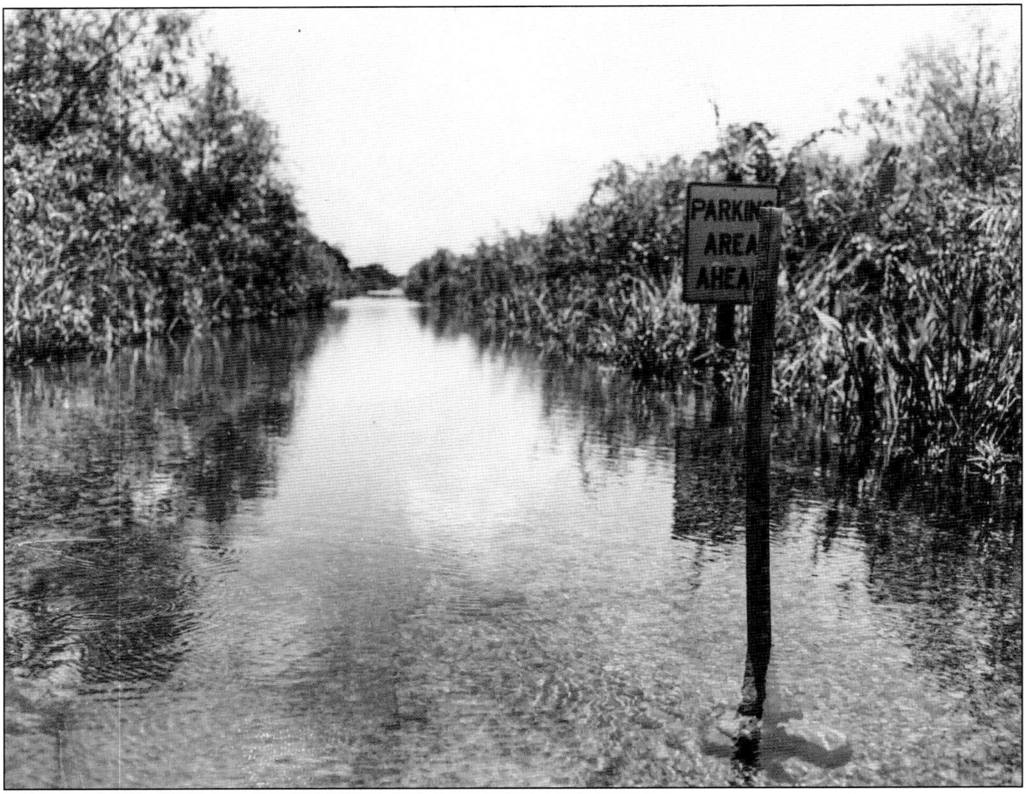

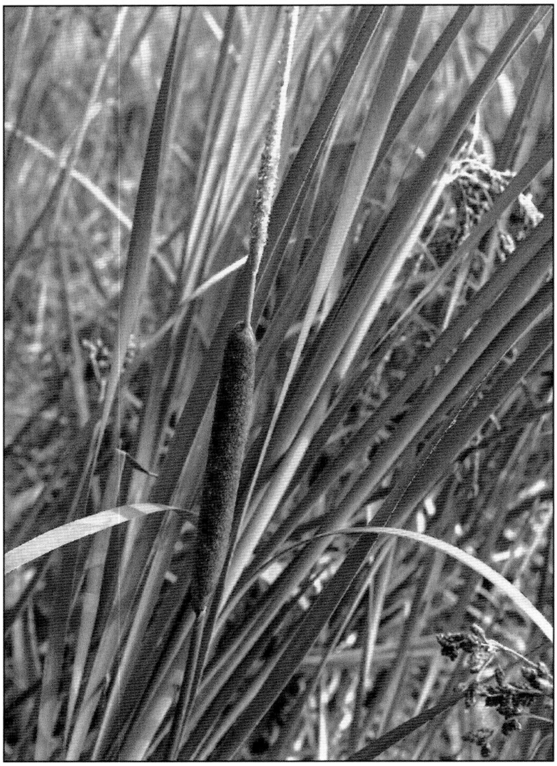

Then came, as is naturally the case, high rainfall years; floodgates at the park's northern boundary were opened. Tree islands and sawgrass strands, as well as roads, flooded long and deeply, natural fires stopped, alligator nests flooded, and wading birds could not nest. It became clear the park needed a guaranteed supply of appropriately delivered water. After much deliberation, the park was provided a seasonal schedule of water delivery. (NPS.)

Not only did water quantity and seasonality become an issue, so did water quality in this naturally phosphorous-limited environment. Cattail, an indicator of high nutrients, expanded in the northern Everglades. After significant litigation, in 1992, an agreement was reached to achieve low levels of phosphorus in the water entering Everglades National Park. To meet this goal, many structural and operational modifications were to follow. (NPS.)

Another crucial issue was the Everglades jetport. Begun in 1968 to accommodate future supersonic airplanes, it was to be the largest in the world. In opposition, Marjory Stoneman Douglas came back to Everglades advocacy 40 years after publishing *The River of Grass*. Reviews concluded that the airport, along with attendant development, would adversely impact the park. Work halted in 1970, and the surrounding land became the Big Cypress National Preserve. (NPS.)

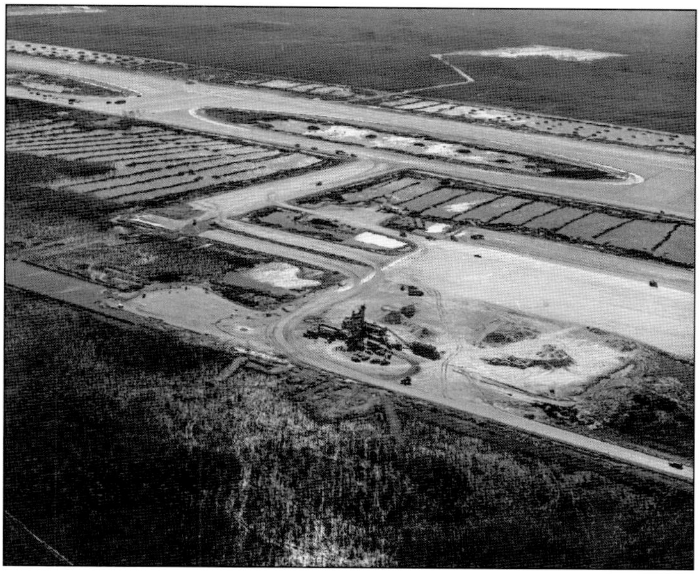

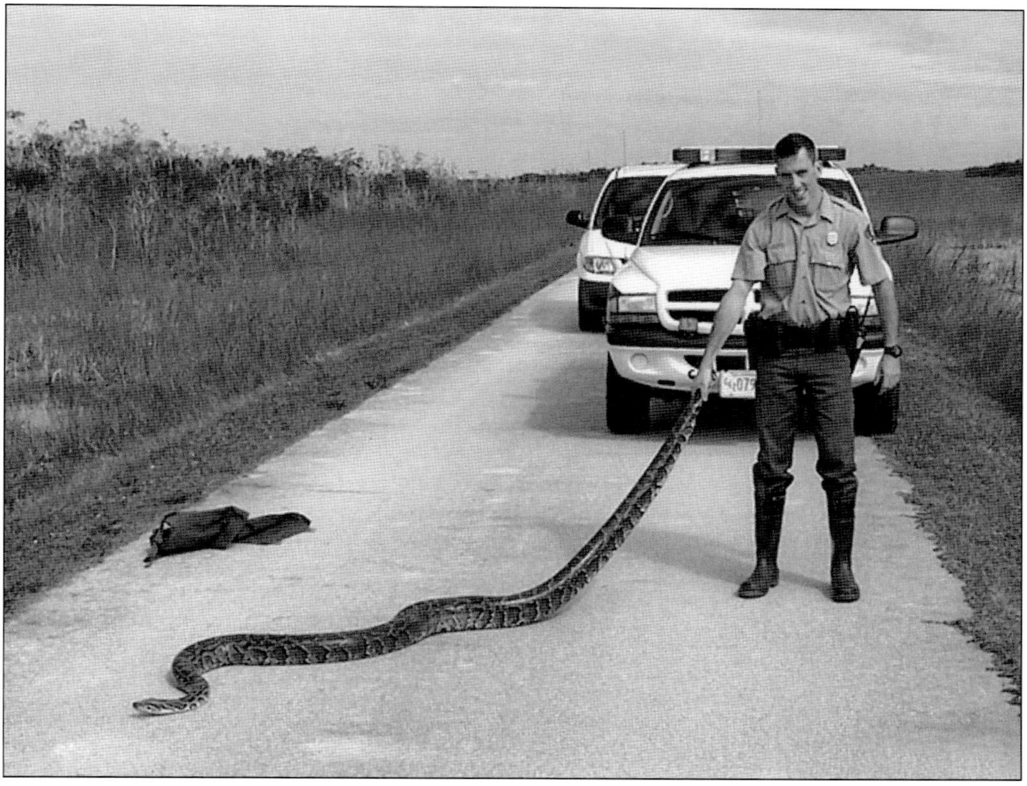

Non-native animals posed a considerable threat to the national park's environment. Non-native fish from Africa and South America—adapted to seasonal tropical Everglades-like marsh—became prominent at Anhinga Trail and Shark Valley. The most famous of the invaders have been Burmese pythons, descended from former pets. They have been found to eat dozens of species and are blamed for decreases in other animals in the Everglades. (NPS.)

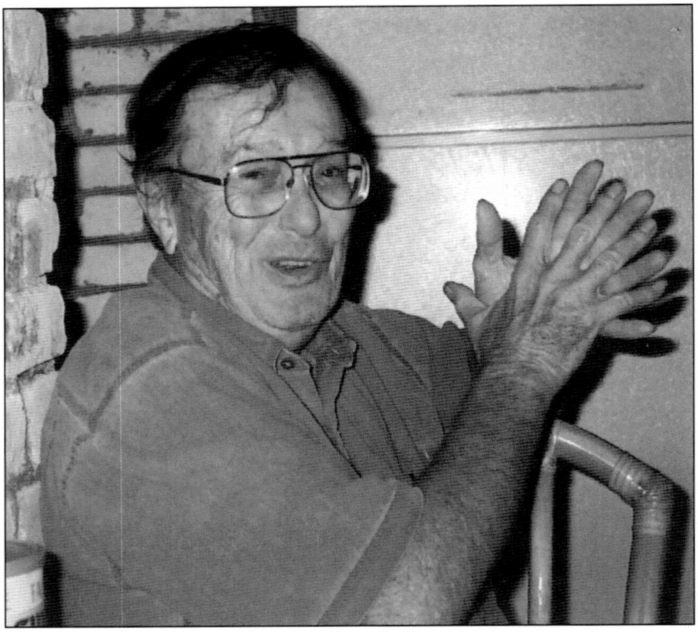

The Everglades became one of the most studied ecosystems anywhere owing to decades of scientific research. William B. Robertson Jr. came to the park as a student, becoming its second resident PhD biologist. Robertson demonstrated that the pinelands needed fire to persist. His understanding of the Everglades was profound. In his honor, the building housing fire management and the archive collections was named the Dr. Bill Robertson Jr. Center. (KH.)

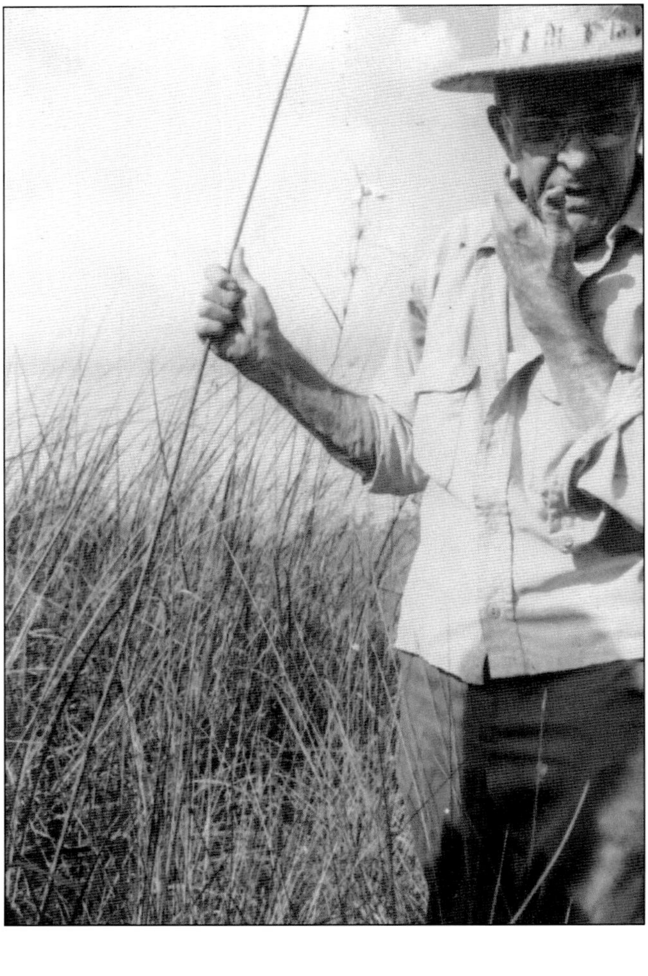

Frank Craighead Sr. first visited the Everglades in 1915. Retiring as the USDA's chief of forest entomology, he came to South Florida in 1956 and spent another two decades studying the Everglades environment and its plants. Indefatigable in the field, he came to be an Everglades expert and advisor on its management. In 1976, Gov. Reubin Askew officially honored him as the Scholar of the Everglades. (KH.)

Starting in 1971, the park's environmental education program was expanded to provide outreach to schoolchildren, camping programs, and ranger-guided and self-guided day trips. Environmental education centers were developed on Loop Road and at Hidden Lake near Royal Palm. This image shows an environmental education ranger introducing a snake to a group during their 1970s camping visit at Flamingo. (NPS.)

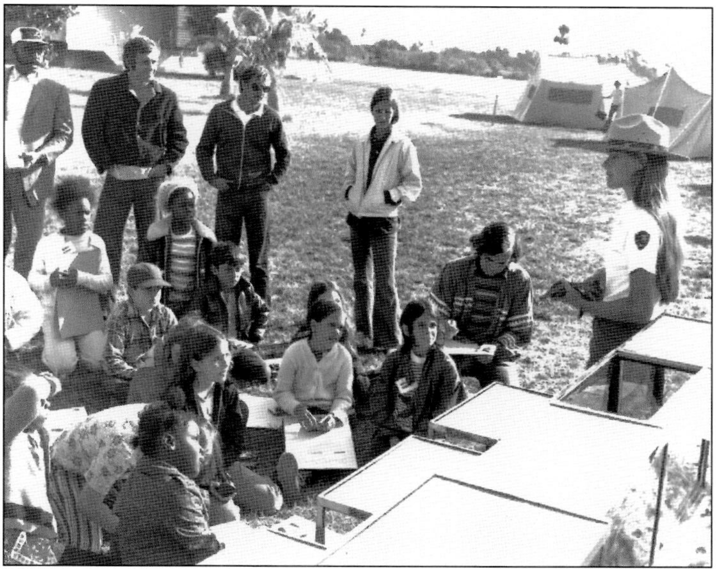

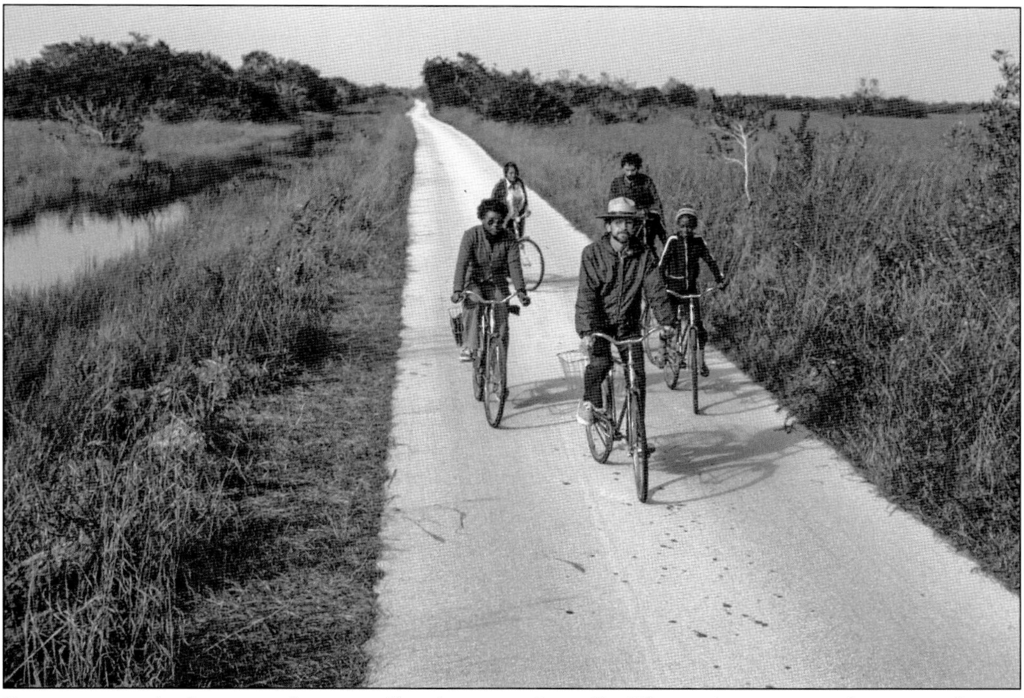

Environmental education also was offered more informally. The park encouraged organized tours so visitors could experience the Everglades and coastal areas that they might not otherwise be able to access on their own. This image shows a ranger-led bicycle tour at Shark Valley. Visitors could also participate in interpretive programs offered by concessionaires on the trams and boat tours at Flamingo and Everglades City. (NPSMWW.)

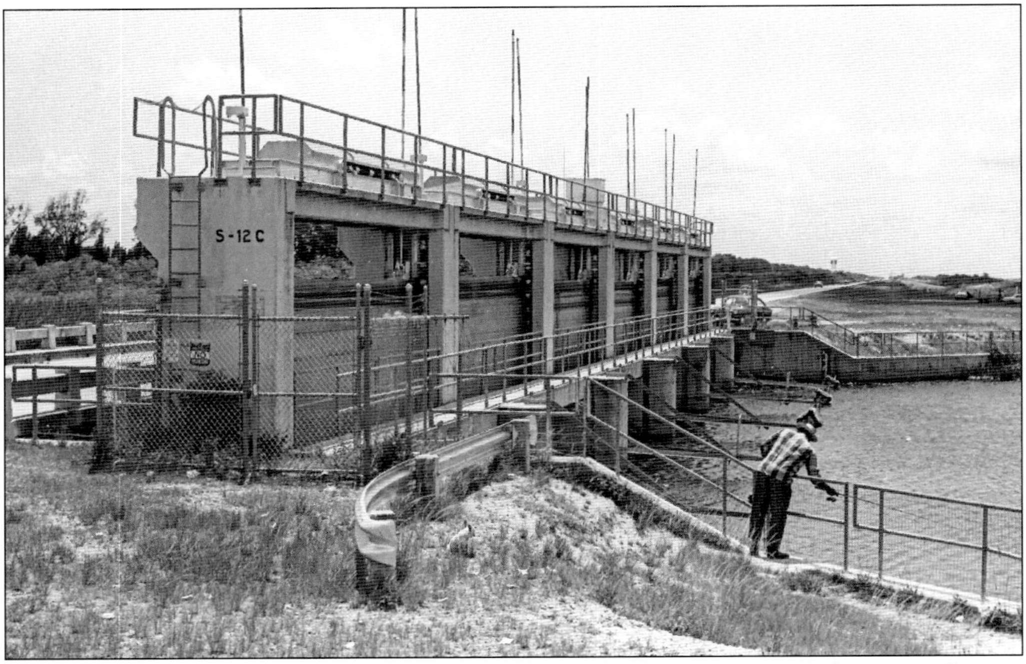

Protection of Everglades National Park's environment required managing surface water flowing into the park, now controlled by levees and flood gates (above). When the park's boundaries were fixed in the 1950s, the center of the park's natural flow way, where the Everglades narrowed into Shark River Slough, was omitted. This was remedied in 1989 with the addition of over 100,000 acres to provide an opportunity to reestablish more natural surface water flows into the park. In 2000, Congress authorized the Comprehensive Everglades Restoration Plan, which became the largest ecosystem restoration plan ever undertaken, intended to eliminate barriers to more natural water flow. A bridge replacing part of the Tamiami Trail roadbed was approved in 2009 to restore water flows to the park through its natural pathway (below). (Both, NPS.)

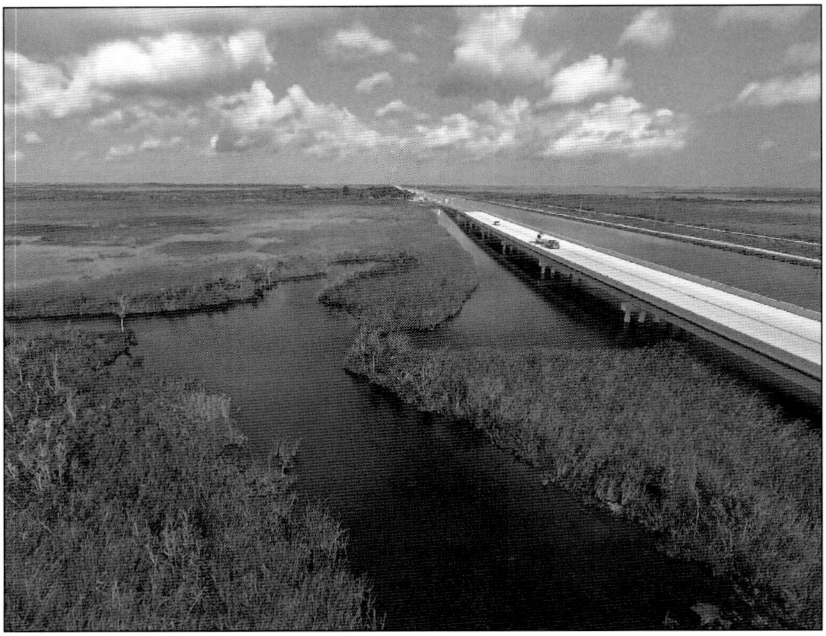

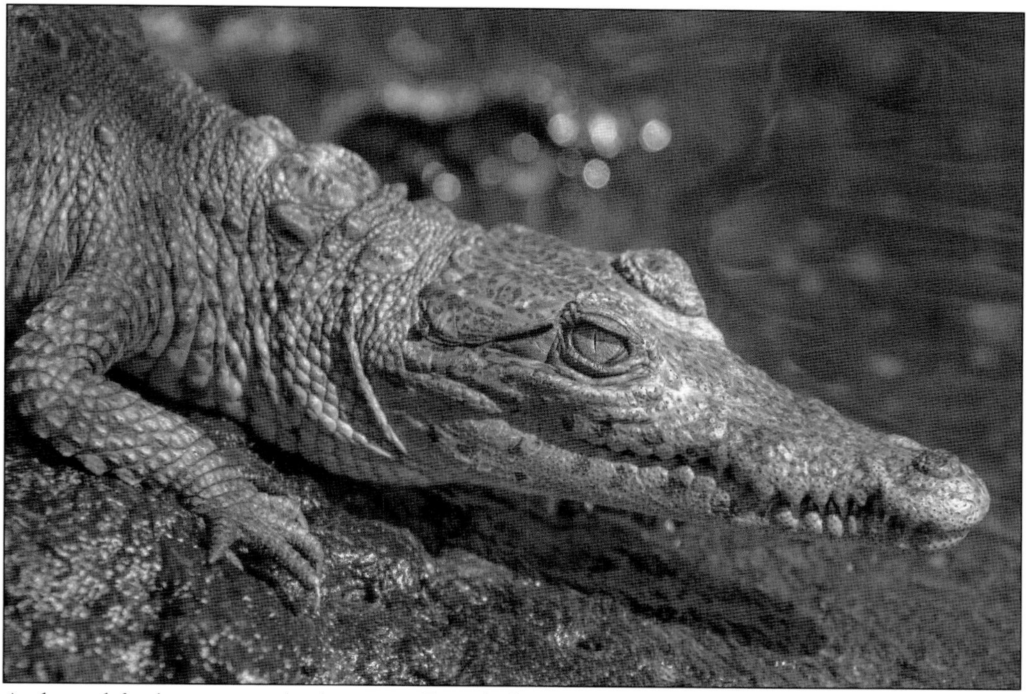

As hoped-for by its initial advocates, Everglades National Park has benefitted wildlife. The American crocodile is one example. In 1975, population declines resulted in its being listed as an endangered species. The park set aside habitat in the north of Florida Bay as a crocodile sanctuary, and a national wildlife refuge was established on Key Largo. A conservation success story, the crocodile's federal status was upgraded in 2007. (KH.)

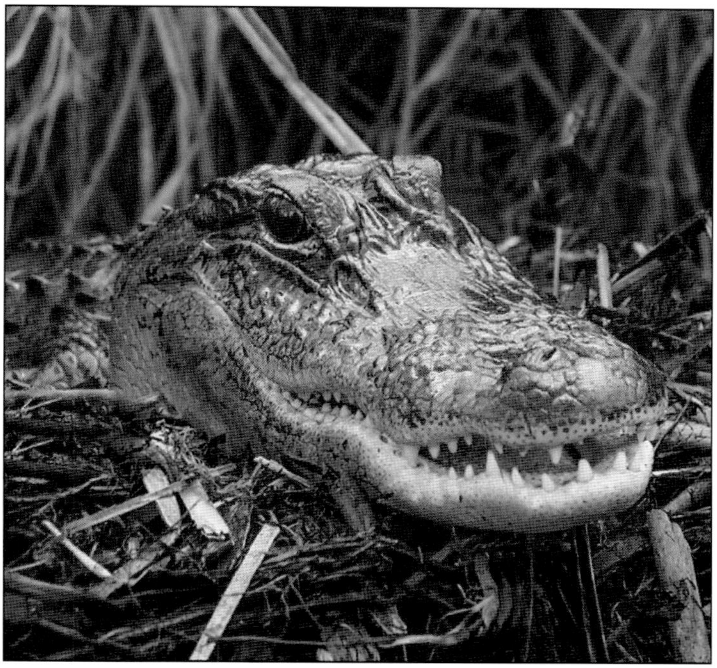

Synonymous with Everglades National Park, the American alligator's population crashed by the 1950s, mostly due to market hunting, including poaching in the park. The alligator was declared an endangered species in 1967, but by 1987, its population had fully recovered, a conservation success story like that of the crocodile. Seeing this symbol of the Everglades is a nearly guaranteed experience for park visitors. (NPSLO.)

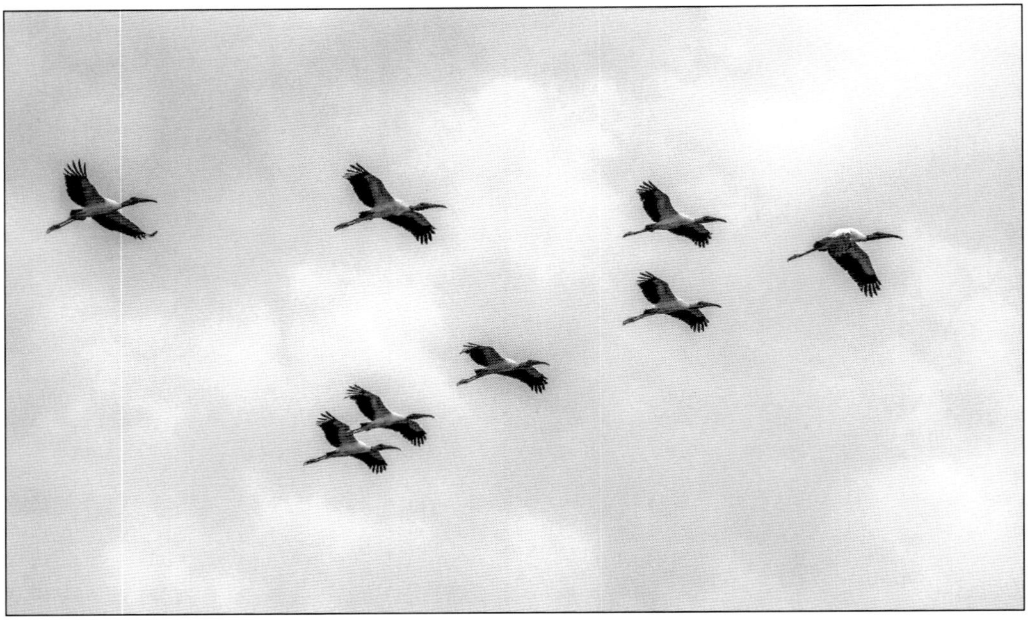

Such conservation success stories abound. This national park's ground-breaking mandate was to preserve intact its unique flora and fauna and the essential environmental conditions that support them. Its waterbirds are indicators of success. Secure within the park and other South Florida protected areas, waterbird populations recovered after plume-hunting, and although facing new challenges of water management, most species have fared well. The white ibis greatly expanded its range; in some years, tens of thousands nest in the Everglades. The US population of the wood stork, pictured here, is no longer listed as endangered as of 2014. In the years ahead, restoration will further return the Everglades to its more natural ecological condition while Everglades National Park will continue to provide an opportunity for visitors from all over the world to experience America's Everglades. (Both, KH.)

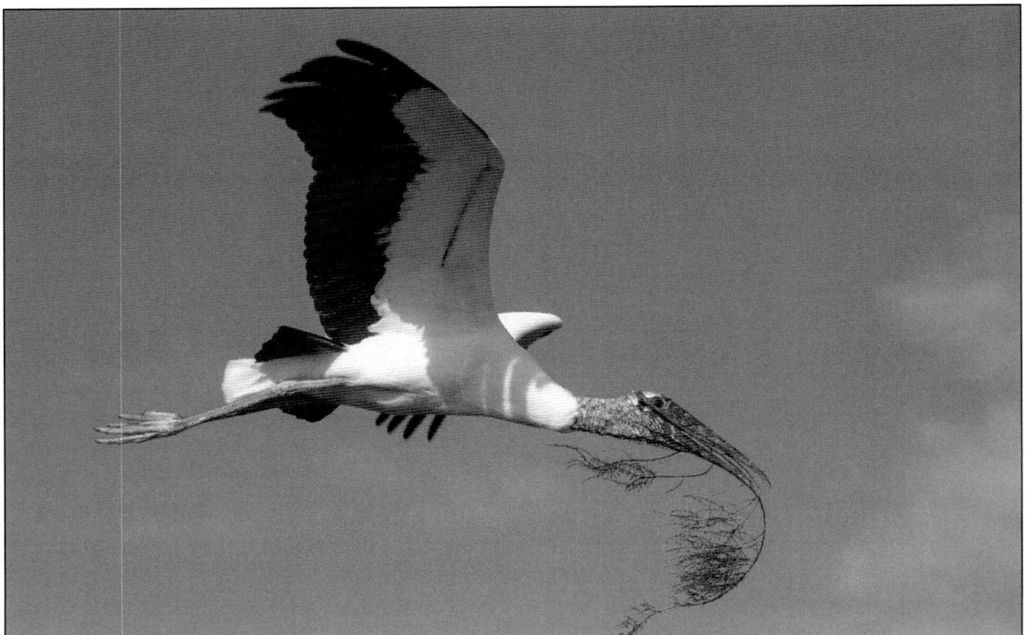

Key to Courtesy Lines

AMNH	American Museum of Natural History
DPL	Denver Public Library, National Parks Association Collection
EF	Everglades Foundation
HM	HistoryMiami Museum, Archives and Research Center
KB	Kelly Balmes, photographer
KH	Kushlan-Hines Collection
LOC	Library of Congress
MCPL	Monroe County Public Library
MDPLS	Miami-Dade Public Library System, Digital Collections, Gleason Waite Romer Photographs Collection
NPS	National Park Service, South Florida Collections Management Center, Open Parks Network, NPS Historic Photo Collection, and NPGallery
NPSLO	National Park Service, Lori Oberhofer, photographer
NPSMWW	National Park Service, M. Woodbridge Williams, photographer
NPSWRE	National Park Service, William R. Eads, photographer
RWB	Robert W. Blythe, photographer
SLAF	State Library and Archives of Florida, Florida Memory
UFMMJ	University of Florida, P.K. Yonge Library of Florida History, Special and Area Studies Collection, George A. Smathers Libraries, May Mann Jennings Papers
UFTEW	University of Florida, P.K. Yonge Library of Florida History, Special and Area Studies Collection, George A. Smathers Libraries, Thomas E. Will Papers
USNA	US National Archives
USNLM	US National Library of Medicine, Digital Collections
UUL	University of Utah, Special Collections, J. Willard Marriott Library

Discover Thousands of Local History Books Featuring Millions of Vintage Images

Arcadia Publishing, the leading local history publisher in the United States, is committed to making history accessible and meaningful through publishing books that celebrate and preserve the heritage of America's people and places.

Find more books like this at
www.arcadiapublishing.com

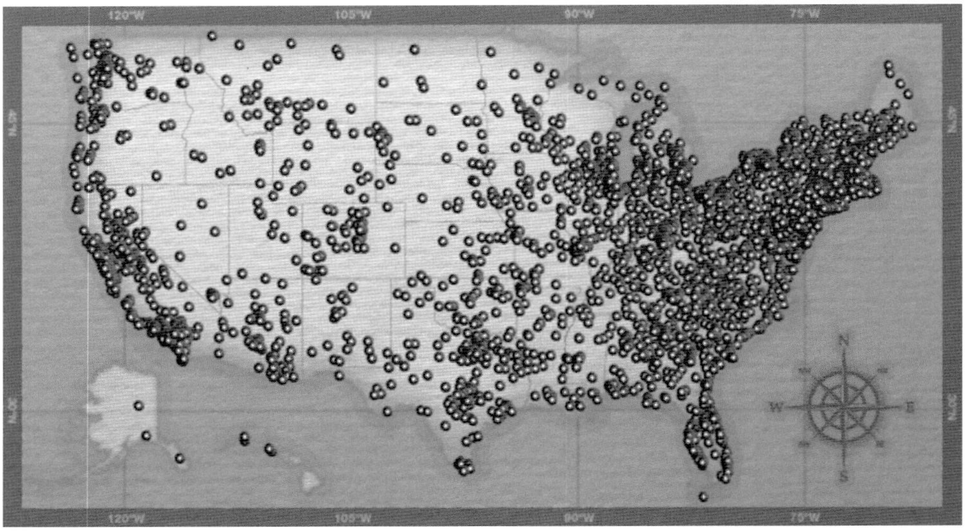

Search for your hometown history, your old stomping grounds, and even your favorite sports team.

Consistent with our mission to preserve history on a local level, this book was printed in South Carolina on American-made paper and manufactured entirely in the United States. Products carrying the accredited Forest Stewardship Council (FSC) label are printed on 100 percent FSC-certified paper.

MADE IN THE USA